Heaven's Gates and Hell's Flames

Heaven's Gates
and
Hell's Flames

A Sociological Study of
New Christian Movements in
Contemporary Goa

Savio Abreu

OXFORD
UNIVERSITY PRESS

OXFORD
UNIVERSITY PRESS

Oxford University Press is a department of the University of Oxford.
It furthers the University's objective of excellence in research, scholarship,
and education by publishing worldwide. Oxford is a registered trademark of
Oxford University Press in the UK and in certain other countries.

Published in India by
Oxford University Press
22 Workspace, 2nd Floor, 1/22 Asaf Ali Road, New Delhi 110 002

ISBN-13 (print edition): 978-0-19-012069-6
ISBN-10 (print edition): 0-19-012069-X

ISBN-13 (eBook): 978-0-19-909985-6
ISBN-10 (eBook): 0-19-909985-5

Typeset in ITC Giovanni Std 9.5/13
by Tranistics Data Technologies, Kolkata 700 091
Printed in India by Replika Press Pvt. Ltd

Dedicated to my
adorable and lively niece,
Jenny Abreu.

Contents

PLATE SECTION BETWEEN PAGES 14 AND 15.

Tables and Figures

Tables

Figures

Abbreviations

AIC	African-initiated Church
AG	Assemblies of God
BJP	Bharatiya Janata Party
CBCI	Catholic Bishops' Conference of India
CCR	Catholic Charismatic Renewal
CMS	Church Mission Society
CNI	Church of North India
CSI	Church of South India
DCST	Diocesan Charismatic Service Team
GST	Goa Service Team
ICCRS	International Catholic Charismatic Renewal Services
IPC	Indian Pentecostal Church
MGP	Maharashtrawadi Gomantak Party
NCCRS	National Catholic Charismatic Renewal Services
NFI	New Frontiers International
NGO	non-governmental organization
NRM	new religious movement
NST	National Service Team
NTC	New Testament Church
ROLC	River of Life Church
RSS	Rashtriya Swayamsevak Sangh

SEZ	special economic zone
UGP	United Goans Party
WRM	World Revival Ministries
YWAM	Youth with a Mission

Foreword

This work is a culmination of the author's doctoral studies, which he completed under my supervision at IIT Bombay. If I recollect correctly, when he first came to do research he had in mind a socio-historical study of Catholicism in Goa. Over several discussions, I urged him to think about new religious movements in the state and whether these might not constitute an interesting and novel subject for research. It is pleasing that the study is now out in print. Indeed, it is even more commendable that despite his initial struggles, Dr Abreu was gradually able to set aside his identity as a Jesuit priest and not allow that to colour his observations in the field and his analysis.

Despite the rapid growth of such movements across the world, there are few book-length studies of Pentecostal–Charismatic cults and groups in India, and it is refreshing to have one from a region of the country, Goa, that has had a strong and long-standing Christian tradition. This has enabled Dr Abreu to examine the new Christian movements in relation to a wider Hindu or non-Christian culture as well as in their contestation and conflict with the existing largely Catholic tradition of the region. Indeed, as is not always appreciated, large numbers of Pentecostal–Charismatics are erstwhile members of mainstream Christian Churches, rather than new converts to Christianity.

Drawing on established sociological concepts, Dr Abreu examines the forms of organization and leadership of these groups, the routinization of the charisma of the founding members, recruitment patterns, and modes of conversion. Further, he looks at how these groups con-struct their boundaries with other religious traditions within the state, how individuals negotiate their identities, and in what forms does solidarity manifest itself internally. Using the notion of the habitus, he has paid attention to ideas of sin, space, time, and the rites of passage in these new Christian groupings. While looking at marriages, he finds that neo-Pentecostals have instituted a practice of endogamy, while this is not strictly the case with Catholic Charismatics. For the most part, notions of patriarchy, ideal womanhood, and the subservience of women to male authority continue to flourish among the Pentecostal-Charismatic groups and are sanctioned by references in biblical texts. At the same time, however, certain forms of liberation have become available for women and they can—to an extent unavailable in main-stream Churches—access a degree of status and recognition in the Pentecostal-Charismatic groups. Certainly, according to Dr Abreu, these Churches have been more successful in terms of gender inclusion than of caste inclusion.

As Dr Abreu points out, neo-Pentecostals are largely cut off from consanguinity and kinship ties. This results in a greater reliance on the Church as a provider of a life plan for them. They depend on the teachings and support of the Church and its members to cope with daily suffering, trials, and pain. He perceives the forms of power among the Pentecostal-Charismatics along the lines of Foucault's notion of pastoral power that, according to him, ensures individual salvation, is not merely commanding but also sacrificing, extends its care collec-tively as well as to each individual separately and for his or her entire life, and, finally, depends for its exercise on an intimate understanding and knowledge of the inner minds and souls of those encompassed within its domain.

The author's research points out that the attempts of Pentecostal-Charismatic Churches to reform practices of mainstream Catholicism as well as their efforts at proselytism and understanding of themselves as set apart and exclusive have created several conflicts in different local areas. There is opposition to these groups both from Catholics as well as Hindus. At the same time, as Dr Abreu argues, these conflicts and contestations are not the result of some grand universal plan of Pentecostal-Charismatic groups to take over the religious space in Goa. They can be understood more accurately as particular discordances occurring in specific contexts and explained by local power tussles. These tussles have involved contestations over land, physical and institutional resources, notions of spiritual grace and authority, and a variety of social contexts. They have involved ruptures within families and villages and played themselves out in struggles over schools and cemetery spaces as well as in media reportage.

What the book shows us is that the Pentecostal–Charismatic movements have, in turn, had an influence over mainstream Catholicism, forcing it, in a sense, to respond to their critique. Thus, Catholic Churches have tried to incorporate Charismatic elements and to reduce some of their formality. At the same time, as Dr Abreu notes, throughout the country one is seeing more violence against Christians. Even more ominously, as the book asserts, a great deal of this violence is actually targeted towards Pentecostals, perhaps because they are more visible and their techniques of recruitment and conversion more direct and intrusive. We certainly need more such studies if we are to understand better the relationship of the spread of Pentecostal–Charismatic movements to global shifts and changes, including the altering dynamics of migration, politics (which has seen an increasing ascendancy of the Right), and the aspirations and expectations spurred by the extension of neoliberal capitalist ideologies across the world.

Rowena Robinson
Department of Humanities and Social Sciences
Indian Institute of Technology Bombay
20 November 2019

Acknowledgements

To acknowledge the numerous contributions to this book in a few lines is no small task, but I will try my best to express in a succinct manner the feelings of gratitude that are welling within my heart. First of all, I would like to thank Almighty God for giving me the grace and perseverance to not only complete this doctoral research in 2010, but also, despite my busy work schedule, to publish my PhD thesis in book form in subsequent years. My gratitude goes to my guide, Professor Rowena Robinson, who has been a source of great support and encouragement to me. It is due to her constant reminders over the years about the importance of publishing my thesis that it is finally getting published. On the one hand she has been quite strict and demanding and has ensured that the thesis is of the highest quality, and on the other hand she has been kind and understanding and has provided me with enough freedom to be creative. I would also like to thank my family, especially my father, Xavier, who has painstakingly edited all my rough drafts, my mother, Aurora, and brother, Sholet, for their patience, understanding, and encouragement.

I am grateful to my Jesuit provincials: Anthony Da Silva SJ for backing me and relieving me of other demanding responsibilities while I was conducting my PhD research so that I could fully concentrate on it, and Rosario Rocha SJ for granting my request for a three-month research break in 2017 to edit my thesis for publication. I also thank my external guide, Delio Menconca SJ, former director of the Xavier Centre of Historical Research, Goa, for his insightful conversations, valuable advice, and other academic assistance. I would also like to remember with special gratitude Ashok Kumar, my fellow PhD student, who was a great companion to me during the years I spent as a PhD scholar at the Indian Institute of Technology (IIT) Bombay. Professor C.D. Sebastian, Department of Humanities and Social Sciences, IIT Bombay, was a great friend and companion during my years there and I cherish the enriching discussions we had over the many meals I ate in his home. I am also indebted to the other faculty members of the department, especially Professors D. Parthasarathy and Kushal Deb, for their guidance and encouragement.

My gratitude goes out to all the members of the Catholic Charismatic groups of Mapusa and Merces and the members of the New Frontiers International (NFI) Church and World Revival Ministries (WRM) Church, who have shared not only information but also their warmth and hospitality. I gratefully acknowledge the assistance I have received from the staff of different libraries, especially those at Jnana Deepa Vidyapeeth, Pune, Vidya Jyoti, Delhi, and Dharmaram Vidya Kshetram, Bengaluru. I would like to thank my Jesuit community at Xavier Centre of Historical Research and also the Jesuit communities at Vinayalaya, Andheri, Mumbai, and Ashirwad, Bengaluru, for their support and Jesuit companionship during the years of my research. I am grateful to everyone at Oxford University Press for their patience and assistance during the entire production process of the book. Finally, I would like to thank the staff and students of the humanities and social sciences department at IIT Bombay and all others who have helped me in my research work, all of whose names cannot be taken here.

Savio Abreu
20 November 2019

Introduction

This work focuses on religious groups that are at the periphery of the religious space in Goa. 'Be careful, they may convert you and you may end up becoming a "Believer"[1]' These anxious words of my mother when she came to know that I was doing fieldwork among the new Christian groups in Goa reflect the common perception of the Catholics regarding the Born-Again Christians or Believers. Many of my companions and colleagues made snide remarks on my choice of such a 'frivolous', 'quaint', and 'peripheral' topic for this volume, which seemed far removed from relevant sociopolitical and economic issues of development such as tourism, mining, or real estate, 'where the action was' (Robbins 2000: 515). Having been brought up in a traditional and orthodox Catholic family in Goa, I was never exposed to the new Christian sects, though occasionally one heard stories of Catholics joining these groups; people who were generally unhappy with the Catholic Church and were thus lured by the money offered by these well-financed Protestant groups. My interest in these groups was first aroused when I noticed changes in my cousin, who had become a Believer. She was quoting with ease from the Bible and aggressively questioned me about my faith and my understanding of the priestly vocation. It made me curious to know what were the beliefs and

---

[1] Believer is the name commonly used for the independent Born-Again Pentecostal–Charismatic Christians.

practices followed in these religious groups and the reasons they were looked down upon by the Catholics. This was the starting point of my interest in the new Christian groups in Goa.

This book is both a descriptive and analytical commentary on the everyday practices of the Pentecostal–Charismatic Christians in Goa. Since the subjects of my ethnographic fieldwork belong to the Pentecostal–Charismatic branch of Christianity, it is necessary to understand what this form of Christianity is all about and how it is different from other forms of Christianity. Pentecostalism, according to Synan (1987: 97–8), is a twentieth-century phenomenon with roots in the Evangelical, Methodist, and Perfectionist movements of the nineteenth century. The crucial difference between Pentecostals and other Christians is the Pentecostals' unique emphasis on the person, work, and gifts of the Holy Spirit. Hollenweger (1972: xix) includes as Pentecostals all the groups that profess at least two religious crisis experiences—water baptism or rebirth and baptism of the spirit—the second being different from the first one and usually, but not always, being accompanied with speaking in tongues. Martin (2002: 4) links Pentecostalism with the pneumatic Christianity of the Primitive Church by defining Pentecostalism as 'primitive' Christianity, which emerged two millennia ago on the despised margins of the Roman Empire, believing in lay empowerments of the spirit in alliance with aspirations to holiness and wholeness. To many, Pentecostalism was and remains a 'tongues movement', but McDonnell (1987) stresses the Trinitarian aspect of the movement by defining Pentecostals as those Christians who stress the power and presence of the Holy Spirit and the gifts of the spirit directed toward the proclamation that Jesus Christ is Lord to the glory of God the Father.

What is so significant about the Pentecostal–Charismatic move-ment that warrants another book to be written on it? In the southern state of Kerala from 27–30 December 2006, more than 20,000 people from all over India and also from other countries gathered for the XIII National Catholic Charismatic Convention organized by the National Catholic Charismatic Renewal (NCCR) to commemorate the 40th anniversary of the beginning of the Catholic Charismatic Renewal (CCR) in the universal Church and the 35th anniversary of its beginning in India. Pentecostalism within the Catholic Church has spread in just three decades to almost every corner of the Christian world, numbering around 119 million Catholic Charismatics in 2000 (Barrett et al. 2001). This is a remarkable achievement for a movement just over 30 years old. The rapid growth and expansion of various types and forms of Pentecostal and Charismatic groups and Churches worldwide during the past few decades have drawn the attention of theologians and social scientists alike. According to Hollenweger (1986), one of the leading authorities on Pentecostalism, in the near future the combined total of classical Pentecostals—those in the Charismatic movements within the traditional Churches and those belonging to the indigenous non-white Churches—will number almost as many as all other Protestant Christians together.

Pentecostalism is the most rapidly expanding religion of our times (Cox 1996: 120). A similar view is expressed by Coleman (2000: 3), who quotes Berger that there are two global religions of enormous vitality—conservative Islam and conservative Protestantism. In the words of Synan (1997: xi), a renowned Pentecostal historian and author of books such as The Holiness-Pentecostal Movement and The Holiness-Pentecostal Tradition, 'The rise and development of Pentecostalism could well be the major story of Christianity in the twentieth century.' 'In all of human history, no other non-political, non-militaristic, voluntary human movement has grown as rapidly as the Pentecostal, Charismatic movement in the last 25 years.' Quoting these words of Peter Wagner, Synan argues that Pentecostalism deserves to be seen as a major Christian tradition alongside the Roman Catholic, Orthodox, and Protestant Reformation traditions (Synan 1997). The variety of its theological and societal views is practically as broad as that of Christianity itself.

Thus, any work on Pentecostal–Charismatic Christianity will have to address the reasons for the rapid growth and proliferation of these groups all over the world. A lot of studies on Pentecostalism have analysed the factors that have led to the rapid expansion of Charismatic Christianity and its implications both at the global and local level. Many sociologists suggest that new forms of religiosity such as Pentecostalism appear as a religious antidote to the conditions of anomie caused in a society in transition brought about, in this case, by the process of rapid urbanization (Caplan 1983; D'Epinay 1969; L. D'Souza 1999; Martin 2002; Wilson 1970). McDonnell (1976: 17–40), in a detailed analysis of different theories of movements, concludes that relative deprivation, social and economic development, social disorganization, and Church–sect theories are useful in understanding the growth of movements such as Pentecostalism; they point to favourable conditions and to facilitating factors, but they are not causal theories of the origin of the movement.

The sheer diversity of the Pentecostal experience, the accent on experience and not doctrine, its de-centralized, non-territorial nature, and its focus on bettering the personal morality of its individual members have led to its extraordinary outgrowth in every corner of the world (Thomas 2008: 60). Hollenweger (1972: 458–67) similarly points out that the Pentecostal movement provides for the poor a home, relative economic security, care when they are sick, and basic educational opportunities. 'It helps the managers of large factories, engineers, diplomats, artists and university professors, overloaded with responsibility, to discover the other side of their personality, the original, spontaneous, and individually human element, and to experience it in the framework of a liturgy which controls it, but which is spontaneous in form' (Hollenweger 1972: 467). Martin (2002: 169–70) points out the ability of Pentecostalism to constantly adjust on the ground in order to meet varied needs and the ability to combine indigenization and autonomy or acculturation as reasons for its acceptance in different social formations. Anderson (2004: 281–3), who makes a point similar to Martin's, argues that Pentecostalism with its 'flexibility or freedom in the Spirit' has an innate ability to develop its own culturally relevant forms of expression and thus make itself at home in almost any context. One explanation given by the locals for the rise of Pentecostalism is the affiliation of Pentecostal groups with overseas funding agencies with vast financial resources (Caplan 1983: 33). All these explanations and other factors that have led to the eruption of the Pentecostal movement on the religious landscape of Goa are explored in this book.

While the literature on Pentecostalism is constantly on the rise, most of the Pentecostal studies have been on Western societies and in Christian contexts. Only more recently has there been a proliferation of such studies in Latin America and other continents. As a result, there are very few well-researched and scientific empirical studies on the Pentecostal–Charismatic phenomenon in Asia, and especially in India, that critically analyse this religious phenomenon from a social science perspective.[2] *Heaven's Gates and Hell's Flames* is an attempt to fill in this gap, to satisfy the need for understanding the rapidly expanding and overtly evangelistic movement of Pentecostalism in pluralist, non-Christian societies, both as a social process and as an embodied everyday practice—'as a living factor inside the social structure'—and also its sociocultural implications in the twenty-first century (Guiart quoted in Robinson 1998: 215). In this endeavour, this work primarily draws from the fields of sociology and anthropology, apart from history and theology.

The flow within the Introduction is not a linear one, moving from the personal to the academic or from the geographical to the intellectual, but rather takes on a spiral movement. It starts with the author's motivation for choosing this area of study and then steps into a conceptual space by locating the themes of the study within the context of related literature. The literature review narrows down the theoretical area from the broader field of new religious movements (NRM) to Pentecostal–Charismatic Christianity to the neo-Pentecostal movement specifically. Then, briefly, the basic premises that gird this study and the reasons for the choice of the theoretical and geographical fields of the study are highlighted. The physical area is then explored by locating the field-work. The narration of the author's field experiences takes us deeper into the personal space of the identity of the author both as a native anthropologist and an outsider. Finally, we turn to the theoretical scheme of the book by outlining the chapters.

Locating the Pentecostal–Charismatic Movement within New Religious Movements

In order to understand Pentecostal–Charismatic Christianity it is necessary to locate its theoretical locus. As it will be shown in this section, this work at the theoretical level is situated in the area of NRMs, a relatively new field that is part of the broader field of sociology of religion and religious studies. According to Harvey Cox (1996: 299), for

[2] Bauman (2015), Bayly (1994), Caplan (1987a), L. D'Souza (1999), Mathew (2009), and Parathazham (1996) are the studies on Pentecostal–Charismatic Christianity in India that I have come across.

the past few centuries, two principal contenders—scientific modernity and traditional religion—have clashed over the privilege of being the ultimate source of meaning and value and have reached an exhausted stalemate. Since both scientific modernity and conventional religion have progressively lost their ability to provide a source of spiritual meaning, two new contenders—'fundamentalism' and 'experientialism' are stepping forward to present themselves as authentic links to the sacred past (Cox 1996: 300). The field of study of NRMs, which Cox characterizes as fundamentalist and experientialist, is concerned with a group of religious bodies or movements that, though they do not share any particular set of attributes, have been assigned an 'outsider' or 'fringe' status by the dominant religious culture and secondarily by elements within the secular culture (Melton 2004: 17). Hence, they are a set of religions that exist in a relatively contested space within society. Pentecostal–Charismatic Christianity, as seen in my work, exhibits both fundamentalist and experientialist characteristics and occupies a contested religious space, which results in them being looked down upon by the mainstream Hindu and Catholic religions. According to Cox (1996: 308), 'the stakes are very high and the battle between the fundamentalist and the experientialist impulses is raging on several fronts at once'.

The sudden visibility of a new generation of NRMs in the early 1970s and the controversy they generated in the United States of America (USA) led to the emergence of studies on NRMs as a separate sub-discipline within religious studies. The NRM scholarship in the 1970s and 1980s debated on issues such as the conceptual boundary problem of NRMs and the implications of NRMs for the premise of secularization. Ever since the non-denominational and independent Pentecostal-like Churches burst on the scene in the 1970s and complicated issues of definition and taxonomy there has been much debate in scholarly circles about how to define Pentecostals and differentiate them from other similar groups. There has also been lot of debate on whether the rapid growth of Pentecostal–Charismatic Christianity has undermined or even refuted the theory of secularization.

There has been a lot of literature on the appropriate nomenclature of NRMs. According to Saliba (1995: 9–10), it is fitting to call the cults of the second half of the twentieth century NRMs since they occurred in a period of Western history when the process of secularization was interpreted as the decline of religion. The new religions are perceived as a novelty since their emergence has surprised many observers of the religious scene. The rapid growth and expansion of Pentecostal–Charismatic Christianity across the world has surprised most scholars of religion. They might also be considered new since, till very recently, those who joined them were first-generation converts: people who were first brought up and socialized in a traditional Church and who then took the important step of abandoning the faith of their parents. L. D'Souza (1999) in her doctoral thesis on the Catholic Charismatic movement in the excessively materialist and consumerist city of Mumbai connects the emergence of the movement to the reversal of the process of secularization. She finds that emerging religious movements such as the Charismatic movement are 'new' since they exhibit a new type of religious consciousness.

What exactly is a *new* religious movement is a question explored by many religious scholars. Hexham and Poewe in their work *New Religions as Global Cultures* (1997) argue that authentic new religions are theologically innovative or at least broadly and globally syncretic (quoted in Robbins 2000: 518). Kranenborg in his 1999 conference paper 'Brahma Kumaris: A New Religion?' suggests that a genuine 'new religion' is innovative in terms of content; its doctrinal and praxis break is recognized by both the new group and the tradition it breaks from (Robbins 2000). In my fieldwork, both the members of the neo-Pentecostal groups that I studied and the Catholics I interviewed agreed that the neo-Pentecostal groups were different and had nothing to do with the Catholic Church. According to Saliba (1995: 9–10), if one looks at the major constituents of religion—namely, belief in a sacred and transcendental power and guidance, and the concern for ultimate matters in human life—then the cults have to be called 'religious'. The data from my fieldwork reveals that all the groups under Pentecostal–Charismatic Christianity accept the broad understanding of a Christian God with special emphasis on the role of the Holy Spirit and a soteriological orientation towards life and mission. The new religions can also be appropriately called 'movements' in the sense that they reflect important transitions in people's lives. They cause a shift not only in the convert's previous religious allegiance, but also in the behaviour of people who are affected by the change. Martin (2002: 23) views Pentecostalism as a religious 'movement' accompanying and facilitating the movement of people in contemporary global society characterized by a radical disturbance of roots and the accelerating compression of time and space. As a 'movement' it provides reception centres as the Believers arrive in impersonal megacities, or else provides a depot to which they gravitate after experiencing such corrosive places (Martin 2002: 24).

In the previous discussion, I have tried to locate Pentecostal–Charismatic Christianity within the field of NRMs by showing that the Pentecostal–Charismatic groups I studied are new and religious and are movements. Now an attempt will be made to classify the new Christian groups that are the focus of this study using Melton's typology of religions. In order to describe and analyse the belief systems and rites and rituals of these groups, it is important to first classify and distinguish these groups from other Christian groups using Melton's criteria of classifying religions. His typology of religions that is used in the *Encyclopedia of American Religions*[3] is one of the most comprehensive and widely used classifications of religions (Melton 1993). Drawing from major religious family traditions and the Church–sect–cult trichotomy, Melton divides the different religious groups in the West into four types (2004: 26–7).

The first type includes 'Churches' or 'established religions'—those Christian denominations that form the religious establishment of several Western countries, besides those religious groups in non-Western countries that dominate the landscape in their own country. This category includes the Roman Catholic Church, the many Protestant state Churches of Europe, Orthodox Judaism in Israel, Theravada Buddhism in Sri Lanka, and so forth. The second category, termed 'ethnic religions', includes in the West those religions that are not Christian but that serve a particular ethnic constituency. Ethnic religions operate outside of the religious establishment and will not become Churches, but are seen by the establishment as somewhat analogous to them. Examples are the several large Jewish synagogue associations, as well as Asian Hindu, Muslim, Buddhist, Sikh, and Jain groups. The 'sects' make up the third type. They are primarily Christian and Jewish groups that

---

[3] In his introductory historical essays, Melton divides the religious families of the world into 22 groups, about half of which belong to the Christian tradition.

are perceived as stricter than the larger Churches and the synagogue associations on matters of belief, more diligent in practice and more fervent in worship. Sect groups are seen as existing along a spectrum of movement towards becoming a Church, with new sects continually arising to protest the tendency of the older sects to adopt Church-like characteristics (less strict, less diligent, less fervent). In the West, many of the more Church-like sects are affiliated with the World Evangelical Alliance and its associated national councils, while most of the less Church-like sects are free from any ecumenical alignments at all.

After setting aside the established religions (the first type), the ethnic religious groups (the second type), and the sects (the third type), those groups that remain are the 'new religions'. While both ethnic religions and the sects have some recognized legitimacy in the eyes of the religious establishment, the new religions are yet to prove themselves and are under constant scrutiny. Thus Melton (2004: 26–7) defines NRMs 'not by any characteristic(s) that they share, but by their relationship to the other forms of religious life represented by the dominant Churches, the ethnic religions and the sects'. Melton's methodology to classify a new religion is to locate it initially within its particular religious tradition, then to determine where it fits when compared to the mainstream of that tradition, and finally to determine its relation to whatever tradition is dominant in that country in which the group operates.

The new Christian movements in Goa that are the focus of this study, namely the CCR and the neo-Pentecostal groups fall within the Pentecostal family, one of the 22 different family groups identified by Melton in *The Encyclopedia of American Religions*. Chapter 1 situates these groups within Pentecostal–Charismatic Christianity by tracing the origin and history of modern Pentecostalism up to the mushrooming of independent Pentecostal–Charismatic Churches all over the world, including the present-day Born-Again Christian groups operating in Goa. While the CCR and neo-Pentecostal groups exhibit characteristics similar to Classical Pentecostalism, which is mainstream Pentecostalism, this study also shows many points of dissimilarity.

Since Melton (2004: 25) defines new religions always in relation with the dominant religious community, the list of religions that would be considered under the rubric of NRMs would differ from country to country and always be under negotiation. In Goa, orthodox Hinduism would fit Melton's first category of established religions, while Roman Catholicism can be classified as an ethnic religion. The various forms of popular Hinduism, including syncretic traditions, practised by the lower-caste Hindus can also be cited as examples of ethnic religions. The Orthodox Church, the few Protestant Churches, and the classical Pentecostal denominations would also fall under the category of ethnic religions as they cater mainly to the migrant population belonging to a particular linguistic constituency. The numerous independent neo-Pentecostal Churches would fit in with Melton's categories of sects and new religions. Most of them advocate a stricter, more biblical reading of the Christian faith and are critical of mainstream Christianity. They are perceived to be more rigid and exclusive in practice and more fervent in worship. Most of them are not acceptable to the dominant Catholic Church and the majority Hindu community—both part of the mainstream religious tradition in Goa—due to their clashing ideologies, and especially due to their practice of aggressive and in-your-face type of proselytization aimed at the Catholics and Hindus. The tense relations and occasional conflicts between the new Christian groups and the Catholics and Hindus are analysed throughout the book, but more specifically in Chapters 3 and 6. Thus, the new Christian groups studied in this book are classified as falling in the Pentecostal family tradition and exhibiting characteristics of Melton's typology of the third and fourth types, that is, sects and new religions.

Classification of Pentecostal–Charismatic Movements

In the previous section, a review of the literature on NRMs and the use of Melton's typology of religions has shown that the new Christian groups, the object of this study, belong to the broader field of NRMs and more specifically to the family of Pentecostal–Charismatic Christianity. Before taking up a detailed descriptive analysis of the field data gathered from these groups, it is necessary to understand the classification of the often bewildering multitude of denominations and Churches that fall under the broad umbrella of Pentecostalism. It is important for theoretical clarity to define and demarcate Pentecostals and Charismatics from other Christians belonging to the historic Churches. While there is no absolute consensus among scholars of Pentecostalism about its taxonomical nature, all of them would distinguish between (*a*) Classical Pentecostalism, the older Pentecostal movement generally linked with the outbreak of tongues at Azusa Street, Los Angeles, in the early 1900s and which has produced its own denominations on a global basis such as Assemblies of God, Church of God, and so on, and (*b*) the Charismatic Renewal or neo-Pentecostalism, the more contemporary Pentecostal movement, which occurred within the mainline historic Churches in the 1960s and which spread from the 1970s onwards to independent, non-denominational Churches. Most of the studies, especially all the recent works on the Pentecostal–Charismatic movement, while classifying Pentecostalism from a historical point of view, trace three waves in the development of the global Pentecostal movement:

1. Classical Pentecostalism that emerged as the religion of the dispossessed in the beginning of the twentieth century.
2. Emergence in the 1960s among middle-class members of mainline Churches, of a new, or neo-Pentecostalism that was re-christened the Charismatic Renewal. A member in the Charismatic Renewal was a Renewalist and still remained a committed Anglican or Catholic, Baptist or Presbyterian.
3. Emergence of numerous independent ministries and new non-denominational Churches and para-Church groups from the late 1970s that have been called neo-Pentecostal or neo-Charismatic Churches did not destroy the Renewal Movement, but penetrated it and eventually altered its nature. Those included in the third wave such as the so-called Restorationist house churches were not Renewalists since they taught a radical separationist doctrine and condemned the historical Churches as moribund. Mathew (2009: 695) terms these Churches as 'post-denominational' in a sense, and 'New Generation Churches'. According to Cox (1996: 312), these Churches claimed the gifts of healing and prophecy, but did not want to bear the onus of the 'Pentecostal' label.

Hollenweger (1986: 3) would add a third stream, namely 'Indigenous non-White Churches', to the earlier mentioned streams of classical Pentecostalism and the Charismatic Renewal. These Third-World indigenous movements are independent of Western mission boards. Writers such as Synan (1987), McGee (1994), and others question whether all these Churches really belong to the Pentecostal–Charismatic movement. Hollenweger, however, argues that most of them belong to this family since they fulfil the criteria, which he used to define the original Pentecostal movement, namely orality of liturgy, narrativity of theology, maximum participation at all levels, and inclusion of dreams and visions into public ritual. The findings of this study corroborate Hollenweger's (1986) and Anderson's (2001; 2004) position that the overwhelming part of Pentecostal Christianity belongs to the non-white, Third-World Pentecostal Churches, indicating that in the near future Christianity as a whole will no longer be a predominantly white person's religion. Besides the widely accepted classification of Pentecostal–Charismatic Christianity into three waves, there have been other modes of classification such as that of Nwaobi (1993), which classifies Pentecostalism into three categories, namely classical Pentecostalism, neo-Pentecostalism, and the Catholic Charismatic movement. The inclusion of the CCR as an additional category and its distinction from neo-Pentecostalism is relevant in the context of Goa and is followed in this book. Besides the classification of Pentecostal–Charismatic Christianity into three chronological waves with their distinct characteristics, another classification, relevant to this study, is based on whether it is anti-modern, modern, or postmodern. Then another distinction relevant to Indian Pentecostalism is the distinction between Evangelicalism and Pentecostalism. Scholars generally distinguish Pentecostalism, conceived as a species from other non-Pentecostal species of Evangelicalism, which is regarded as a genus. However, in the Indian context it is not easy to distinguish between the hybrid species produced by Evangelicalism and Pentecostalism and so the term 'Pentecostalised Evangelicals' is used to refer to Evangelicals that are heavily influenced by Pentecostalism (Bauman 2015: 25).

Pentecostal–Charismatic Christianity and the Process of Modernization

Many of the studies on NRMs by sociologists of religion have tried to analyse their response to the process of 'modernization'.[4] A contradiction

---

[4] All the articles in Stephen Hunt, Tony Walter, and Malcolm Hamilton (1997) analyse the relation of neo-Pentecostalism to modernization. See also Dawson 1998.

in Pentecostalism is that it appears to resist secularizing forces while simultaneously endorsing some aspects of present-day culture. Hunt, Walter, and Hamilton (1997: 3), while defining modernization as the interrelated processes of industrialization, rationalism, the break-up of community, and pluralism—processes that engender disbelief and the decline of religious faith—state that neo-Pentecostalism displays attributes that are, sometimes simultaneously, anti-modern, modern, and postmodern.

The Charismatics in the historic Churches reject that their movement is backward-looking, reactionary, and fundamentalist, that is, having anti-modern characteristics, but Hollenweger (1972), Thomas (2008), and others have argued that neo-Pentecostalism is fundamentalist since it adheres to the inerrancy of the Bible, opposes theological liberalism, and embraces a complex and systematic world view in its own right. The characteristics of Christian fundamentalism will be analysed in detail in Chapter 6. Cox (1996: 303), on the other hand, identifies Christian fundamentalists with their prosaic view of the Bible and their cognitive conception of faith in the modern camp as modern by-products of the religious crisis of the twentieth century. McGuire looks at neo-Pentecostalism as 'a deviant religious minority with a distinct uncompromising worldview' (Hunt, Walter, and Hamilton 1997: 5). Neo-Pentecostalism is also interpreted as providing a sub-culture into which people could occasionally or permanently retreat from the intellectual and rational control of the impersonal modern world (Hunt, Walter, and Hamilton 1997). L. D'Souza (1996: 313) highlights the anti-modern nature of the Charismatic movement by classifying it as a socio-religious protest and a challenge to the dependence on the modern primacy of reason in the Churches. At the same time she does not term the Charismatic movement simply as an anti-institutional movement, but points out certain postmodern attributes such as the development of a 'new religious awareness' that acknowledges the need of individuals for an emotional and subjective experience of the supernatural in a rationally dominated world that has failed to provide answers.

Another backward-looking characteristic of Pentecostalism described by Cox (1996: 81–3) is its 'primal spirituality', along with primal speech, primal piety, and primal hope. This is an attempt by Pentecostals to restore the spiritual experience that began the Christian faith. Dawson (1998: 137) cites the works of Hunter and other commentators on

NRMs to indicate that NRMs represent a de-modernizing impulse, an attempt to provide a holistic sense of self in theory and in practice that transcends the constellation of limited instrumental roles recognized by modern mass society.

Walker, on the other hand, is convinced that the entire Pentecostal movement has been thoroughly modern, especially neo-Pentecostalism, which has been more open than its classical counterpart to the cultural obsessions of late-modernity (Hunt, Walter, and Hamilton 1997: 17–42). An important reason among the many he gives to emphasize this point is that Charismatics have unwittingly followed liberalism by allowing experience to become the touchstone of orthodoxy. This touchstone is not a return to New Testament Christianity, as is believed, but a thoroughly late-modern concern with the self and its satisfaction (Hunt, Walter, and Hamilton 1997: 36). One of the aims of Coleman's study of Protestant Charismatics (2000: 3) is to show that though earlier it was tempting to see them as an anti-modern and anachronistic revival of tradition, many features of their ideology and practice are well-adapted to modern and even postmodern cultural conditions.

While describing the Charismatic Renewal among the Baptists, McBain (Hunt, Walter, and Hamilton 1997: 43–59) points to the opposition that the Renewal faced from conservative forces within the Church as a sign that the Renewal was getting too modern. Hunt, Walter, and Hamilton (1997: 8) link ecumenism with liberalism and point out that with the emergence of the Charismatic movement in the 1960s, as Christians began to discover that they were brothers and sisters in the spirit, the Protestant–Roman Catholic divide began to reduce. Since the Charismatic movement brought in ecumenism, it is an indication of its modernizing tendency. While normally religious groups must either choose between their fundamentalist beliefs or compromise them by accepting modernizing trends, the Charismatics are very proficient in holding this tension—reacting against society while simultaneously celebrating a number of its major features (Hunt, Walter, and Hamilton 1997: 10).

Dawson (1998: 146–7) rejects the standard ways of differentiating anti-modernist NRMs from modernist NRMs by demonstrating how seemingly anti-modernist and modernist NRMs are as much alike as different. To illustrate this point, he cites Lucas's (1994) work that

Image 1 Teaching aid in the form of a wheel used by one of the Charismatic leaders to explain Christian life.

Source: These pictures regarding the daily lives of Pentecostal-Charismatic Christians have been taken by the author.

Image 2 Teaching aid in the form of a chart used by one of the Charismatic leaders to explain Christian family life.

Image 3 Pastor explaining the rite of water baptism to those who wish to become members of the church.

Image 4 Pastor praying over the person to be baptized.

Image 5 Water baptism being carried out through complete immersion in sea water.

Image 6 The baptized coming out as a new person.

Image 7 Depiction of heaven from the drama 'Heaven's Gates and Hell's Flames', which was staged in Panjim, Goa, in April 2008 by several neo-Pentecostal groups. The angel at the top of the stairs reads from the book of life and only if your name is in it you are permitted to enter the gates of heaven.

Image 8 Another depiction of Heaven from the play.

delineates the marked convergence and parallels between the orienta-tions of two seemingly very contrary NRMs, the Pentecostal–Charismatic revival and the New Age movements. If the Charismatic movement fits neither the anti-modern nor the modern mould, then is it a postmod-ern phenomenon? Richter (Hunt, Walter, and Hamilton 1997: 97–119) characterizes the 'Toronto Blessing' that broke out around 1994 at the Airport Vineyard Church, Toronto, as an attempt to prevent the Charismatic movement from ossifying and becoming like a formal Church organization dominated by a rational bureaucratic setup. The issue of the stagnation of the Catholic Charismatic movement is taken up in Chapter 2 in the section titled 'Routinization of Charisma and the Web-Like Structure of the Catholic Charismatic Renewal'. The much-reported and discussed Toronto Blessing was characterized by many unusual physical phenomena such as bodily weakness and falling to the ground; shaking, trembling, and convulsive bodily movements; uncontrollable laughter or wailing and inconsolable weeping; animal sounds; besides a heightened sense of the presence of God, prophetic insights into the future, and 'out of the body' mystical experiences (Hunt, Walter, and Hamilton 1997: 97). The Toronto Blessing, referred to as ultra- or hyper-modern by Walker (Hunt, Walter, and Hamilton 1997: 34), appears to indicate that the Pentecostal–Charismatic move-ment has journeyed a lot from the Charismatic outbreak in the main-line Churches in the 1960s and is indulging in spiritual innovations matching the social conditions of the contemporary world.

Those who argue about the postmodern nature of Pentecostal–Charismatic Christianity emphasize that it has become part of the entertainment industry of Western culture, and in order to compete in a postmodern world, it offers eye-catching wares and satisfies the impatient urge for religious experiences that give immediate gratifica-tion (Hunt, Walter, and Hamilton 1997: 12, 13). At the same time, the ecstatic religious experiences of 'now' can appear both ways—postmodern and anti-modern. Anderson (2004: 284) finds that a stress on 'Church planting' and the rampant individualism that creates a proliferation of new 'Churches' in Pentecostalism, some of which are no more than a handful of people, is a feature of this postmod-ern age. Martin (2002: 169) argues that one can either insist that Pentecostalism belongs to a wave of fundamentalism that is sweeping world religions in a last ditch defence against modernity or see it as an adaptable form of heart-work[5] and spiritual self-exploration breaking free of the restrictive protocols of enlightened reason into a new age of post-modernity.

Thus, Pentecostal–Charismatic Christianity today is a very complex religious phenomenon that has a variety of differing, often contradictory appraisals, by scholars of religion. Dawson (1998: 148–9) quotes from Beckford's study to show that Christian fundamentalist, Pentecostal, and Charismatic movements do not possess the hallmarks of the postmodernist sensibility such as immanence, playfulness, fragmentation, and so on. The question that arises from the discussion until now is whether the sociological frameworks of modernization or postmodernization are adequate to describe Pentecostal–Charismatic Christianity, which seems to sometimes possess simultaneously anti-modern, modern, and postmodern traits and which differs significantly from established, mainline Christianity. Questions such as whether the Pentecostal–Charismatic movement emerged in response to the process of modernization and whether Pentecostalism is anti-modern, modern, or postmodern will be taken up in the book, but my approach to these matters of definitions and 'isms' is similar to Beckford's position: 'My preference is to examine the emerging forms of the new spirituality and the range of occasions and places where it has an impact without worrying too much about definitional matters' (quoted in Dawson 1998: 148). The beliefs and ideology, the rites and rituals of the new Pentecostal–Charismatic Churches examined in this book exhibit features that appear at different times anti-modern, modern, and postmodern.

Locating the Geographical Area of Fieldwork

Having delved into a conceptual space through the analysis of relevant literature and having located NRMs of the Pentecostal–Charismatic type as the theoretical field of this study, I chose the state of Goa in India as the geographical area of my ethnographic fieldwork. I chose Goa because both the CCR, which entered Goa in 1974, and the numerous independent neo-Pentecostal groups that have sprung up in Goa since

[5] Heart-work constitutes ecstatic religious experiences that appeal to the heart of the Believer.

the 1980s have grown rapidly and spread all over Goa. Another reason for choosing Goa is that with its long colonial history of nearly 450 years of Portuguese rule with a distinct Latin Catholic influence, and a near total absence of Protestant Christianity, which strongly influenced the rest of India, Goa represents a rather unique religio-cultural case. The fact that I was born and brought up in Goa and am also interested in issues concerning Goan society, religion, and culture played an important part in my choice of Goa as the area of fieldwork.

Goa is a very small state with a total area of only 3,702 square kilometres, located on the west coast of India and bound by Maharashtra in the north, Karnataka in the south and east and the Arabian Sea in the west. Goa is a land of great natural beauty with many sun-kissed beaches, natural coves and lagoons, rivers, cascading waterfalls and gurgling streams, and a reasonably good though fast-declining forest cover.[6] The name 'Goa' seems to have been derived from Gomanta, which the Madras glossary connects with the Sanskrit 'go' (cow), making Goa mean 'cowherd's country' (Bhandari 1999: 7–8). Being rich in natural resources, the land has seen generations of human settlements. Various chieftains and kingdoms, both Hindu and Muslim, had held sway over the land of Goa till the Portuguese, under the leadership of Afonso de Albuquerque, in 1510, succeeded in capturing the city of Goa (present-day Old Goa). By the middle of the sixteenth century, the Portuguese extended their rule to four talukas known as Velhas Conquistas (Old Conquests), which became predominantly Christian (D'Costa 1965; Gune 1979). The Portuguese annexed the remaining seven talukas of Goa, known as Novas Conquistas (New Conquests) only by the end of the eighteenth century (Xavier 1993). The New Conquests are predominantly Hindu since the Portuguese, who were in a period of political and economic decline made no efforts to carry out large-scale conversions (Robinson 1998). Even today, the Old Conquests, where the bulk of industry and most of the educational, medical, banking, and other facilities are located, are more developed than the New Conquests, which are sparsely populated and contain the mines and forests that keep the coastal districts prospering (Newman 2001). All four new

---

[6] The government forests measure about 28.4 per cent of the total land area of Goa and are mostly confined to Satari, Sanguem, and Canacona talukas (Gune 1979: 34).

Christian groups belonging to the Catholic Charismatic movement and neo-Pentecostalism, from where ethnographic data for this study was gathered, are from the Old Conquests, where most of the Christians are found.

The twentieth century saw a lot of political uprising in Goa and the liberation of Dadra and Nagar Haveli in 1954 gave a further fillip to the Goan freedom movement (Bhandari 1999; Gomes 2004). Nearly 450 years of Portuguese rule came to an end on 19 December 1961 and Goa became part of India as the Union Territory of Goa, Daman and Diu till 30 May 1987 when it attained statehood. The same year, the Goa, Daman and Diu Official Language Act, 1987, was passed and Konkani in Devanagiri script was declared as the official language of Goa. Newman (2001: 71) describes this event as *Konkani Mai* (Mother Konkani) ascending her rightful throne at last after centuries of suppression by the Portuguese and 25 years of neglect by Goan governments. All the Hindus and the majority of Christians in Goa speak Konkani, with the Christians using the Roman script. An increasingly large number of people from the urban and also from rural areas speak English, while a few of them still speak Portuguese.

Administratively, Goa is divided into two districts—North Goa and South Goa—with a total of 11 talukas comprising 359 villages and 44 towns. Goa's population of 1,458,545 accounts for only 0.12 per cent of the country's population (Census of India 2011). The rapid urbanization of Goa since the 1960s is seen in the difference between the portion of the population residing in urban areas (62.2 per cent) and in rural areas (37.8 per cent). That is why two out of the four new Christian groups (50 per cent) that I chose for my ethnographic study are urban groups. Although the popular perception of Goa is that it is Christian, only 25.1 per cent of the total population are Christians, while Hindus (66.1 per cent) constitute the majority (Census of India 2011). Muslims (8.3 per cent) are a small but rapidly growing minority. Despite the high literacy rate of 87.4 per cent, the sex ratio is rather low—968 women per 1,000 men. It is interesting to note that the sex ratio for Christians is 1,129, much higher than the state average, while it is much lower for Hindus (929), and still lower for Muslims (905). The religion-based differentials in the sex ratio assume significance when we study the Catholic Charismatic movement in Goa, which has more than 80 per cent women.

The caste composition of Goa is not analysed here since caste is not one of the important threads of discussion in the book. The chief castes found in Goa are in no way different from other states of India. One finds in Goa the Brahmins (such as the Gaud Saraswats and Chittapavans), who are 15 per cent; Kshatriyas (such as the Marathas, Bhandaris, and Gomantak Marathas), who are 12 per cent; Vaishyas or Vanis, who are 9 per cent, and the lower Shudras (such as the Kharvi, Gaudas, Kunbis, and Velips), who are 41 per cent (Singh 1993). The main Scheduled Castes in Goa are Bhangi, Chambar, Mahars, and Mang (Singh 1993). The main issues that occur in many of the studies on Goan history, society, and culture, with specific reference to Christianity in Goa, are debates on conversions, caste among Christians, questions of Goan identity vis-à-vis Indian identity and its link with Catholic identity, questions of representation in the various forms of print media, language issues, migration and the insider–outsider issue, and so forth.[7] Many of these issues come up in this study in relation to the new Christian groups in Goa.

Personal Space of the Author: Both Native Anthropologist and Outsider

At one level, this is an anthropological study of the Catholic Charismatics and neo-Pentecostals in Goa. However, it is not a conventional ethnography as has been practised in anthropology, but a multi-sited ethnography (Marcus 1995). Ethnography moves from its conventional single-site location, usually a village, a town, or a slum, contextualized by macroconstructions of a larger social order, to multiple sites of observation and participation that cross-cut 'dichotomies such as the "local" and the "global", the "life-world" and the "system"' (Marcus 1995: 95). Multi-sited ethnography, which arises in response to empirical changes in the postmodern world and therefore to transformed locations of cultural production claims that any ethnography of a cultural formation in the world system cannot be understood only in terms of the conventional 'single-site mise-en-scène' of ethnographic research (Marcus 1995: 97).

[7] See Bhandari 1999; Cabral 1986; Costa 2002; D'Costa 1965; D'Souza 1975; Gomes 2003; 2004; Larsen 1998; Malekandathil 2008; Mendonca 2002; Newman 2001; R. Pinto 2007; Robinson 1998; Sinha 2002.

This mode of ethnography is located within the new spheres of inter-disciplinary work, including media studies, science and technology studies, and cultural studies broadly. Thus, this study of production of globalized forms of Christianity and the Charismatic habitus that move smoothly from the local to the global in a postmodern world operate simultaneously at several different physical locales—Siolim, Mapusa, Merces, and Panaji in the state of Goa. This is not an ethnographic study of a particular village or a single site but is an exercise in mapping out a terrain at different levels and in different locales. This multi-sited eth-nographic approach is used right through the study. This study is thus a contribution to the expanding ethnographic literature on non-Hindu communities in India and to the sociology of religion in India.

The fact that I was a 'local' meant that I shared the identity of a 'native' anthropologist with my respondents (Madan 1989; Mascarenhas-Keyes 1987; Narayan 1993; Robinson 1998), but my identity as a Catholic priest proved to be both a boon and a bane in the field. During the fieldwork, spread over nearly two years, I visited and interacted with people of different backgrounds, many of whom became good friends and shared much more than the necessary information. In the case of the neo-Pentecostals, I attended their Sunday Praise and Worship, their small prayer cell meetings in different houses, accompanied them on their evangelization trips, and attended their social and family func-tions, including weddings, birthdays, baptisms, and picnics. In the case of the Catholic Charismatics, I attended their weekly prayer meetings that are normally held in the Church and other programmes of the Goa Service Team (explained in Chapters 1 and 2), such as Leader's camp, night vigils, and so forth. On all these occasions, I keenly observed things around and talked informally with the people present. These participant observations, informal conversations, and formal inter-views with prayer group leaders, pastors, priests, and other members, besides access to the printed magazines, newsletters, pamphlets, and audio-visual material on the movement became the main source of my ethnographic data. At the same time, I was cautious to avoid 'objectify-ing' or 'reading' the given reality of the Charismatic world, but was alert to the interplay of voices in the field. When a movement is still young, as neo-Pentecostalism or the CCR in Goa, written sources are not easily available and dependence upon oral tradition and personal observa-tion is so much the greater. Although neo-Pentecostal and Catholic

Charismatic groups have now been in existence for over 20 years, their written sources are still largely informal in nature. Thus, corroborating the field data with objective and dependable written texts remains a problem in the study of NRMs.

In my dealings with the members of the CCR, my identity as a priest, who was ready to visit their homes and spend time listening to their everyday problems, their hopes and aspirations, and their views on how the Catholic Church should be run immediately brought me closer to them and many of them shared much more information than I expected. On the other hand, my identity as a Catholic priest did separate me from the members of the neo-Pentecostal Churches, since mutual animosity and tension exists between the old, politically and socially dominant Catholic community and the new Pentecostal 'upstarts', and this is aggravated by the rather unflattering manner in which the Catholic clergy portray the neo-Pentecostals from the pulpits. One of the methodological assumptions with which I had entered the field was that my identity as an 'outsider' belonging to a competing religious organization would not come in the way of collecting reliable ethnographic data. According to Robinson (1998: 29), 'even "outsiders" may establish valuable and sensitive ties with persons in the societies they study over a period of time'. While my neo-Pentecostal respondents treated me intimately, like a friend, sharing warmly their hospitality with me, when it came to discussions on religion many of them would become argumentative and attack Roman Catholicism and sharply criticize Catholics, including me.

There were several occasions when I was sharply questioned on my 'non-biblical' Catholic beliefs and practices and I had to restrain myself from retorting with a theological riposte. Once at a prayer cell meeting, one of the women participants, who was a former Catholic, in a rather agitated tone asked me (during an interview at Porvorim on 1 August 2008):

> How can you, a Catholic priest, attend our Sunday worship? If I had to attend mass in a Catholic Church I would be like fish out of water. I would feel strong opposition and disagreement within me and would find all that meaningless. How can you accept our worship which is so different from Catholic worship?

To this provocative query, my rather diplomatic answer was, 'Both of us worship the same Jesus Christ. I look for similarities and not differences between us.' When I was in the field, I always tried to keep in mind that the ethnographer is not the experienced observer who holds unquestionable rights of authorship, but is a scribe and archivist who dialogues with the informants, who are co-authors. The disposition to be non-judgemental and to listen with patience to my respondents, to put on the attitude of an empathetic observer by putting myself in their shoes, was not very easy. Initially, I found myself evaluating all the field data and my respondents from my Catholic background, and it was only gradually that I learnt to understand their beliefs and practices from their perspective, without any comparisons. At the same time, my identity as a member of the Catholic Church and thus a 'suspicious outsider' had unfortunate repercussions on my fieldwork. The pastors of both the neo-Pentecostal groups from which I gathered data refused to allow me to administer questionnaires to the members of their groups during the Sunday prayer meeting to elicit a socio-economic profile of each member. Both of them were afraid that the information I would gather through the questionnaires might fall into the wrong hands, in other words, either in the hands of the Catholic Church hierarchy or the right-wing Hindu nationalist forces. This brings me to an important point concerning the relationship between the new Christian groups and the Hindus. This was referred to in the earlier section in which the new Christian groups were being classified using Melton's typology of religions. According to Melton's methodology, to classify a new religion it is necessary to determine its relation to the religious tradition that is dominant in that society. In the case of Pentecostal–Charismatic Christianity in Goa, the dominant religious tradition is Hinduism.

New Christian Groups and Hindutva Forces[8]

Right-wing Hindu nationalism in India began with the formation of an organization called Rashtriya Swayamsevak Sangh (RSS), the mother of

---

[8] Hindutva is the essence of the Hindu faith and the Hindu identity, the 'Hinduness'. The Supreme Court in a judgement in 1995 has held that Hindutva is a way of life of the Indian people and not just a religious practice. In this book, Hindutva implies right-wing Hindu fundamentalism, different from Hinduism or the definition of the Supreme Court.

the Sangh Parivar,[9] at Nagpur, Maharashtra, in 1925 by Keshav Baliram Hedgewar, who was profoundly influenced by Vinayak Damodar Savarkar's work 'Hindutva: Who is a Hindu?', one of the basic texts defining 'Hindutva' ideology.[10] Already before the founding of the RSS, organizations such as Arya Samaj (1875), the All-India Hindu Mahasabha (1915), and advocates of Hinduism such as U.N. Mukherji, writer of a series of articles in 1909 in *The Bengales* titled 'Hindus—A Dying Race', began propagating the idea that the growth of Christianity and the challenge of Christian proselytization by foreign missionaries represented a serious threat to Hinduism. The RSS grew and gave rise to several other important organizations, constituting the Sangh Parivar, including the political party of BJP. Though the Hindutva movement began nearly a century ago, it is only from the 1980s that it found its moorings and crystallized itself as a social, political, and ideological force by mobilizing the new urban middle class, the predominantly upper-caste traders, professionals, and the petty bourgeoisie that was spreading in the cities and small towns of the Hindi heartland of India. The growth and expansion of the Hindutva forces is built around the dream of a 'Hindu Rashtra' (Hindu nation), in which an external enemy in the form of the foreign 'Muslims' and, more recently, the 'Christians' is identified. This foreign enemy has to be excluded, hated, and fought against, and the rest of the Indians are projected as a homogenous, model, Indian (Hindu) society with emphasis on each one's 'dharma'[11] for the harmonious running of society (Jaffrelot 2017). Madhav Sadashiv Golwalkar (1966: 155–9),[12] the high priest and theoretician of Hindutva ideology, held that the Church, as a worldwide organization

---

[9] Sangh Parivar is the family or umbrella body of different militant Hindu nationalist organizations such as RSS, Vishwa Hindu Parishad, Bajrang Dal, Bharatiya Janata Party (BJP; the political wing), and other recent organizations.

[10] Most of the analysis on Hindutva is taken from 'Hindu Rashtra: Dream or Nightmare', unpublished paper submitted by Savio Abreu as partial fulfilment of the requirements for the degree of B.Th., Vidya Jyoti College of Theology, New Delhi, 2001.

[11] Dharma has multiple meanings in Hinduism, but here it means religious duty.

[12] Madhav Sadashiv Golwalkar, also known as Shri Guruji, was the second Sarsanghchalak of the RSS.

with the intention of increasing its membership in the name of Christ, is a political power and thus is a threat to Hinduism and the dream of Hindu Rashtra. Though the primary concern of most Hindutvadis in the twentieth century was the Muslim threat, fears about Christianity never faded away completely and from the late 1990s there has been a sharp increase in Hindu–Christian conflict. The rising anti-Christian violence from the 1990s was accompanied by an increasingly promi-nent, sophisticated, and standardized intellectual critique of Indian Christianity. Beginning with Gandhi, who was the first to popularize a principled critique of conversion, and later Swarup, Goel, Shourie, and others, this intellectual critique of Christian evangelism articulated several grievances such as: (*a*) evangelism and the attempt to convert another person to one's faith is a socially disruptive endeavour; (*b*) evangelistic Christians in India use their superior access to Western wealth and technology to lure non-Christians into the fold; and (*c*) that Christianization entails a process of denationalization (Bauman 2015: 55–69).

In the light of militant, well-organized, and well-financed Hindutva forces, and a prominent and sophisticated intellectual critique of Indian Christianity, the mainline Protestant, Catholic, and Syrian Orthodox Churches tend to appear as a minority that is divided, compromising, and weak,[13] and thus the new Pentecostal–Charismatic movements 'represent a defence of a fragile but genuine Christian stake in the social order, a marking out of identities and a very Indian reclamation of living presences and concrete powers even if some of the organizational mod-els were clearly made in the USA' (Martin 2002: 155). Newman (2001: 5) believes that distortions and corruption of communal politics is the worst enemy of modern India and his book *Of Umbrellas, Goddesses and Dreams: Essays on Goan Culture and Society* is a refutation of the view that Goa is merely a land where Catholics, Hindus, and Muslims of a large number of sects and castes happen to find themselves living; that Catholics are 'foreign-elements', Hindus are all Maharashtrians, and Muslims potential Pakistanis. Newman's views on communal politics are similar to my own views, which shape and influence this study. In a sense, this study is a rebuttal to the communal propaganda and divisive

[13] For more details on the Christian minority discourse in India see Abreu (2009).

politics that threaten an inclusive and accommodating Indian identity. In several parts of India, Christian fundamentalism has emerged and grown as a reaction to the rise of Hindu fundamentalism that has targeted the Christian community and their institutions across the nation. This uneasy and tense relationship between the Pentecostal–Charismatic Churches and the Hindutva forces, and its implications for these Churches is one of the important themes analysed in this book.

This work deals with the impact of the fastest growing religious movement of the twentieth century on the history, society, culture, and everyday life-practices of the Goans. Before studying how Pentecostal–Charismatic Christianity has impacted and has been influenced by Goan society and culture, we need to analyse the causes—both local and global—and the historical roots of the emerging movement. Chapter 1 is a historical account of the emergence of the Pentecostal–Charismatic movement in Goa. Chapter 2 shifts back to the present structure and organization of the Catholic Charismatic and neo-Pentecostal move-ments. The chapter also describes the profile of their members. Chapters 3 to 6 deal with the ethnographic data on the two movements. Chapter 3 is an elucidation of the process of identity formation among the Catholic Charismatics and the neo-Pentecostals with the recreation of the New Testament Church (NTC) as the guiding motif. The world of symbols of the Charismatics with their concepts of sacred and profane and the structuring Charismatic habitus are important to understand in order to make sense of their world view and ethos. This is done in the next chapter. Chapter 5 deals with the use of authoritative symbols and discourses while analysing and comparing the life-cycle rituals of the Catholic Charismatics and the neo-Pentecostals. Chapter 6 deals with a different strand of the Pentecostal movement—its exclusivist and fundamentalist notions and the resultant terrains of conflict in Goan society. The final chapter attempts to bring all these different themes together and build a cohesive, though not necessarily conclusive, mosaic of Pentecostal–Charismatic Christianity in a pluralist and non-Christian context.

1 Entry of New Christian Movements in Goa

This chapter deals with the emergence of Pentecostal–Charismatic movements in the state of Goa. It is carried out in the revealing light of the historical encounter of the Goan people with Portuguese colonial rule, which established and expanded Roman Catholicism in the region. The narration of the tale of the Pentecostal–Charismatic movement found in Goa today compels one to analyse the historical context of Christianity in Goa and locate the proper place of these more recent movements in the historical trajectory of Goan Christianity. This chapter will commence with the entry of the Portuguese into Goa and the subsequent Christianization of the region. The subsequent section, while briefly narrating the history of Christianity in post-liberation Goa, will locate the entry of Charismatic Christianity into Goa in its proper sociopolitical and historical context. The existing Pentecostal–Charismatic Churches in Goa cannot be understood without a historical exploration of the origins and growth of the worldwide Pentecostal movement, which will be dealt with in later sections of the chapter. This chapter, which begins with the local and then turns to the universal, will also focus towards the end on the local oral history of the Pentecostal–Charismatic groups in Goa.

While there is much debate among scholars of Pentecostalism about how to differentiate between 'Pentecostal' and 'Charismatic', there is general consensus that the term 'Charismatic Movement' refers to the phenomenon of baptism of the spirit and manifestation of spiritual gifts that occurred in the older, historic, or mainline Churches since the 1960s, known as the 'second wave', as opposed to the Pentecostal denominations that emerged in the first wave of Pentecostalism known as Classical Pentecostalism. With the development of 'non-denominational' Charismatic Churches and organizations a decade or so later (the 'third wave'), the term was expanded to include all those movements outside denominational or classical Pentecostalism that exhibited the manifestation of spiritual gifts. Also, the terms neo-Pentecostals and neo-Charismatics have been used to describe these latter Churches. For the sake of clarity, in my work I will be using the terms neo-Pentecostals, Catholic Charismatics, Charismatics, and Pentecostals with specific fixed meanings (see Table 1.1). All the non-denominational and independent Pentecostal groups (the third wave) that emerged from the 1970s onwards and the manifestation of the Pentecostal phenomenon within the historic or mainline Churches since the 1960s, except the Catholic Church, will be referred to as neo-Pentecostals or Born-Again Christians. The term Believers commonly used by the Catholics in Goa to refer to the neo-Pentecostals will also

Table 1.1 Nomenclature of Pentecostal–Charismatic Movement

Sr. no.	Name	Meaning
1.	Neo-Pentecostals, also Born-Again Christians or Believers	Members of the non-denominational, independent Pentecostal–Charismatic groups (third wave) that came up from 1970s onwards and Pentecostalism which started within the Protestant Churches since 1950s (second wave)
2.	Catholic Charismatics	Members of the Catholic Charismatic Renewal, Pentecostalism within the Catholic Church (second wave)
3.	Charismatics	Both Neo-Pentecostals and Catholic Charismatics
4.	Pentecostals	Usually Classical Pentecostals (first wave), but in certain contexts could mean all members of Pentecostal–Charismatic Christianity, all three waves

Source: Author.

be used occasionally, depending on the context. Since the major focus of this work is a comparison between the trajectories of the Pentecostal phenomenon within the highly structured Catholic Church and within the highly flexible and unstructured independent Churches and sects, the Pentecostal phenomenon in the Catholic Church is treated separately. It will be referred to as the CCR and its members will be called 'Catholic Charismatics' as opposed to neo-Pentecostals. Whenever the term 'Charismatics' is used, it includes both neo-Pentecostals and Catholic Charismatics, that is, people belonging to both the second wave and third wave. 'Pentecostals' would normally imply the older Classical Pentecostals or people belonging to the first wave, but depending on the context it could also have a much broader meaning, namely all the members of the Pentecostal–Charismatic Christianity, that is, people belonging to the first, second, and third waves.

Christianization of Goa by the Portuguese

Most historians tend to associate Christianity in Goa with the advent of the Portuguese in 1510, though some historians such as Cosme Costa, Pius Malekandathil, and H.O. Mascarenhas argue that Christianity was present in Goa before the Portuguese arrived. While archaeological and other evidence indicate some Christian presence in pre-Portuguese Goa (Costa 2002: 10–11,122–3; Moraes 1964: 154–5), hardly anything can be ascertained about the nature and extent of that presence, given the lack of historical documents and the absence of any well-established Christian community when the Portuguese arrived in Goa. So, the present-day Christian community in Goa traces its roots to the advent of the Portuguese, whose colonial ventures were in the form of a mercantile expansion couched in a military and ecclesiastical mould. Fired with the great colonial dream of serving the Crown and the Cross, Afonso de Albuquerque, at the invitation of the admiral of the Vijayanagara fleet captured the island of Goa (present-day Tiswadi) in 1510. The Portuguese acquired Bardez, Mormugao, and Salcete in 1543 and the New Conquests of Bicholim, Pernem, Ponda, Sanguem, Quepem, Canacona, and Satari by 1788 (Cabral 1986: ix–xvi; B.G. D'Souza 1975). The close link between the missionary activities and the political interests of the Portuguese is noticed in the functioning of the Padroado system, which made the Portuguese king the effective head of the Catholic Church within his overseas territories with the power to nominate bishops, endow religious institutions with funds from royal revenues, and license religious orders and individual clergy who sought passage to his colonies. Most of the early missionary work in Goa was done by religious orders such as the Franciscans (1517), the Jesuits (1540), the Dominicans (1548), and the Augustinians (1572).

The Portuguese world view that saw the world as two—Christians and pagans or infidels—resulted in a close linking of conversions and the establishment of Portuguese rule in a foreign land. This link can be seen in Albuquerque's efforts at indirectly promoting conversions to Catholicism through the system of *casados*. Casados were Portuguese nationals who married local women and settled down in Goa or elsewhere in other Portuguese colonies. The local women, mostly the young wives and daughters of slain Muslim officers, were converted and married. Albuquerque's aim was that the offspring of such marriages, who would be Catholic, would be loyal to the Portuguese Crown and in due course of time there would be a substantial number of loyal subjects, who could be drawn into the armed forces. He knew that territorial expansion would necessitate more and more recruitment to the armed forces. Regarding the question of conversion, some authors argue from the perspective of the converting missionaries that conversions were genuine as they arose out of true commitment to the faith and not out of force or out of a desire to gain material benefits (D'Costa 1965; Heras 1935). Other writers emphasize that conversions were based on force, the threat of violence, and the lure of material rewards, with the local population helpless in the face of the missionaries (B.G. D'Souza 1975; Pereira 1978; Priolkar 1961). Then those writers, who attempt to strike a balance between these two opposing views, do not make this distinction between temporal and spiritual motivations for conversions, arguing that whereas the Portuguese closed in on the Hindu society with force, choice was exercised by those tracked down to adopt Catholicism, if only within the limits of the given situation (Gomes 2003; Mendonca 2002; Robinson 1998). In order to bring about conversions, the Portuguese used a system of privileges to attract Believers to the faith, which involved setting aside jobs and offices for those who converted, while denying them to those who refused to do so. Since this method of conversion succeeded only in small measure, the Portuguese launched a stronger attack on Hinduism, destroying all places of worship and idols and prohibiting religious practices.

The Church and the missionaries taught the converts about Catholic liturgical celebrations, feasts of Christian saints and Mother Mary, Church-centred celebrations of the life-cycle rites of the individual, Christian symbols and prayers, and Catholic mysticism and spirituality. Gradually among the converts, the Hindu religious rites and symbols were replaced by Catholic ones. Villages constituted parishes and each parish had a parish Church with one or more priests looking after its pastoral governance. The debate on conversions and methods of evangelism and missiology that have been briefly discussed previously in relation to the Catholicization of Portuguese Goa are issues that will be discussed in detail in this book with respect to the Pentecostal–Charismatic Churches and which will highlight several characteristics of these Churches.

Christianity in Post-colonial Goa

While the history of Christianity in Portuguese Goa was a narrative of the entry and expansion of Roman Catholicism, Christianity in post-colonial Goa has expanded to include Protestant and Pentecostal denominations and non-denominational forms of Christianity such as neo-Pentecostals. The Catholic Church in post-liberation Goa has undergone a discernible shift in its image and public presence. While the colonial Church tried to be where the ruler was, the post-colonial Church has tried to be where the laity was (Sinha 2002: 118). Since the liberation of Goa in 1961, the Catholic Church got involved in many social, economic, and political issues and struggles. The first major struggle that the Catholic Church participated in was the anti-merger movement. In December 1962, general elections were held for 30 assembly and 2 parliamentary seats with a local party, the Maharashtrawadi Gomantak Party (MGP), emerging successful, winning 16 assembly seats and both the parliamentary seats. Since the MGP, portraying an image of the champion of the lower-caste Hindus, got elected on the election plank of 'immediate merger of Goa with the state of Maharashtra', they, along with the help of Congress supporters in Maharashtra, began agitating for the merger of Goa with Maharashtra. In the agitations that followed, the Goans got crystallized into two camps, mergerists and anti-mergerists, Marathiwadis and Konkaniwadis, Hindus and Christians. To calm down the highly polarized situation, the central government decided to have a referendum on the political status of Goa in 1967.

The Church fully supported the stand of the anti-mergerists, which included the Christians and the main opposition party, United Goans Party (UGP), demanding separate political status for Goa. In this campaign against merger, the priests gave political speeches from the pulpits and marched in the streets with the laity, often working along with the Hindu Saraswat Brahmins who also vociferously opposed the merger. During the one month of campaigning before the opinion poll, the MGP almost wholly concentrated on the Hindu electorate advocating the stand that a merger with the huge Hindu majority of Maharashtra would put an end to Catholic domination forever (Newman 2001). However, the MGP dream came crashing down with 54.20 per cent voting against the merger. While the Christians and Saraswat Brahmins opposed the merger along expected lines, what surprised the MGP was that a significant number of non-Saraswat lower-caste Hindus had also voted against merger as seen from the voting patterns. In Bicholim taluka, where Christians constituted only 6 per cent of the population, about 30 per cent of the votes went against the merger (Sinha 2002: 119). This campaign against merger with Maharashtra made the Church realize the importance of Christian–Hindu solidarity for the protection of Goa's separate culture and identity.

As a follow-up to the victory in the opinion poll, the Catholic Church backed the Konkani movement, with the aim of carving a separate identity for Goa. The MGP dominated Goan politics for the first decade and a half and received its major support from the Hindu areas. It vigorously promoted Marathi, the language of Maharashtrian expansionism, and there was a fear that the expansionists would enter and occupy Goa through the back door. To counter this threat the Church strove to build a stronger Christian–Hindu solidarity to defeat the Marathiwadis and this solidarity got strengthened with a lot of non-Brahmin Hindus joining the language movement. Shenoi Goembab, who later came to be regarded as the father of the Konkani Movement, addressed his first gathering at the Rachol Seminary. Sinha (2002) holds that the Konkani movement was a political movement, not a linguistic one with the Church using it to ensure a separate status for Goa. In pursuit of this goal of securing a separate political status for Goa, the Church backed Christian political leaders and other Goans in campaigning for the grant of statehood to Goa. While the language struggle culminated in the passing of the Official Language Act that declared Konkani as the official language of Goa on 4 February 1987, Prime Minister Rajiv Gandhi, fulfilling the implicit promise his grandfather had made in 1963 regarding Goa's distinctive personality, granted Goa full statehood on 30 May 1987. In spite of the withdrawal of political patronage and economic support with the exit of the Portuguese rulers in 1961, the Catholic Church continued to exert sociopolitical influence in post-liberation Goa through its involvement in social and political issues by collaborating with non-governmental organizations (NGOs) and the majority Hindu community. This involvement and influence of the Catholic Church in post-colonial Goan society and polity is criticized by the more recent Pentecostal–Charismatic movement as a sign of worldly corruption of the original sacred message given by Jesus in the New Testament.

Entry of Syrian Christians in Goa

From 1961 onwards, the state experienced rapid economic growth. With the departure of the Portuguese, massive public funding was earmarked for development projects and, as a result, industry, mining, tourism, agricultural productivity, mechanized fishing, banking, real estate, education, health care, and business all started to develop and expand. All these new industries and public sector ventures required a lot of skilled workers and the period after liberation witnessed a huge influx of migrant workers into the state. The mining boom, which began in the 1950s and got further boost after 1961, also led to an inflow of workers, especially from neighbouring states. This is reflected in the sudden increase in the population of Goa from 1961 to 1971. From 589,997 in 1961, the total population rose to 795,120, an increase of 34.8 per cent. This is much higher than the subsequent decadal growth rates of the total population: 26.7 per cent from 1971 to 1981, 16 per cent from 1981 to 1991, and 15.2 per cent from 1991 to 2001.[1] Among

[1] The population analysis is taken from various censuses and other works such as *Censo da Populacao* 1903; 1916; *Anuario Estatistico* 1950; 1955; Census of India 1991; 2001; Christovam 1882; Fonseca 1878.

the people who came to Goa seeking their fortunes were a few Syrian Christians from Kerala. Initially a priest would come from Mangalore to cater to their religious needs. For many years, their liturgical services were conducted in St Inez Church and Bathlem Chapel. The first Syrian Christian congregation was established on 17 January 1967 and named St Mary's Orthodox Syrian Church. The present building of St Mary's Orthodox Syrian Church, located at Ribandar, was ready only in 1979. Just before that, in 1978, another Syrian Christian Church came up in the town of Vasco da Gama. This Church, which came up on military area, mainly caters to the Keralites who work in the Navy. The Orthodox Syrian Christians belong to the Orthodox or Eastern Churches, which separated from the Catholic Church in 1054 AD. The current membership of the Orthodox or Eastern Churches worldwide is around 215 million (Barrett et al. 2001: 4, 12). The number of Orthodox Syrian Christians in Goa is small, as they comprise only migrants from Kerala. This number keeps fluctuating due to transfers and new arrivals.

Entry of Evangelical Christian Groups in Goa

According to oral sources, the Methodists came to Goa in 1969 and did evangelical work in a few areas of Goa under the leadership of a lady pastor. Today the Methodist Church is located at Campal, Panaji, with a congregation of nearly 500 people catering mainly to settlers from South India. The Seventh Day Adventist Church also came to Goa around 1967–72 and two pastors, Dawn and Burns, were actively preaching the gospel in Panaji and Vasco.[2] The Indian Pentecostal Church arrived in Goa in 1971 and initially focused only on the diaspora of the Keralites until 1981. Due to financial difficulties and cultural barriers, the work was not effective and began to decline. From 1989 onwards, with new pastors coming to Goa, they began to cater to the natives of Goa and slowly the ministry began to expand. At present, the Indian Pentecostal Church has seven Churches in Goa and caters mainly to migrants from South India. All their leaders and pastors continue to come mainly from the South. Around the same time, in 1972, an independent evangelical group called the Vasco Brethren Assembly was started by a Keralite, C. John.

---

[2] Most of the data in this section on various Christian Churches is taken from Fernandes (2007).

This group began with five members, grew to large numbers, and has subsequently witnessed splits and divisions with members moving to other congregations in Goa. Bethel House of Worship was the first independent Church started by a pastor of Goan origin, Evangelista Dias, in 1979. He began with just three families at Assolna, South Goa, and has presently grown to 150 members and has shifted to the town of Margao.

The 1980s can be described as the decade of the mushrooming of neo-Pentecostal Churches. The year 1987 saw the emergence of two prominent neo-Pentecostal Churches, the New Life Fellowship and New Frontiers International. The former under the banner of New Life Fellowship, Mumbai, began simultaneously in Vasco under Pastor Joseph D'Cruz and in Panaji under Pastor Arc D'Cruz. At present, New Life Fellowship has five Churches in Goa catering mainly to Goans and have services mainly in Konkani and English. The other prominent neo-Pentecostal Church, the New Frontiers International was launched in Gogol, Margao, by Pastor Duncan from the UK with the help of a team from Mumbai. Today, they have spread all over Goa having Churches in the major towns of Mapusa, Vasco, Panaji, and two in Margao and cater to all sections of society. The 1990s and 2000s have seen a lot of expansion and many new neo-Pentecostal Churches coming into Goa. Among the prominent ones are the Assemblies of God, which came in 1993 and have five congregations at present and the Believer's Church, which came in 1999 and have 11 congregations at present. Most of these Churches cater to the migrant community and their services are in Hindi, Telegu, Kannada, or Malayalam.

Changing Image of the Catholic Church in Post-colonial Goa

The transportation network of roads, bridges, and public transport that developed after 1961 brought every part of the state within a few hours' bus journey. By 1985–86 every village in Goa had been connected by electricity and by all-weather roads. Goa's per capita income was ₹17,406 against the national average of ₹10,151 in 1999–2000 (Sinha 2002: 174). However, all this progress came at a price. Tourism became the main industry in Goa generating lot of employment and foreign exchange, the tourism boom reflected in the growth from 450 hotel beds in 1961 to 30,617 beds in 2000, but there were a lot of unhealthy side effects (Statistical Hand Book of Goa 2001). Since the early 1980s the Catholic Church had directly or indirectly backed several NGOs that were speaking out against the ill effects of tourism on local culture. One such social struggle was the large agitation launched by the Church against the commercialized Carnival festival. After three years of campaigning against the vulgarity and obscenity in the Carnival floats that were against traditional Goan moral values, the Church and the NGOs backed by it forced the government to withdraw its patronage to corporate-sponsored Carnival floats, though the sponsored parade reappeared in 1993. In recent years, the Catholic Church has also been taking up struggles and programmes for raising awareness among clergy and the laity about human rights, environmental protection, rights of children, women and the marginalized, need for a peaceful and just society, corruption, religious freedom, and inter-religious dialogue.

Two images of the Catholic Church that have emerged in postcolonial Goa and which have fed into each other are: first, a Church that is socially active and ready to tackle the roots rather than the effects of social injustice and inequality; and second, a Church with the laity that promotes inter-religious dialogue and tries to build Hindu–Christian solidarity in the fight against social injustice. The traditional Church, which had enjoyed state patronage in Portuguese Goa, had been involved in charitable service to the poor without ever tackling the system of exploitation, which gave rise to poverty, inequality, and discrimination. In post-liberation Goa, especially since the 1990s, the Church has periodically attacked the class of 'unscrupulous' politicians, who it claims are out to destroy Goa's ecology, culture, and identity. Both the previous and the present Archbishops have issued circulars and statements during the elections warning people against the monster of corruption and asking them to support 'good' candidates, those who were not tainted by corruption and communalism.[3] Two of the diocesan bodies, the Council for Social Justice and Peace and Diocesan Centre for Social Communications Media have served as the arms of the radical Church involved in fighting for people's issues and in the process have assisted in the metamorphosis of the Church

[3] See *Renewal* (2007). Also Barbosa (2004).

from a pro-state, conservative, highly institutionalized, and hierarchical institution to a people's Church that is more radical and egalitarian, and less institutionalized. At the same time, a popular perception that emerges from newspaper articles and letters to the editor is that the Catholic Church is too conservative and cautious in its approach to issues of social and economic inequality.

Changing Religious Composition and Caste Equations

The changing face of the Church has met with strong resistance not only inside the Church but also outside it. The Church has tried to make the Hindus join its fight against social injustice but the Hindus have been wary of the intentions of the Catholic Church, given its role in history. This situation has been changing in the present century with increased collaboration and participation of people from both the communities in the recent agitations against the regional plan and special economic zones (SEZs). The Church's attempt to build a Hindu–Christian solidarity and promote inter-religious dialogue between the Hindus and Christians is partly a compulsion of the dramatically changing demographic profile of Goa, which has changed from a Christian Goa to a Hindu Goa. Though statistics are merely indicative, the census data from the 1851 census until the 2011 census indicate that the religious composition of Goa has changed a lot. In 1851 Goa was a Christian state with 63.8 per cent of the population being Christian. Christians were reduced to just 42.2 per cent in 1950, and they were further reduced to 25.1 per cent in 2011. The Hindus, on the other hand, increased from 35.4 per cent in 1851 to 66.1 per cent in 2011.[4] In such a changed environment, the efforts of the Catholic Church to build Hindu–Christian solidarity and promote inter-religious dialogue is at some level a struggle for survival and for remaining relevant.

Another impulse for promoting inter-religious dialogue has been the emergence of the ecumenical movement in the post-Vatican II Catholic Church, which recognized that there were divine elements in

---

[4] All analysis of the population statistics of Goa is taken from various censuses and other works such as *Censo da Populacao* 1903; 1916; *Anuario Estatistico* 1950; 1955; Census of India 1991; 2011; Christovam 1882; Fonseca 1878.

other faiths. Caplan (1987b: 161–2) in his study on Protestantism in South India found that the strong commitment to the 'social gospel', a direct legacy of the dominant liberal theological emphasis within missionary circles which gained ascendancy in the early twentieth century, led to a more positive conceiving of relationships to persons of other faiths. Though the post-colonial Church does not enjoy state patronage like the Church in colonial Goa and Christians have been reduced to a minority compared to the Hindus, the Church has repeatedly demonstrated its clout in being able to bring out on the streets thousands of lay Christians, whenever it has wanted to demonstrate about any sociocultural issues that it has taken up.

With the end of Portuguese rule, many of the agricultural workers and small farmers started working on ships, in foreign countries or filling lower-level government jobs in Goa's cities. Migration had begun to some extent in the mid- and late-nineteenth century and picked up in the first few decades of the twentieth century. This process of mostly Christian men going out to work on ships or in the Gulf or taking up other jobs unrelated to their earlier occupations within the agrarian economy accelerated after 1960. Access to material wealth has led to occupational mobility and has enabled these groups occupying the lower levels of the social ladder to challenge the traditional social order. This occupational mobility of the Shudras is one of the factors that has led to a relaxation of the rigidity of the caste system not just among Catholics, but even among Hindus. Though caste ideas and practices persist among Catholics, many changes are noticed. While pollution practices have been given up, the operation of caste is still noticed in endogamy and ideas about social precedence and status. Even endogamy is changing with a closer coalescence between the Christian Bamonns and Chardos and intermarrying is much more common, especially if the economic and educational status and social ranking are found to be compatible. There is also no separation in the Church or in the cemetery based on social status.

Thus, the all-powerful, state-backed, hierarchical, and highly institutionalized colonial Catholic Church has undergone a decline in its political power and influence after 1961. The post-colonial Church has been demographically reduced to a minority, enjoys no state patronage, and has seen the declining influence of caste in the Church, and all these factors have led to the Church projecting an image of being with the laity and not with the rulers, and ready to build bridges with people of other religious communities. The new Christian movements, which are less hierarchical and institutionalized, which emphasize laity participation and empowerment, and are more personal, entered Goa at such a time that was conducive to their entry. It was a period that witnessed the changing face of the post-colonial Church and changing religious composition and caste equations. The CCR, which is predominantly a movement of lay Catholics, has grown tremendously since its entry into Goa in 1974, enhancing this image of the Catholic Church being with the laity.

Locating the Pentecostal–Charismatic Movement in Goa within the History of Global Pentecostalism

Reasons for Moving from the Local to the Global

For a better understanding of the CCR and the neo-Pentecostal groups existing in contemporary Goa, it is necessary to trace the origins and history of these groups, which, though distinct from each other and having their own self-identities, belong to the same global Pentecostal–Charismatic movement. Since the neo-Pentecostals have been influenced by Pentecostal spirituality and theology and have borrowed and adapted many Pentecostal beliefs and practices, the tale of the Pentecostal–Charismatic movement in Goa will have to include the history of the classical Pentecostal movement from the late nineteenth century onwards. In many ways the present-day Charismatic movement has selectively borrowed and integrated into its belief system ideas and doctrine from different Pentecostal sources, which will be seen in more detail in the following chapters. Great efforts have been put in by the Charismatics to interpret Pentecostal spirituality and theology within the categories of their own denominational traditions in a bid to resolve the conflict of the theology of Pentecostalism, which they initially accepted, with their own theological tradition. This fits in with Fenn's definition of religion as a way of tying together multiple experiences and memories of the sacred into a single system of belief and practice (Fenn 2001: 6).

The Catholic Charismatic Renewal in India has been closely connected with the Charismatic movement in the USA in several ways.

Catholic Pentecostalism came to India in 1972 through Minoo and Luz Maria Engineer,[5] both committed Pentecostals, who had just returned from the USA. A cursory glance at the first few National Catholic Charismatic Conventions held in different parts of the country show that key speakers at most of them were from the USA. George Otis from the USA was a key speaker at the first Convention in 1974 (Engineer 2008b: 29), while Ralph Martin from the USA, one of the pioneers of the CCR, was the main speaker for the second Convention held in 1976. For the third Convention held in 1978, the theme of healing was developed in detail by a large team from the USA, while the well-known American evangelist Bobbie Cavnar was the main speaker for the fourth Convention in 1980 (Souvenir of the XI National 'Great Jubilee' CCR Convention 1999: 22–4). The strong embryonic connection between the Charismatic movement in India and in the USA is why we now briefly undertake a historical investigation of the Pentecostal movement in the USA.

Origins and Early History of Pentecostalism

Pentecostalism is a contested scholarly terrain and so it is not surprising that the exact origin of Pentecostalism is disputed. Pentecostal history-writing and Pentecostal historiography have undergone a lot of changes in recent years. Voices from around the world, which have not been heard from previously or have been ignored by earlier Pentecostal historians, are increasingly involved in these worldwide discussions. They have challenged, and in some cases even set aside, the findings of earlier historians, originating mainly from the USA that are biased in favour of the West, in favour of the USA, and in favour of white males. Women and indigenous people who carried the message and transformed it into something indigenous to various cultures have been overlooked, marginalized, or forgotten altogether. Many of the early Pentecostal historians, especially Walter Hollenweger and his researchers at Birmingham in the 1970s, had regarded the Azusa street revival that took place in Los Angeles

---

[5] For more details on the origin of Catholic Charismatic Renewal in India, see Minoo Engineer's articles in several issues of *Charisindia*, from April 2008 onwards.

in 1906 as the heart or cradle of Pentecostalism and that the Pentecostal–Charismatic Churches existing today trace their lineage to the Azusa mission.

The black preacher of the Azusa street revival, William James Seymour (1870–1922), learnt the new Pentecostal theology from Charles Parham, often described as a pioneer of Pentecostalism but ignored by the later generations of Pentecostal preachers. At the Azusa street revival that began on 18 April 1906, scores of people began to 'fall under the power', speak in other tongues and experience the baptism of the spirit, and for three years without interruption prayer meetings took place there with speaking and singing in tongues and prophecy. Since Pentecostalism came as a division within the older Holiness movement, leading many Holiness followers to embrace the new movement, some of its earliest and bitterest critics were from the Holiness and Methodist Churches (its mother Churches).[6] Many works such as W.B. Godbey's *Commentary on the New Testament* (1896), Alma White's *Demons and Tongues* (1949), and H.J. Stolee's *Speaking in Tongues* (1963) represent the chorus of criticisms of the Pentecostal movement.

As mentioned earlier, scholars more recently have begun to stress the polycentric origins of Pentecostalism. Seen this way, Pentecostalism is neither a movement that has a distinct beginning in USA or any- where else nor a movement that is based on a particular doctrine, but rather a series of movements that took several years and several forma- tive ideas and events to emerge. Thus, besides the Azusa street revival in Los Angeles, several revival movements of the late nineteenth and early twentieth centuries in evangelical circles, both in the West and in other places led to the birth of Pentecostalism (see Figure 1.1). Besides the Pietist, Methodist, and Holiness antecedents of Pentecostalism, revivals, and outpourings with manifestations (including tongues) occurred in different parts of the world such as Wales (1904–5), the Khasi hills of north-east India (1905), Pandita Ramabai's mission in Pune, India (1905–6), pietistic Scandinavians in North Dakota and Minnesota, USA (1906), the Hebden Mission in Toronto (1906), the Korean Pentecost of Pyongyang, Korea (1907), and so on, indirectly

---

[6] For a detailed account of the Holiness movement in the USA, please see Synan (1997).

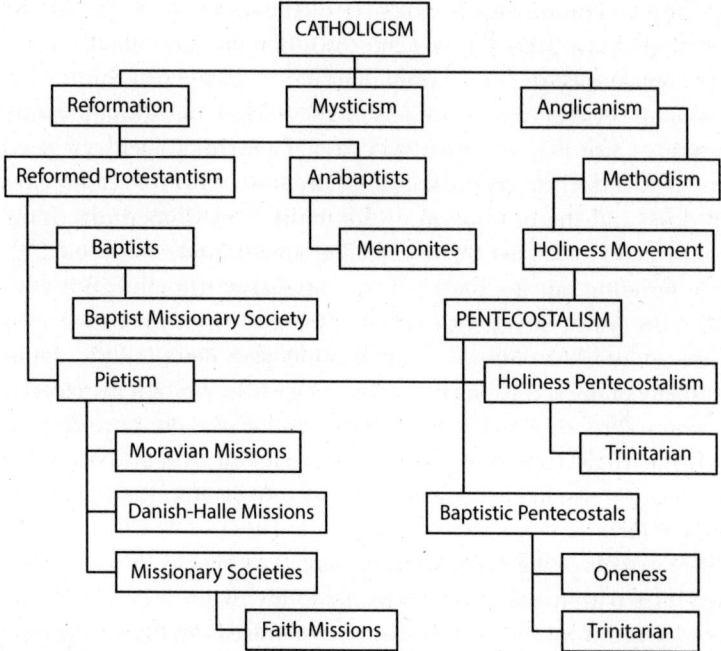

Figure 1.1   Precursors of the Pentecostal Mission
Source: Anderson 2007: 17.

preparing the ground for the Pentecostal revival of the twentieth century. Thus the Pentecostal revival of the twentieth century was a series of revivals that occurred within a few years of each other in the first decade of the twentieth century having a 'Pentecostal' character, with gifts of the spirit such as healings, tongues, prophecy, and other miraculous signs with the Azusa street revival being one such revival, regarded by most Classical Pentecostals as the main centre of origin for early Pentecostalism.

Pentecostalism began as an inter-racial movement, attracting people from all over the nation, regardless of race, and boasting of a much higher proportion of women than any other form of Christianity at the time—white bishops and black workers, Asians and Mexicans, white professors and black laundry women mixed equally— and with white Church leaders being ready to have hands laid on them in a community led by blacks (Hollenweger 1986: 5). When the Assemblies of God, the largest Pentecostal denomination in the world today, was formed in 1914, a third of its ministers and two-thirds of its missionaries were women (Anderson 2004: 274). But social pressure soon prompted the emerging Pentecostal Churches to get segregated into black and white organizations just as most of the other Churches had done and the promotion of the ministry of women practically disappeared in the later Pentecostal movement. Anderson (2007: 9), while pointing out the unconscious imperialist attitude which convinced the white missionaries of the innate superiority of their own European and Euro-American 'civilization' says there is little doubt that many of the secessions that occurred early in Western Pentecostal mission efforts in Africa, China, India, and elsewhere were at least partly the result of cultural and social insensitivities on the part of the missionaries, and in some cases there was racism, ethnocentrism, and ethical failure.

Pentecostals of the Azusa street mission, Los Angeles, professed the three-stage path to salvation compared to the majority of the groups that emerged from this revival who soon reduced the three-stage pattern to a two-stage one. The early Pentecostals held that sanctification was a sudden and distinct second work of God's grace, which followed the stage of conversion. Baptism of the spirit, accompanied by speaking in tongues, was then added to these two stages (conversion and sanctification) to make a three-stage path to salvation. It was W.H. Durham, an evangelist in Los Angeles and Chicago, who reduced this three-stage pattern to a two-stage one. Under the influence of the Baptists, he regarded conversion and sanctification as simultaneous. Most of the neo-Pentecostal groups in Goa accept a two-stage path to salvation. The other group that I studied in Goa, the Catholic Charismatics, have a different understanding of baptism of the spirit as a separate stage in the path to salvation, which is explained in Chapter 5. They have rejected the cultural trappings of classical Pentecostalism with its rigid exclusivism, accept infant water baptism, and downplay the importance of speaking in tongues. However, despite all these theological disagreements or rather because of the capacity to accommodate differing views and various types of peoples and cultures, the Pentecostal movement has spread rapidly to nearly every part of the world.

Spread of Pentecostalism to Other Parts of the World, Especially to India

We have seen in the previous section that Pentecostalism is not a movement with a single precursor in the USA, but arose through a series of movements spread over several years and in different parts of the world. Thus, the revivals and movements in other parts of the world, especially in India, assume significance in the tale of the Pentecostal–Charismatic movement. Also, present-day statistics show that there has been an explosive growth of Pentecostals and Charismatics in several parts of Asia with an estimated 135 million in Asia comparing favourably with 80 million in North America and 38 million in Europe (Barrett and Johnson in Burgess and Van Der Maas 2003: 284–302; Barrett et al. 2001). Latin America, which has the largest number of Pentecostals at 141 million, along with Africa (126 million) and Asia contain more than three quarters of all the Pentecostals in the world (524 million), marking a significant geographical shift in global Christianity. The Eurocentric image of Christianity as predominantly a white man's religion has undergone a dramatic change with the rapid growth of Pentecostal–Charismatic Christianity. This change is seen through the growth of Pentecostalism in Latin America as a mass popular movement that is transforming the religious landscape of the region. In Latin America, it is an indigenous movement, distinctly different from North American forms of Pentecostalism and it should not be regarded as a North American creation or importation (Anderson 2004: 63–4). Similarly, in Africa, Pentecostalism has assumed a distinct African identity through the mushrooming of thousands of African-initiated Churches (AICs) known collectively as spirit Churches or spiritual Churches. In a study on Charismatic Churches in Ghana, Cephas Omenyo (2002: 252–77) concluded that the rapid growth of Charismatic Churches in Africa was due to their attempt to fit the gospel with the African primal world view, thus redefining African Christianity in terms of African culture. Today Pentecostalism is fast becoming the dominant form of Christianity on the continent with an estimated 11 per cent of Africa's population being Charismatic in 2000 (Anderson 2004: 103–5).

As seen earlier, there were a series of Indian Christian revivals in the late nineteenth and early twentieth centuries that manifested Pentecostal-like features similar to the Azusa street revival. The most significant and talked-about revival in the early history of Indian Pentecostalism occurred in 1905 at the Mukti Mission in Pune of Pandita Sarasvati Ramabai (1858–1922), a Christian-Brahmin woman. The residents of a girls' orphanage and other women saw visions and spoke in tongues at this revival that had all the characteristics of the Azusa revival, lasted for a year and a half, and resulted in 1,100 baptisms (Anderson 2007: 77–9). Even before the Mukti Mission, there were earlier Pentecostal revivals in India such as the revival in Tirunelveli, Tamil Nadu, in 1860–1, where the Tamil Anglican evangelist John Christian Aroolappen and his followers experienced many charismatic gifts and other paranormal and Pentecostal phenomena, followed by another revival in neighbouring Travancore, Kerala, in 1874–5 among Church Mission Society (CMS) congregations and those of the Syrian Church of Malabar (Anderson 2004: 124). Another Pentecostal-like revival occurred among the tribals in the Welsh Presbyterian missions in the Khasi hills in north-east India in 1905. The above-mentioned Pentecostal revivals in late nineteenth and early twentieth centuries support the argument of Anderson that the Pentecostal phenomena in Asia have existed long before the arrival of Western Pentecostalism, and the Charismatic movement in Asia must not be interpreted in the light of the familiar themes of American Pentecostalism (Anderson 2004: 123). Ramabai's revival did not result directly in the formation of Pentecostal Churches but rather foreign Pentecostal missionaries, some of whom got baptized in the spirit at Azusa Street, began establishing Pentecostal missions in different parts of India with the first Pentecostal Church established at Thuyavur, Kerala, in 1911.

The first indigenous Pentecostal Church, that is, the Indian Pentecostal Church of God (IPC), was started by K.E. Abraham (1899–1974) along with other Indian leaders in 1933. Abraham also started the Hebron Bible School for training of Indian pastors. Pentecostalism has seen steady growth in India till independence and has experienced rapid expansion from the 1970s with the emergence of independent neo-Pentecostal and Charismatic Churches, leading R. Frykenberg, a distinguished commentator of religion, to suggest that the single most sweeping movement of conversion in India is Pentecostal (Martin 2002: 154). Similarly, the Pentecostal historian Allan Anderson (2004: 128) says Pentecostalism is clearly the fastest growing form of Christianity in India. The IPC and Assemblies of God (AG) are the two largest Classical Pentecostal denominations in India with around 750,000 members each in 2000 (Anderson 2004: 127). In 2000, India contained around 33 million Pentecostals and Charismatics with only four other nations—Brazil, the USA, China, and Nigeria—having more followers. Of this nearly 15 million are neo-Pentecostals and Catholic Charismatics, which include prominent Churches such as the New Life Fellowship founded in 1968 by S. Joseph in Mumbai and the Nagaland Christian Revival Churches founded in 1952.

While several factors are attributed to the international expansion of Pentecostalism in the early twentieth century, probably the most important reason for the rapid worldwide growth was the willingness of the early Pentecostal missionaries to travel to any part of the world and undergo any hardship. They were called 'missionaries of the one way ticket' since most of them went out with only enough money to get to the mission field and with little or no promise of support to return. This willingness to risk such long and hazardous journeys stemmed from their pre-millennial eschatological belief that the period they lived in was the end of time, so there was an urgent need to evangelize the world before the imminent return of Christ. Their readiness to travel to far and strange lands was also motivated from their experience of spirit baptism, where they spoke in tongues. They firmly believed that the gift of tongues enabled them to speak in different foreign languages and thus preach the gospel to the nations of the world (Anderson 2007: 46–68).

History of the Charismatic Renewal within the Historic Churches

The movement was returning with a new fire and vigour to find a place of acceptance among its former critics and enemies. The new wine of the spirit was now pouring into the old bottles of traditional Churches. (Synan 1997: 233)

After the spread and growth of Classical Pentecostalism to various parts of the world in the early half of the twentieth century, the experience of baptism in the spirit with speaking in tongues entered the mainline Protestant Churches from the 1960s. Since the beginning of Pentecostalism, many clergy and lay members of the traditional Churches received the Pentecostal experience and spoke in tongues. But they were forced to remain silent about it, since they were afraid of sanctions from the Episcopal hierarchy. Hundreds of Methodist, Baptist, Presbyterian ministers, and laypersons who were baptized in the spirit were forced to leave their Churches and join Pentecostal denominations. By 1960, the Charismatic movement starting with Episcopalians such as Fr Richard Winkler and Fr Dennis Bennett began spreading to other Protestant denominations such as Presbyterians, Lutherans, Baptists, and Methodists. In spite of opposition from conservative denominations such as the Southern Baptist Convention, the Church of Nazarene, Lutheran Church, and the Missouri Synod, the Charismatic movement continued to engulf the traditional Churches, because of the publicity that this new movement got through television broadcasts, particularly those of Oral Roberts and Pat Robertson, both well-known TV evangelists. The traditional view of the American origin of the Charismatic Renewal in 1960 in California with Dennis Bennett has been questioned by other Pentecostal scholars, who have written about Pentecostalism in Third-World countries in light of reports of similar phenomena among Baptists in Brazil by the late 1950s and among black Anglicans in South Africa in the 1940s (Freston in Hunt, Walter, and Hamilton 1997: 184–204).

History of the Catholic Charismatic Renewal

Since this work is a comparative study of the Pentecostal phenomenon within the Catholic Church and the independent neo-Pentecostal Churches, the history of Pentecostalism within the Catholic Church is treated separately from the history of Pentecostalism within the mainline Protestant Churches. While the phenomenon of Pentecostalism in the Catholic Church may appear as an unexpected and sudden event that took off from the first outpouring of the spirit at Duquesne University, Pennsylvania, in 1967, several developments over a long period of time prepared the ground for this phenomenon. Pope Leo XIII's encyclical titled 'On the Holy Spirit' and his dedication of the newborn century to the Holy Spirit on 1 January 1901—at the suggestion of Elena Guerra, a nun from Lucca, Italy—led to millions of Catholics, from theologians to the faithful, turning their attention to the Holy Spirit in a manner not seen before in the Church.

Another development that laid the groundwork for the entry of Pentecostalism in the Catholic Church was the Vatican Council II convened by Pope John XXIII for the purpose of 'opening the windows so that the Church could get a breath of fresh air' (Synan 1997: 235). Due to Vatican II, for the first time Catholic priests began to share in Protestant services and Protestant pastors were invited to speak during Catholic services. Thus, Vatican II prepared the Catholic mindset to accept Protestants as 'separated brethren' (Pope John XXIII's words) and look with openness at Protestant teachings and doctrines, after centuries of mutual distrust and suspicion (Synan 1997: 237). Other developments, which laid the ground for the entry of Pentecostalism in the Catholic Church were the emergence of the ecumenical movement and resurgence in Catholic biblical scholarship, both after World War II. If the Charismatic Renewal had happened in the Catholic Church before Vatican II, it would have most likely been interpreted as a Protestant phenomenon and, therefore, forbidden to Catholics, but due to the influence of Vatican II, it was seen positively: as one of the treasures of the Church to be freely shared by everyone.

Origin of the Catholic Charismatic Renewal in the United States of America

The American beginnings of the CCR are traced to the 'Duquesne weekend' in February 1967 where some students and faculty of the Duquesne University in Pittsburgh, USA, experienced an outpouring of the Holy Spirit. The catalyst for this Pentecostal experience began with two lay theology professors of Duquesne University, Ralph Kiefer and Bill Storey, reading the books, David Wilkerson's *The Cross and the Switchblade* and John Sherrill's *They Speak with Other Tongues*, which kindled an interest in the topic of baptism of the Holy Spirit. The leaders of the early Catholic Pentecostalism, such as Steve Clark, Ralph Martin, Ralph Keifer, Bill Storey, and others were all highly educated intellectuals who had achieved considerable academic distinction. Most were orthodox Catholics, who were concerned about personal and liturgical spiritual Renewal. None of those who received baptism of the Holy Spirit on the Duquesne and Notre Dame University, Indiana, campuses ever thought of leaving the Catholic Church and joining a Pentecostal one.

The climax of the North American Charismatic Renewal was seen in 1977 at an ecumenical meeting of nearly 50,000 Charismatics from almost all the denominational Renewals in Kansas City, regarded as 'the largest ecumenical meeting in the history of the nation' (Synan 1997: 261). Soon the Charismatic Renewal became the fastest growing movement in the Catholic Church and present estimates reveal that there are around 120 million Catholic Charismatics in the world (Barrett and Johnson in Burgess and Van Der Maas 2003: 286). Many scholars of religion were surprised by the manner in which the CCR was accepted within the Catholic Church in great contrast to other liturgical and non-liturgical Churches. An important reason for the acceptance of the CCR was the position of its leaders in perceiving it not as a movement within the Church, but as the Church in movement (McDonnell 1980: 516–17). This position that the CCR had no structure apart from the Church facilitated its blending with the existing structures of the Church and its submission to the guidance and monitoring by the Church hierarchy.

Another important reason for the rapid growth and acceptance of this movement within the Catholic Church was the serious study done by scholars of religion right from its inception in 1967, resulting in works such as *The Catholic Cult of the Paraclete* by the well-known Christian sociologist Joseph Fichter, Edward O'Connor's *The Pentecostal Movement in the Catholic Church*, Kevin Ranaghan and Dorothy Ranaghan's *Catholic Pentecostals*, and the path-breaking three-volume *Presence, Power, Praise: Documents on the Charismatic Renewal* by Kilian McDonnell, in which she presents 104 documents relating to the Charismatic Renewal produced by various historic Churches and also national and international ecclesial bodies. The serious analysis on the theological meaning of the Renewal by well-known theologians such as Donald Gelpi, Francis Sullivan, and others helped the CCR get public recognition and develop its own unique style, which led it to abandon the term 'Pentecostal' in favour of the more neutral 'Charismatic', marking it as an 'indigenous' Catholic movement with little of the theology and cultural baggage of Classical Pentecostalism.

Also, Cardinal Leon J. Suenens of Belgium, the first Episcopal advisor to the CCR, played a key role in relating the Renewal to the mainstream of Catholic life, thereby ensuring its acceptance and growth both in Rome and internationally (Mascarenhas 1996). An area of conflict in any religious organization is about control over power and decision-making. The question that often leads to disputes and schisms is whether the prophet—the individual bearer of charisma (in this case the founding leaders of the new charismatic movement)—accepts the authority of the priests—a specialized group involved in regular organization of religious worship that seeks to protect established doctrine (in this case the episcopal hierarchy). Suenens, being part of the Church authority structure and also an important figure in the Renewal, was able to allay any doubts and fears about the CCR posing any challenge to Church authority and thus prevent any clashes over authority. The CCR is served by an International Office, founded in Belgium in 1974 and moved to Rome in 1981. This office is overseen by an International Council of leaders from the five continents, and is funded by voluntary contributions from prayer groups and communities all over the world. The Vatican formally granted pontifical recognition to the International Catholic Charismatic Renewal Services (ICCRS) in September 1993, as an international body for the promotion of the CCR.

Entry of the Catholic Charismatic Renewal into India and Goa

The historical account of the CCR now moves from the global scene to the national scene and from there to the local level. The CCR first came to India through Minoo Engineer, a Parsi civil engineer who had converted to Christianity, and his Puerto Rican wife Luz Maria: the Pentecostalized couple who returned from USA to Bombay, presently called Mumbai, in February 1972. Four or five Charismatic groups sprang up in the city in the first year itself, and within two years there were about 25 prayer groups in the city. Individuals and teams from these groups were invited to other dioceses for retreats and so the CCR began spreading rapidly throughout the country. A National Office was started in Bombay in 1974, and it organized the First National Convention in Bombay from 29 December 1974 till 5 January 1975, and also started publishing the national magazine *Charisindia*. In 1977, a National Service Team (NST) was elected by the First National Leaders Conference held in Bangalore, and attended by leaders of the then existing Charismatic groups of India. Local service teams have been formed in many places in cooperation with the NST to help unite and foster a genuine CCR. Also, various publications in the regional languages are published by these service teams. The CCR has now spread to many dioceses in India and 16 National Conventions have been held so far, the last being in Pune in 2015. There are no official statistics showing the number of members of the CCR in India, though people in the movement estimate around 5 per cent of the Catholics in India are Charismatic. The official statistics of the Catholics in India are 17.5 million (*Catholic Directory* 2013: 77–83), so the number of Catholic Charismatics in India are estimated to be around 900,000 (5 per cent of the total Catholics).

The Charismatic movement in Goa began not with priests or nuns or theologians, but with a housewife from Aldona village, Teresa Muniz, who had gone to East Africa and had an experience of the Charismatic Renewal there. She came back with stories of people being touched by the Holy Spirit. One of her neighbours, Fr James D'Souza, who was very much involved in the Charismatic movement in Bombay, had come down for his holidays and suggested to Teresa that they could have a prayer meeting in her house. She contacted a few friends and the first ever Charismatic prayer meeting in Goa was held in Aldona in 1974. In the same week, another prayer meeting was held in her friend Phyllis Dias's house in the city of Mapusa. While the Aldona prayer group discontinued after some years, the Mapusa group has continued to function vibrantly and is one of the two prayer groups from which I have drawn my ethnographic data. Soon after this, people began meeting elsewhere and prayer groups started in Panaji and other parts of Goa. There was a need felt for coordination and some of the early leaders used to meet once in a while in Panaji. This was the origin of the Goa Service Team (GST), the regional body that oversees all Catholic Charismatic phenomena in the state of Goa. The GST was formed at a Night Vigil at the St Francis Xavier Convent, Mapusa, on 18 December 1978 and its statutes received provisional recognition on 15 June 1997. One of the major activities that gave a boost to the Renewal in Goa was the English retreats preached by Fr Rufus Pereira and Fr James D'Souza, both actively involved in the CCR in Bombay.

Most of the early Charismatics were from urban, English-educated, middle-class backgrounds and so all the early Charismatic prayer groups were urban, English-speaking groups. The diversity and de facto plural-ism of religious traditions in cities, the density of populations, and the patterns of first generation immigration to cities have made American urban locations places of religious vitality, creative adaptation, and cultural synthesis according to a study by Rhys Williams (2005). His analysis shows that changes across space (geographic mobility) and the changes over time (adaptation, pluralism, and assimilation) produce new religious forms and this explains why the Catholic Charismatic movement in the USA and also in India and Goa originated in cities. Gradually, the Charismatic movement in Goa spread to rural areas and the first Konkani prayer group was started in the village of Merces in 1982, by a teacher from Panaji, Alzira Antao. The first Konkani retreat was preached by a team comprising Alzira Antao, Rosy Alphonso, Peter D'Souza, and Anthony Lobo in 1983. Today the CCR has spread to most of the parishes in the archdiocese of Goa and Daman and the number of Catholic Charismatics is estimated to be around 32,000 (estimated at 5 per cent of the total number of Catholics).

History of Mapusa and Merces Charismatic Prayer Groups

The sample of the CCR in Goa that I drew for my fieldwork comprised two prayer groups from Mapusa and Merces. The Mapusa Charismatic prayer group is the oldest existing prayer group of the CCR in Goa. The first meeting of the Mapusa prayer group, held in 1974 in Phyllis Dias' house had about 12 people. Initially all the members were women, who were mainly housewives. Slowly more people, including young-sters, began coming from nearby villages such as Siolim, Moira, and from cities such as Panaji and even Margao till it grew to around 70 people. While the first meeting was conducted by Fr James D'Souza, in general the prayer meetings were managed by the laypeople them-selves. They would conduct the praise and worship and some among them even gave talks on different spiritual topics. Phyllis, who was the founding leader of the group, used to also call Jesuit priests from St Britto's School, Mapusa, and a Pallotine priest from Assagao to come and give talks to the group. Also, American Charismatics came and conducted healing sessions for the group, though some of them were not Catholics. In many ways, Phyllis can be regarded as the mother of the Charismatic movement in Goa. Phyllis and some others from Goa attended the first National Charismatic Convention held at St Mary's School grounds, Bombay, in December 1974. She played a crucial role in the forming of the GST and became its first chairperson from 1978 to 1981. The prayer meetings of the Mapusa group were held in the house of Phyllis till 1991 when she and her husband went abroad to see their daughters and the meeting had to be shifted to Swiss Chapel, Mapusa. It was there for a short while before it was shifted to St Jerome's Church, Mapusa, where it is held at present. The day of the meeting too was shifted from Wednesday to Saturday since many of the members were working people.

The other group from which I have drawn my ethnographic data is the one at Merces, which is the oldest Konkani prayer group in Goa. It was started in September 1980 by Alzira Antao, who was at that time teaching in the government primary school in Merces. Alzira had entered the Renewal in 1978 and was attending the prayer meetings of the Aldona prayer group, which was started by Teresa Muniz. She felt God telling her repeatedly, 'Alzira, look after my sheep.'[7] So she collected all the Catholic housewives in Merces who were interested and curious to know about the Holy Spirit. Thus, the Merces prayer group began. However, shortly after that, the group died out since Alzira got busy with other work and so stopped going to the group. She realized she had made a mistake and the group needed her leadership, so she restarted the group in 1982. Initially, for more than a year they met in one of the women's house, which was close to the school. Later, the parish priest gave them permission to have the prayer meetings in the parish Church, but slowly the numbers of the group declined, apparently due to lack of leadership in the group and lack of support from the parish priest. Then in 1992, Flora Rodrigues, a woman from Salcete who got married in Vaddy, one of the wards in Merces, was chosen as the leader of the group. She already had experience of the Charismatic Renewal before marriage when she was in the group of Fr Savio Gama, a well-known Charismatic preacher. With the support of the parish priest, Fr Imidio Pinto, and another woman from Vaddy, she was able to revive the prayer group. Though Flora was only a housewife with education up to senior school certificate (SSC), her charismatic personality combined with a natural gift of teaching and preaching helped her lead the group successfully for nearly eight years till she had to hand over the leadership to another woman due to maternity reasons. Many of the Charismatics in Merces also mention the role of the then parish priest, Fr Imidio Pinto, who is a well-known Charismatic preacher, in

[7]   Interview with Alzira Antao on 27 August 2008.

popularizing the Charismatic Renewal and ensuring that it did not die out. It was only in 2001, under the present leader, Clara Fernandes, that the Merces prayer group got registered under the GST.

Rise of Pentecostalism in Independent Neo-Pentecostal Churches

Besides the two CCR prayer groups of Mapusa and Merces, I chose two neo-Pentecostal Churches for my ethnographic fieldwork, both belonging to the independent, neo-Pentecostal wave of the Pentecostal–Charismatic movement (third wave). For a better understanding of these Churches in contemporary Goa, it is necessary to carefully analyse their historical antecedents and so this history is treated separately. As the Charismatic Renewal in the mainline Churches began to decline in the late 1970s, a new independent Charismatic movement with much weaker links with older Pentecostal Churches began to emerge. Associations of independent Churches were formed and they soon became the fastest growing segment in the Pentecostal–Charismatic movement in the English-speaking world. In the US, the 'shepherding' or 'discipleship' movement began with strong emphasis on submission to 'shepherds' or Church leaders. This shepherding movement, which attracted large numbers of independent Charismatic pastors, closed in 1986.

Parallel to the shepherding movement was the British 'restoration' or 'house church' movement[8], which arose in the late 1950s with Arthur Wallis and Dennis Lillie as its first leaders (Wright in Hunt, Walter, and Hamilton 1997: 60–76). Many of their leaders were former brethren who had been expelled because of their Pentecostal experience. This movement, presently known as 'New Churches' has become the fastest growing and largest Pentecostal–Charismatic Church group in the UK with over 400,000 affiliates (Anderson 2004: 157). Several major new Church networks such as that of Terry Virgo, founder of New Frontiers

[8] House church movement is an inappropriate label, a hopeless misnomer to describe Churches in houses outside existing denominations, which have now become full-blown Churches with house groups attached (Walker in Caplan 1987b: 199).

International (NFI), Bryn Jones of Covenant Ministries International, and Tony Morton of Cornerstone Ministries have emerged, of which NFI is now the largest.

Both the neo-Pentecostal Churches in Goa chosen for my fieldwork belong to the above-mentioned New Churches. The first Church, known as the River of Life Church (ROLC), belongs to the UK-based NFI.[9] New Frontiers International, which entered Goa in 1987, with one congregation in Margao has gradually spread to other towns of Goa. On 10 August 1999, Wellington Gomes along with his family shifted from Margao to Panaji, in answer to God's call. There were already a few families in Panaji being looked after by Colin, a Bible trainee, for about a year. Since Colin had to suddenly leave for the Gulf, Wellington was asked by Pastor Melwin, who was leading the NFI Church at Margao, to go to Panaji. For some months, they met first in Wellington's house at Miramar and then in the hall of a city hotel. The Panjim Church plant became the ROLC on 4 June 2000, when they met for the first time in the hall of another city hotel. Today ROLC comprises nearly 150 members and has two services on Sunday, meeting in the hall of yet another city hotel.

The other neo-Pentecostal Church, called World Revival Ministries (WRM) is an independent Church started by a Goan couple, Domnic and Joan D'Souza, in the small village of Sodiem in Siolim situated in the north-west of Goa. Domnic, a former Catholic and businessman, owned a private factory manufacturing aerated water and ran a bar and restaurant. He had a life-changing experience at the Catholic Divine Retreat Centre, Potta, in Kerala and decided to give up all his businesses and serve God through full-time ministry. He got involved in the CCR and became the leader of the Konkani prayer group at Mapusa. Due to differences with the parish priest, he left the Catholic Church and began a small prayer meeting in his house in 2000. Slowly people began flocking there, including Hindus. Despite many challenges and conflicts with the local Catholic community and the village officials, WRM has grown into an independent Church with a membership of nearly 500 people and is associated with the New Covenant Family of Ministries, an apostolic network of nondenominational and independent Churches,

---

[9] Most of the data that follows is taken from interviews with the leaders and members of the ROLC and WRM.

based in the USA. It has ministries in three centres in Goa—Siolim, Panaji, and Margao. The main centre at Siolim is known as Five Pillars Christian Church.[10]

This chapter, by engaging in 'a continuous process of interaction between the historian and his facts, an unending dialogue between the present and the past', has recounted the history of the Pentecostal–Charismatic movement from its origin through the revival movements of the nineteenth and twentieth centuries to present-day Goa (Carr 1964: 30). Both Freston and Anderson in their analysis of Pentecostal and Charismatic Churches in Asia, Africa, and Latin America have questioned the commonly held view that Charismatic Christianity has spread from the USA, which they term as part of an agenda to make Third-World people more subservient to American interests. Asia, Africa, and Latin America have their own Christian heroes, who should be more visible in the writings of Pentecostal histories (Anderson 2007: 290). This has been the aim of this historical chapter: to unearth the polycentric origins and the global history of the Pentecostal–Charismatic movement.

Similarly, the new Christian groups in Goa being studied in this work, namely the CCR and the neo-Pentecostal Churches, distance themselves from global Pentecostalism and claim to be indigenous movements. The subsequent chapters will analyse the similarities and differences they have with the global Pentecostal–Charismatic movement in their religious beliefs, symbols, ritualistic practices, and world views. Given the polygenetic nature of neo-Pentecostalism and the state of flux of the movement, the difficult question that arises is whether these seemingly disparate new Christian groups can be viewed as part of a single Pentecostal–Charismatic movement. Another interesting question that arises is whether they are representative of the new direction that Christianity in Goa and in the world is taking. These and other questions will be studied in the following chapters, which will focus on the ethnographic picture of the neo-Pentecostal and Catholic Charismatic movements in present-day Goa.

[10] For more details, see the website for the Five Pillars Christian Church, available at: http://www.fivepillarscc.org/index.php (accessed on 1 February 2017).

2 The Pentecostal–Charismatic Movement in Goa Today
People, Organization, and Membership

In the previous chapter, we were able to acquire a historical picture of the Pentecostal–Charismatic movement and in this chapter the narrative of our study moves towards the present status of the movement in Goa. The flow of the study is from the past to the present, from the universal to the local. This chapter will deal with the Pentecostal–Charismatic movement in Goa today—the profile of its members, its organization, structure, and activities. From this chapter onwards, the study will draw more specifically from the fieldwork data on the Merces and Mapusa prayer groups of the CCR, and the two neo-Pentecostal Churches, namely ROLC, Panaji, and WRM, Siolim.

Overview of the Catholic Charismatic Revival in Goa Today

Today the CCR in Goa has grown into a large movement of around 32,000 Catholic Charismatics and has spread to almost every parish in Goa with 118 prayer groups now registered with the GST, which oversees the movement in Goa. The movement is divided into four zones—North Zone A, North Zone B, South Zone A, and South Zone B, which are further subdivided into 23 sectors (see Figure 2.1). Each zone has a zonal leader, while each sector has a sector leader. In each

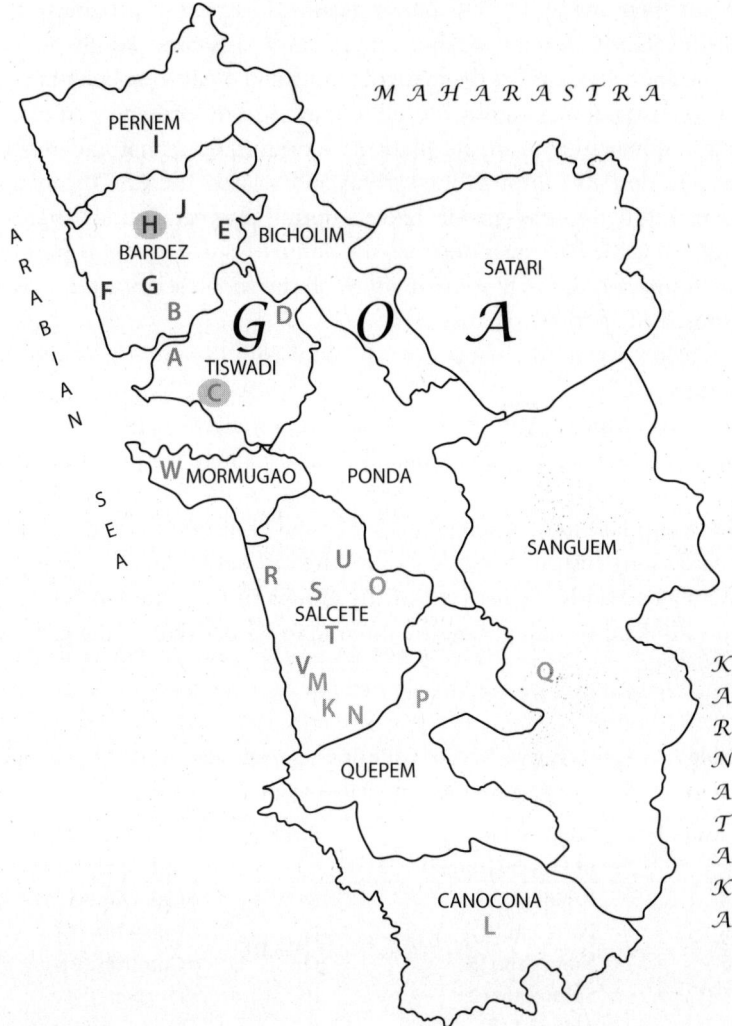

Figure 2.1   Sector-wise Distribution of Catholic Charismatic Renewal Prayer Groups in Goa

Disclaimer: This map is not to scale and is provided for illustrative purposes only.

Note: North Zone I: A, B, C, and D; North Zone II: E, F, G, H, I, and J; South Zone I: K, L, M, N, O, P, and Q; South Zone II: R, S, T, U, V, and W.

Fieldwork done in C and H.

Source: Shalom, CCR Newsletter, October 2006.

sector there are about 5–8 prayer groups. In terms of activities, the GST deals with five apostolates—Intercession, Teaching, Youth, Social Concern, and Music. As the main planning and organizing body of the CCR in Goa, it meets every month to pray, discern, evaluate, and plan. The implementation of the plans is done through zonal and sector leaders, and also through the various apostolates. The GST organizes several initiation-and-growth retreats during the year in both English and Konkani. They also organize the annual leaders' camp as part of the formation of the leaders, at which all the zonal, sector, and prayer group leaders come together.

Table 2.1 gives the name of each sector with the number of prayer groups.

Using purposive sampling, I chose two prayer groups from the CCR in Goa to draw detailed ethnographic data, namely the prayer groups of Merces and Mapusa. They were chosen on the following criteria: the group had to be a representative of the CCR in Goa, had to have a fairly long history of existence, and had to have a large number of members. Nearly 95 per cent of the groups in Goa are parish-based and Konkani-speaking. Besides, more than 75 per cent of the groups

Table 2.1   Location-wise Data of Catholic Charismatic Renewal Prayer Groups in Goa as Depicted in Figure 2.1

Symbol	Sector (Number of Prayer Groups)	Symbol	Sector (Number of Prayer Groups)
A	Panaji (4)	M	Chinchinim (6)
B	Porvorim (2)	N	Cuncolim (5)
C	Santa Cruz (5)	O	Curtorim (6)
D	St Estevam (2)	P	Quepem (8)
E	Aldona (4)	Q	Sanguem (6)
F	Calangute (5)	R	Betalbatim (6)
G	Guirim (6)	S	Margao (5)
H	Mapusa (4)	T	Navelim (6)
I	Pernem (6)	U	Raia (6)
J	Tivim (4)	V	Varca (6)
K	Assolna (7)	W	Vasco (6)
L	Canacona (3)		

Source: Prepared by the author based on data collected during fieldwork.

are rural-based.[1] Keeping the above criteria in mind, I chose the prayer group in Merces, which is Konkani-speaking, rural-based, has a regular attendance of 50–100 people, and is also the first Konkani-speaking prayer group in Goa. The English-speaking prayer group at Mapusa was then chosen since it is the oldest existing prayer group and has a fairly large number of regular members, about 100–120 people from several parishes. It must be noted that the early CCR prayer groups were English-speaking and city-based. Therefore, to get a fuller picture of the Charismatic Movement, it was also necessary to study urban-based, English-speaking groups.

Place: Merces

Merces, just 5 km away from the capital city of Panaji, is not considered a village but rather an outgrowth of Panaji by the 2001 census. It has a population of 11,012 with 5,560 males and 5,452 females (Census of India 2001: 12–13). The sex ratio is 981 females per 1,000 males, while the literacy rate is 78.1 per cent. This is significant given the fact that the Charismatic prayer group at Merces comprises almost entirely women. According to the official records of the Catholic Church, the Catholic population is 8,500, indicating that Catholics constitute the majority in Merces (*Archdiocese of Goa and Daman Directory* 2006: 137). There are very few Orthodox and Born-Again Christians in Merces, and they attend services in Churches outside Merces. This village, which has four *communidades*[2] and a dozen wards, has a Catholic Church, the Church of Our Lady of Merces, and two chapels, both without Chaplains (Rodrigues 2000: 50–3; *Archdiocese of Goa and Daman Directory* 2006: 137). There are also at least six temples in Merces. The main feasts celebrated by the villagers are 'Our Lady of Merces', 'Festa de Novidade' (harvest festival),

[1] Taken from *Shalom*, the newsletter of the National Catholic Charismatic Renewal Services, Goa Branch.

[2] *Communidade*s or village assemblies were peculiar to Goa. Locally called *gaunpon*s or *gauncaria*s, they were at once administrative and socio-economic institutions at the village level. The village elders known as *gauncar*s formed the communidade of the village. The Portuguese allowed the village administration to continue in the hands of the age-old gaunpons and renamed them communidades (Xavier 1993: 67–70).

and the Palki festival at the Sateri temple (Rodrigues 2000: 50–3). The economy of the village mainly depended on agriculture, salt pans, and pisciculture. Today all three have declined. With easily accessible education, many of the villagers have entered the service sector, while a number of them are working abroad. Also, many industries have come to Merces. The rapid development and urbanization of the village is noticed by the number of grocery shops, pharmacies, fast-food joints, restaurants, and many mushrooming apartment buildings.

Mapusa, the second largest town in North Goa District after Panaji, is the nerve centre of Bardez taluka and the main transit point for North Goa traffic. It was considered by Fonseca (1878: 106) 'as one of the most important commercial places in the whole territory of Goa'. Due to the well-known Friday Fair, which is the largest in Goa, it got the name Mapuçá—'map' meaning measure and 'çá' meaning to fill up, that is, a place where goods are measured and bought and sold (Fonseca 1878). The Vani or Vaisha community has ruled the roost here, from trade to politics, though other caste groupings are also jostling for space (D'Souza 1991: 48–51). Mapusa has a population of around 40,000 with a sex ratio of 928 females per 1,000 males and literacy rate of 75.2 per cent, which is lower than the state average (Census of India 2011). Hindus constitute 68.8 per cent, while Christians constitute only 17.1 per cent, which is lower than the state average of 25.1 per cent. The Church of St Jerome, popularly known as the Church of Our Lady of Miracles, was founded in 1594 and is the only Catholic Church in Mapusa (Archdiocese of Goa and Daman Directory 2006: 130). The new Christian groups have at least five Churches, of which one belongs to the NFI. The main temple in Mapusa is the Maruti temple, which is close to the main market and where Hindu devotees from all over Bardez throng on Saturdays to offer oil to the deity (J. D'Souza 1991: 48–51). Huge crowds come for the Bodgeshwar Zatra celebrated with great fanfare at the temple of Kanokeshwar Baba in Mapusa in December/January.

People in the Catholic Charismatic Renewal

While there are no documented statistics regarding the strength of the CCR in Goa, the total number of Catholic Charismatics in Goa is estimated at around 32,000. This total includes all the members of the prayer groups registered under the GST, the prayer groups and independent ministries that do not come under the GST, and the large number of Catholics who are not attached to any prayer group, but who consider themselves as Charismatics.

The data that follows is taken from a questionnaire administered to 362 respondents chosen by random sampling and represents all four zones and 13 different sectors of the CCR. Thus, the findings of the questionnaire present a representative socio-economic profile of the CCR in Goa. Among the 362 respondents, 319 were women (86.5 per cent), while 49 were men (13.5 per cent), but this numerical dominance is not reflected in the decision-making and governing bodies of the CCR. In the GST, which was elected in September 2006, there were only 2 women out of the 11 members. In 2007, out of the 23 sector leaders, only 9 were women. In the 35-year history of the CCR in Goa, only 2 women have been elected chairperson of the GST. All the remaining 11 chairpersons have been men.[3] The preponderance of women in the CCR is in keeping with the demographic trend of Christians in Goa, whose sex ratio of 1,129 women per 1,000 men is much higher than the Hindus (929) and Muslims (905) (Census of India 2011). The feminine character of the CCR is also found in other parts of India. While conducting research in Pune on Pentecostals, Chad Bauman attended a prayer meeting of the CCR and found the group to be very feminine. The women in the group asked more questions than the men and many of them were clearly recognized as leaders (Bauman 2015: 72–3).

Table 2.2 shows that the overwhelming majority of the respondents are married (82.3 per cent). Adding those respondents who are widowed implies that 87 per cent of the respondents were married at some point. Table 2.3 shows that one-third of the Catholic Charismatics fall in the age group of 51–60 years. The CCR is a movement for middle-aged or older people, with 82 per cent of them being above 40 years. One reason for the low percentage of youth—only 7 per cent are 30 years or below—is that the CCR in Goa, right from the beginning, deliberately or inadvertently projected an image of being a family-oriented pious religious movement and so appears to have mainly attracted 'pious' married women. According to Phyllis, the founding leader of the

---

[3] All this data about the CCR is taken from various issues of *Shalom*.

Table 2.2 Marital Status of Catholic Charismatics in Goa

Marital Status	Frequency
Married (82.3%)	298
Single (11%)	40
Divorced (0.3%)	1
Widowed (6.4%)	23
Total Respondents	362

Source: Prepared by the author based on data collected during fieldwork.

Table 2.3 Age-wise Distribution of Catholic Charismatics in Goa

Age	Frequency
Blank (1.1%)	4
Up to 20 years (1.9%)	7
21–30 years (5%)	18
31–40 years (10.2%)	37
41–50 years (23.8%)	86
51–60 years (34%)	123
61 and above (24%)	87
Total Respondents	362

Source: Prepared by the author based on data collected during fieldwork.

Mapusa prayer group, all the members of the Mapusa group initially were women and mainly housewives. As the present data shows, the CCR has a preponderance of married women and so predominantly caters to issues related to piety, religiosity, family, and marriage. This type of a profile has kept children, teenagers, youth, and singles away from the movement.

The educational profile of the CCR from Table 2.4 reveals that a majority of the Charismatics (70 per cent) possess school education up to SSC. Only a small percentage of the respondents are well-educated, at least possessing a college degree (13.5 per cent). Table 2.5 reveals that nearly 71 per cent of the respondents are homemakers, assuming the 42 female blank entries most likely indicate household work. And if we take into consideration those involved in domestic work and those retired, then three-fourths of the members are in the domestic sphere.

Only 12.7 per cent of the Catholic Charismatics are in the service sector (doctors, bankers, engineers, teachers, government servants, and

Table 2.4   Educational Background of Catholic Charismatics in Goa

Educational Level	Frequency
Primary–IV std (14.1%)	41
Middle and High School: V–SSC (55.7%)	162
HSSC–XII (15.4%)	45
Graduate (11.3%)	33
Post graduate (2.1%)	6
Illiterate (1.4%)	4
Total	291

Note: The blank entries numbering 71 are left out since their implications are equivocal. SSC = senior school certificate; HSSC = higher secondary school certificate.

Source: Prepared by the author based on data collected during fieldwork.

Table 2.5   Gender-wise Occupation of Catholic Charismatics in Goa

Occupation of Respondent	Male		Female	
	Frequency	Per Cent	Frequency	Per Cent
Blank/N.A.	5	1.4	42	11.6
Homemakers	1	0.3	215	59.4
Tailor	0	0	2	0.6
Agriculture	0	0	2	0.6
Service (doctor, banker, engineer, teacher, and so on)	22	6.1	24	6.6
Domestic work	0	0	5	1.4
Business	6	1.7	3	0.8
Retired	8	2.2	7	1.9
Student	2	0.6	6	1.7
Artist (musician)	1	0.3	2	0.6
Full-time Evangelist	1	0.3	1	0.3
Social worker	2	0.6	4	1.1
Cook	1	0.3	0	0

Source: Prepared by the author based on data collected during fieldwork.

so forth), while very few of them are involved in business (2.5 per cent). Also very few are students (2.3 per cent), again indicating that the Charismatic prayer groups do not attract many youngsters. Hardly anyone is involved in agriculture in line with the general trend in Goa, which reveals that only 9.6 per cent of the total workers in Goa are involved in cultivation, compared to 31.7 per cent at the national level (Census of India 2001). The above data indicates that the CCR has been able to touch every type of person, from the illiterate to the highly educated and from the farmer to the highly professional. A comparison of the work participation rate (the percentage of total workers to total population) of the Catholic Charismatics with that of the general population of Goa reveals some interesting gender variations, which could explain the paucity of women in the decision-making bodies of the CCR. While the male and female work participation rates for the state of Goa are 54.6 per cent and 22.4 per cent respectively in the 2001 census, the respective figures for the Charismatics are 67.3 per cent and 13.5 per cent. Thus Charismatic men are five times more involved in economically productive work than the women, the majority of whom are homemakers. The preponderance of women in the domestic sphere coupled with the high working rate of men in the public sphere may provide a clue as to why so few leaders in the CCR are women.

Since it was difficult to acquire class data of the Catholic Charismatics through a questionnaire, it was done by analysing the occupation, educational qualifications, and living conditions (condition of the house, ownership of certain household goods, and the like) of the members of the CCR through participant observation, close interaction, and interviews with the Mapusa and Merces Charismatic prayer groups and members of other groups. The results show that on the whole the CCR appears to be a movement of the lower and middle classes with around 10 per cent of the members belonging to the rich class.

Table 2.6 indicates that the overwhelming majority of the Catholic Charismatics are Goans (95 per cent). This observation that the CCR is a movement of locals has important implications for the discussion in later chapters on identity formation of the Pentecostal–Charismatic

Table 2.6   Place of Origin of Catholic Charismatics in Goa

Origin	Males (Per Cent)	Females (Per Cent)	Total (Per Cent)
Blank	3 (0.8%)	6 (1.7%)	9 (2.5%)
Goan	42 (11.6%)	302 (83.4%)	344 (95.0%)
Non-Goan	4 (1.1%)	5 (1.4%)	9 (2.5%)

Source: Prepared by the author based on data collected during fieldwork.

movement and the impact of ethnic and regional differences on religious contestations. From the above analysis, the following socio-economic profile of Catholic Charismatics in Goa emerges: they will most likely be Catholic Goan women, who are married, middle-aged (over 40 years old), with up to high school education, and who are involved in the domestic sphere (household work) and so are not earning. They belong mainly to the lower and middle classes. The above profile matches the assessment of Fr Joseph Silva, the spiritual advisor for the CCR, who claims that the majority of the people in the Renewal are of the masses. A comparison of the above profile with two other studies (Parathazham 1996; Choi 1986) reveals that all three samples have predominantly married people from the middle class. The profile of the followers of the Full Gospel Church in Korea, as described by Choi, matches closely with the profile of the CCR in Goa. The Full Gospel Church members show a preponderance of women who outnumber the men by more than 2 to 1, a preponderance of educational attainment at or below the level of high school, a bipolar age distribution, and a preponderance of belonging to the working and middle classes.

The profile of the members influences the organizational structures of the CCR. For example, the Merces prayer group, which has only married women in their group, has fixed its weekly prayer meeting on Wednesdays at 5 pm. Many working youth want to attend but are able to come only later in the evening after work. However, the late timing does not suit the housewives since they have to go back home and prepare supper. A cursory glance at some other CCR prayer groups in Goa also reveals that most of them slot their weekly prayer meetings between 3.30 pm and 5.30 pm, while only the city groups meet after 6.30 pm.

Sociology of Organization of the Catholic Charismatic Revival

The CCR began in Goa in 1974 with a handful of housewives meeting in one of their houses. There was no structure, no formally appointed leader, or any form of organization. In a short time, people began meeting in other houses, slowly prayer groups started emerging, and soon there was a need felt for coordination. Some of the leaders of these early groups began meeting once in a while to discuss what was happening in their groups and this led to the formation of the first structure of governance in the CCR, namely the GST. Today, the CCR has grown into a large movement within the Catholic Church with various structures of organization such as zones, sectors, prayer groups, apostolates, the GST, the Diocesan Charismatic Service Team (DCST), and the like. In contrast to the Catholic Church, which is hierarchically structured and highly institutionalized, the CCR has tried to maintain the model of a movement with emphasis on charisma and dynamism. The concern that too much preoccupation with structures and institutions will reduce the charismatic and spiritual dimension of the movement is illustrated by the following comment of a Catholic Charismatic: 'God will not ask the Catholic Church how many buildings they have built, how many graveyards did they repair, how much land do they own, how many schools and hospitals they have built, but how many souls have you got for me.'[4] In this section, the development of organizational structures in the Charismatic movement will be examined based on Max Weber's paradigm of charisma.

Weber (1978: 212) identified three types of legitimate control—charismatic authority, traditional authority, and rational–legal authority. Each leads to a particular form of organizational structure. In a system of control based on Weber's charismatic authority, the following characteristics are noticed in the organization: (*a*) obedience derives from the devotion felt by subordinates to what they see as the exceptional qualities of their leader; (*b*) those who occupy positions of authority either share the charisma of the leader or possess a charisma of their own; (*c*) the criteria for selection of leaders is not family ties to the leader or technical qualifications; (*d*) the organizational structures are fluid and ill-defined; (*e*) there is no fixed hierarchy of officials and no legal rules governing the organization; and (*f*) there is no systematically organized economic support for the movement. Weber mentions that after the death of the leader the movement must become routinized in terms of either traditional or rational–legal authority if it is to survive.

---

[4] Interview with a member of the CCR prayer group of Mapusa on 18 September 2007.

Organization of the Catholic Charismatic Revival and Weber's Charismatic Authority

The first three characteristics of an organization, based on Weber's paradigm of charisma, which deal with leadership will be taken up later. We shall now analyse the remaining three characteristics of fluid organizational structures with respect to CCR—lack of fixed hierarchy and legal rules and lack of rational economic conduct. Weber clarifies that charismatic authority does not imply an amorphous condition but it indicates a definite social structure with a staff and an apparatus of services and material means that is adapted to the mission of the leader (Weber 1978: 1119). The CCR is not a single unified worldwide movement with a founder or group of founders like other movements. It is not like other structured organizations within the Catholic Church. The lack of a formal structure and formal hierarchy can lead to disagreements and problems and gives the appearance that the CCR is unruly, but Whitehead would argue that these characteristics draw attention to the fact that the Renewal is not man-made and comes directly and with sovereignty from God.[5] The fluidity of their organizational structures, the lack of emphasis on fixed legal rules, and the importance given to the charismatic and spiritual nature of the movement in most of their talks and writings is brought out well in the following words of a member of the Porvorim prayer group, 'In the CCR you can be yourself and really enjoy yourself. The CCR is like meeting God in a picnic, a very informal, friendly manner. ... The CCR has now converted the Good Friday Christians to Easter Sunday Christians with joyful faces.'[6]

The goals of a movement determine its type of organizational structures, and its followed pattern of membership and leadership. From the data collected through interviews and informal conversations, the main goal of the Charismatic movement is the spiritual and personal transformation of the individual Christian. Since the aim of the CCR is to share the experience of the Holy Spirit (Pentecostal experience) with individuals, it has tried to preserve the charismatic nature of the movement. The CCR ideology has implied spontaneity, emphasis on

[5] *Shalom,* January 2007: 7.

[6] Interview with a member of the CCR prayer group of Porvorim on 1 August 2007.

experience, and orality of tradition. This ideology necessitates a minimum of structures and non-rigid organizational patterns. The belief that all those who experience the spirit and are Born-Again are 'equal' before the Lord, has led to the CCR, at least in theory, to eschew all hierarchical patterns of leadership.

The CCR is neither a hierarchical nor a highly structured organization and has no central leadership. At the international level, the CCR is served by the International Catholic Charismatic Renewal Service (ICCRS), the main coordinating organization of the CCR at the world level. Since the CCR is in the first place a local phenomenon and not an international or national movement, it is directly under the jurisdictional authority of the diocesan bishop. While the ICCRS is there to provide service to all the individuals and groups in the CCR, it does not have the authority to decide for others on the national or diocesan levels as to the direction of the CCR in their areas. It has no juridical authority over the CCR. Similarly, at the national level the CCR is served by the NCCRS, which was officially granted recognition by the Catholic Bishops' Conference of India (CBCI) as a national Catholic organization in September 1996. Like the ICCRS, the NCCRS has no juridical authority over the CCR in India. It is only there to provide service to all the different forms and expressions of the CCR in India.

The decentralized and non-hierarchal nature of the CCR is further noticed in the working of the many independent Charismatic preachers in Goa. Many of these preachers are parish priests who do not submit to the GST, which is mainly a body of laypeople. These priests feel that they are working under the bishop and so submit only to his authority. Meanwhile, the other independent Charismatic preachers, who are mainly laypeople, do not come under the jurisdiction of any of the CCR regulating bodies. They are completely independent and not bound by any Church guidelines for the Charismatic movement. Only when they want to organize any Charismatic programme in the parish do they have to submit to the parish priest. Thus, the CCR, while not having any organizational structures of its own at the parish level except the parish-based prayer groups, has integrated itself within the structures and the modes of authority of the Church.

According to Weber, while bureaucracy depends on continuous income, charisma lives in, not off, this world (1978: 1113–16). Charisma is never a source of private income but receives the requisite means through sponsors or through honorific gifts, dues, and other voluntary contributions of its own following (Weber 1978). The CCR in Goa is a voluntary organization with no fixed source of income. People voluntarily contribute for any charismatic programme. All prayer groups make an annual voluntary contribution to the GST fund; besides that, several individual members and well-wishers contribute. It is not binding that each prayer group should contribute a fixed amount.

The GST organizes nearly two retreats every month in Goa. Though they charge the retreatants, the income they receive is not enough to meet the expenses. Though the CCR is in Goa since 1974, they have so far not been able to have a Charismatic office in Goa with qualified, paid, full-time office staff. Almost all the officials working in different Charismatic bodies work part-time and do not draw any salary. When the National Charismatic Convention was organized in Navelim, Goa, in 1999, the total expenditure for the convention came to around ₹1,000,000–1,500,000. The GST spent ₹100,000, while the NST contributed ₹150,000. The remaining money came from prayer group members and from different persons, some of whom were not even part of the movement. The chairperson of the GST, who was the main organizer of the convention, had to spend a lot of his own money for the convention.

Routinization of Charisma and the Web-Like Structure of the Catholic Charismatic Renewal

Based on Weber's paradigm of charisma, we have seen charismatic elements present in the organization of the CCR, such as lack of fixed hierarchal set-up, decentralized leadership, and few well-defined structures. Weber mentions that charismatic authority is naturally unstable and when the extraordinary situations and events that lifted a charismatically led group out of everyday life flow back into the channels of workaday routines, at least the 'pure' forms of charismatic domination will wane and turn into an 'institution' (Weber 1978). There is no doubt that the present-day CCR in Goa is not the pure form of Weber's charisma but has been routinized and, in the words of Choi, 're-institutionalized' (1986: 116).

The awareness and concern about the bureaucratization and institutionalization of the Charismatic movement, which is leading to stagnation, has been expressed in various fora in the CCR. Jorim Mendonca, who was twice chairperson of the GST, in an article titled 'CCR in Goa—Where are we? Where are we going?',[7] and while speaking to me about the institutionalization of the Renewal said: 'As the CCR has grown it has become more of meetings, structures, and administration and it is becoming more fossilized. Organizations become institutions and institutions have a tendency to fade into irrelevance. Movements become monuments, inspiration becomes institutions, and passion becomes paralysis.'[8]

According to Weber (1978: 1121), the main cause for routinization of charisma is the desire to transform charisma and charismatic blessings from a unique, transitory gift of grace of extraordinary times and persons into a permanent possession of everyday life. The charismatic community of a prophet tends to become a Church or sect. The CCR too has tried to transform the original charisma of the extraordinary experience of the outpouring of the Holy Spirit that occurred among the first Catholic Charismatics into a permanent possession by re-enacting it periodically in the prayer groups and through the various ministries and activities of Charismatic individuals, teams, and centres. The process of the growth of the CCR has led to the mushrooming of a vast diversity of charismatic phenomena in different stages and modes of development, and with differing emphases, often without any common norms or guidelines binding them. The types of relations between the individuals, teams, ministries, and centres of the CCR assume a web-like pattern.

The different parish-based prayer groups operate autonomously in their own parish set-ups and the sense of being a global organization is felt only in the common state-level or national-level programmes and activities. Pentecostalism organizes itself in a web-like network with the various cells bound through intersecting sets of personal relationships (Gerlach and Hine 1970). Many of their programmes and activities are modelled on weaving together web-like networks. One such activity conducted by the ICCRS and NCCRS in May 2007, which reveals the web-like network of the CCR was 'Operation Upper Room 2007'. This nine-day Pentecost novena saw prayer groups/

---

[7] *Shalom*, March 2007: 11–12.
[8] Interview on 11 November 2007.

individuals praying 12 hours a day for nine days, weaving a dense 12-by-9-hour prayer net of adoration and intercession. The purpose of this prayer net was for a 'new outpouring of the Holy Spirit' during the 40th anniversary of the CCR (*Shalom*, June 2007: 10). Thus, the model of umbrella bodies or web-like networks rather than a hier-archal organization with well-defined structures describes the CCR organization best and seems best suited to transform the charisma of the original Pentecostal experience of a few into a permanent posses-sion of the entire movement.

Prayer Groups: Building Blocks of the Catholic Charismatic Revival

The basic structure of the CCR globally and particularly in Goa is the prayer group, which comprises all types of people and are mostly parish-based, though sometimes trans-parish in nature. The dominant form of the neo-Pentecostal movement in New Zealand also consists of prayer groups (Reidy and Richardson 1978: 225). The prayer group is the building block of the CCR. A typical Charismatic prayer group in Goa has around 20–50 members, facilitating both adequate group dynamics leading to fellowship, and personal attention to individual members. Kilian McDonnell (1987), while explaining why the ultra-conservative and highly structured Roman Catholic Church accepted the Charismatic Renewal, gives the reason that the CCR, especially in the US, was either embodied in a trans-parish prayer group or was orga-nized as a parish-based prayer group that coexisted alongside already existing parish societies. The grass-root and distinctly non-clerical (lay) nature of the CCR stem from the prayer groups, which are found in the remotest parishes of Goa. The prayer groups meet at least once a week for a prayer meeting, where all the members come together to pray. The Merces prayer group keeps a register of all its members. Each member is given an identity badge and attendance is taken at the prayer meetings. Considering they are mainly housewives, with little education and coming from a village background, they are quite well-organized. The leadership of the prayer group is managed by a core group. The core group comprises the prayer group leader and few other members chosen through a process of election/appointment. All the parish-based prayer groups in Goa are under the jurisdiction of the local pastor. He regulates the resource persons who give talks to the group and screens the topics for the talks. Occasionally, he himself or his assistant preaches to the group.

There is also a good deal of division of labour within the prayer group. Whenever they organize retreats, talks, recollections, or any other programmes, the leader allots responsibilities to different members, as well as responsibilities for the prayer meeting. The prayer groups are not just pious associations for religious activities but are social groups that organize various activities that build close ties between the members. The members of the Merces group visit hospitals (about once or twice a month), visit people in their neighbourhood, pray at sick and dead people's houses, and perform other works as a group. When someone from the group dies, they all gather together, visit the family, and pray for the dead person.

Goa Service Team

If the ICCRS is the fulcrum, the spider of the web-like organization of the worldwide CCR, the GST is the spider of the CCR in Goa. It coordinates and regulates all the activities of the CCR in Goa. The non-clerical nature of the CCR in Goa can be gauged by the fact that not once has a priest become chairperson of the GST, unlike the service teams in other parts of India. Also, except one, all the chairpersons of the GST have been from the urban areas, though the members of the team have been from both urban and rural areas. The names of the various chairpersons of the GST over the years are as follows:

1978–81	Phyllis Dias
1981–3	Anthony Correia
1983–4	Captain Louis Mendonca
1984–6	Brother Mulligan
1986–9	Brother Mulligan
1989–91	Francis Menezes
1991–3	Noemia Mascarenhas
1993–5	Jorim Mendonca
1995–7	Francisco Dias
1997–2000	Jorim Mendonca
2000–3	Savio Mascarenhas
2003–6	Savio Mascarenhas
2006–	Eric Correia

The GST organizes a lot of programmes during the year. For example, the GST's programme list in 2006 had 58 programmes for the year, while in 2007 it was 46 programmes, including retreats, meetings, training and formation programmes, gospel music nights, lenten missions, youth rallies, family day, national day of intercession, and so on. Besides the programmes of the GST, many other programmes are organized by individual prayer groups and the independent Charismatic preachers and ministries.

Leadership in the Catholic Charismatic Revival

The leadership of the CCR right from its inception did not strictly match Weber's ideal type of charisma. There was no single prophet, hero, or leader who founded the CCR and commanded devotion from his followers due to his exceptional charismatic qualities. From the beginning, the focus of the CCR was on the charismatic qualities of Jesus Christ and the effect of the overwhelming power of the Holy Spirit. In case the charismatic leader is considered a unique incarnation such as Christ, his temporal representative becomes his successor and this process of finding a successor to the prophet channels charisma towards legal regulation and tradition (Weber 1978: 1123–5). The question of whether the Catholic Charismatic leaders are considered representatives of Christ or to be just occupying a legally and rationally defined office will be taken up in this section.

Nature of Leadership in the Catholic Charismatic Revival

An article on leadership that appeared in the October 2007 issue of *Shalom*, the newsletter of the CCR in Goa, listed the following criteria for becoming a leader in the CCR:

1. One should be a 'doer' of the word, and not just a hearer.
2. One has to regularly spend at least one hour in personal prayer, to listen to what God is saying to him/her regarding the group.
3. One has to meditate on scripture, which will confirm the messages heard in prayer. He/She should also be familiar with the teachings of the Church.
4. One has to receive the sacraments, which will provide the necessary grace to live this commitment in service and fellowship.

All the above-stated qualities of a leader are spiritual and charismatic in nature. What is demanded of a leader of the CCR is not any specific technical, academic, or physical qualifications but that he/she shares in the sacred charisma and grace of God and as his representative follows the directives of God regarding the running of the group. An article on leadership in the Charismatic prayer group states that a prayer group leader is supposed to be a leader and not a manager.[9] Leadership in the CCR is more about guiding the heads and hearts of members in the prayer meeting to a close encounter with Jesus and genuine fellowship among members, rather than just efficiently conducting the prayer meeting.

All the independent Catholic Charismatic preachers who draw huge crowds for their programmes possess a charisma of their own. They naturally become the leaders of their respective ministries and centres, not selected by any rational procedure but self-appointed and, as Weber puts it, 'acclaimed' by their followers (1978: 1123–5). A young female Charismatic had this to say about a well-known Charismatic priest: 'You can feel the power of God when he speaks.'[10] Often an increase in the number of followers is taken as proof of the charismatic qualities of the leader. When the present leader of the Merces prayer group, a very charismatic person, took over as leader, the strength of the group was hardly 10–20. After seven years in charge, the number has shot up to nearly 150 members. Another indication that leadership in the CCR is not based on rational–legal authority is that most of the leaders in the CCR in Goa are part-timers, ordinary laypeople with hardly any formal training in spirituality, theology, or management techniques, but with high levels of dedication and commitment. For example, the present chairperson of the GST is an advocate who is busy all day at his practice.

At the same time, the routinization of charisma into rational–legal authority is seen not just in the organizational structures of the CCR but is also noticed in the emphasis on leadership training. The CCR in Goa has regular leadership-formation training for prayer group leaders, core group members, sector and zonal leaders, and apostolate leaders, in which the teachings of the Church, leadership training, the need for

---

[9] Bosco Vaz, *Shalom*, July 2006: 1.

[10] Interview with a member of the CCR prayer group of Mapusa on 11 August 2007.

continuous prayer, sacraments, inner healing, and scripture reading in the lives of the leaders are imparted. Leaders are taught how to conduct and evaluate a core group meeting, how to conduct and evaluate a prayer group meeting, how to devise a plan for the prayer group, and so forth.

Criteria for Choosing a Leader

Modes of choosing a leader in the CCR are diverse: some are simply invited to take up leadership; some are elected or appointed to do so; and some others are self-appointed because they have the vision and commitment to start a new group or ministry. The process of electing leaders for all the prayer groups under the GST follows a general pattern. In the first phase, all the members of the prayer group listen to several teachings on leadership at least a month or so before the election. The teachings are given by a team from the GST. Just as Jesus prayed before choosing his core group (disciples), all prayer group members are asked to pray and they believe the Holy Spirit will show them whom to choose as leader. Weber makes an allusion to this charismatic dimension of the 'election' of a new king, pope, bishop, or priest when he says that this was not an 'election' in the modern sense of a presidential or parliamentary election but was something completely different, namely the recognition of a qualification older than the election: charisma (Weber 1978: 1126).

After the prayer, usually before the Blessed Sacrament, the election is held by secret ballot involving all the members of the prayer group. Every member of the group is eligible to vote and has a chance to be elected as leader. The process of election gives an indicative vote that is then used by the discernment group, which normally consists of an elected member, the outgoing leader, and some GST members to select the leader. It is not necessary that the one getting the maximum votes will be chosen the leader. For example, a former leader of the Mapusa prayer group was chosen as its leader though another member got more votes than him, because that person was new in the group. This is an important recognition of the presence of charisma in the CCR leadership. As Weber acknowledges, once succession is determined by the majority principle, charismatic domination begins to yield to a genuine electoral system (Weber 1978). The term of leadership of the prayer group and also the core group is three years. Once a person is elected for two terms in succession, he/she can be elected again either as leader or as a member of the core group only after a break of three years/one term. The function of the core group is to assist the leader in managing the affairs of the prayer group. While the election of leaders in the CCR appears very rational and systematic, it can be described as a process of discernment since the Charismatics believe that God is guiding them to choose a particular person as leader. This gives a religious legitimization to the leaders, chosen not because of their qualifications, but because they share in the charisma of Jesus.

Membership Recruitment Patterns

For any Catholic, joining the CCR was not a major shift in the traditions of their faith, but was like joining any other parish-based association such as Sodality, Marriage Encounter, or Couples for Christ. In most cases the Catholic Charismatic 'did not undergo what in sociological if not in theological terms would be called a conversion' (McDonnell 1976: 37–8). Charles Harper in his analysis of the Catholic Charismatic movement presents a conversion model that stresses a dramatic 'turning point' event, which is the culmination of 'stressful experiences' (Reidy and Richardson 1978: 223). Full commitment is achieved through the development of personal ties and the gaining of more knowledge about the group and its ideology. Hardly any of the members of the CCR mentioned a dramatic 'turning point' event as in Harper's model, though many of them mentioned some 'crisis event' in their lives, which led them to the Renewal. A man got into alcohol and drugs at a young age. He did not even finish his college, and was involved in drinking and drugs for nearly 25 years. There is a saying among drug addicts, 'Once a junkie, always a junkie.' He had tried a lot to give up drugs but to no avail. Finally, in desperation, he attended a two-day retreat conducted by the Potta Charismatic team at Calangute on the advice of a friend. That was the turning point as he came to realize that God would not forsake him and he began going regularly to Potta, Kerala, for retreats. Slowly he gave up both drugs and alcohol and joined the Mapusa Charismatic prayer group.

A Hindu widow belonging to the Merces prayer group was rather irregular in attending the weekly prayer meetings until once one of her sons had an accident and had to have an operation. He was in a critical condition and she was deeply affected by it. In tears, she fasted and prayed for him on her knees in Church. She also asked the Charismatic group members to pray for him and she believes that due to their prayers he recovered completely. Since then she has been regularly attending the prayer meetings and even shared this experience of healing in the group. Similarly, there are many other stories of people joining the Renewal due to some difficulty or problem in their lives. Thus, the 'problem' or 'crisis event' plays an important role in leading people to join the CCR.

Various studies on religious movements have pointed to the importance of personal and pre-existing networks of social relationships in the recruitment of members (Salazar in Fuss 1998: 497). According to McDonnell (1976: 38), the research of Gerlach and Hine (1968; 1970) and McGuire (1974) all point to the importance of recruitment by a committed participant. The field data on the Mapusa and Merces prayer groups suggests a similar trend. In the Merces prayer group, most of the members were recruited by relatives, friends, or neighbours. Since most of the members of the CCR in Goa are women and are based in villages, they come to know about the Renewal from some neighbour, friend, or relative who is already attending the prayer meetings. In the case of city-based groups such as the Mapusa group, recruitment also takes place through colleagues at the workplace. Once the new members begin attending a prayer group meeting, often they are attracted by the ecstatic style of worship with powerful preaching on the word of God and lively music, besides the testimonies and praying in tongues. The intense group dynamics helps build close personal ties, which increases the attachment to the group.

Another important mechanism of sustaining and increasing the commitment of the neophyte, once the initial contact has been made, is the Charismatic retreats—the Potta retreat and the Life in the Spirit retreat. Most of the Charismatics I interviewed have gone for a retreat to the Divine Retreat Centre, Potta, Kerala. The Potta Centre is an independent Charismatic Centre started by the Vincentian priests in the 1980s. This centre, which began on a small note has grown tremendously and is today one of the largest retreat centres in the world. Many Goans began going to Potta from the mid-1990s and were bitten by the Charismatic bug. The 'Potta effect' is illustrated in the following cases.

A woman belonging to the Mapusa prayer group went to Potta because of her son. She found the retreat very good and felt the presence of God there, and within a few months she went again with her younger son. Soon after going to Potta she joined the CCR. So far, she has been to Potta 14 times, each time taking with her different people who have had problems in their lives.

Another member of the Mapusa prayer group described the Potta effect in the following words: 'I came in contact with the Renewal through my mother who went to Potta for a retreat. There she heard someone taking her husband's name and also my name. I was studying medicine at that time and had a fear of going to Potta. I was afraid that by going to Potta I would end up becoming a priest or becoming psychotic. But after going there, Potta turned out to be a new world for me and I came back with the feeling that I could conquer the world. At that moment I was filled with frenzy, a feeling that I could heal the world. I immediately joined the Mapusa prayer group.'[11]

Thus, the Potta effect was a major catalyst for joining the movement for many members of the CCR in Goa. It can be compared to the dramatic 'turning point' event found in Charles Harper's conversion model.

A key technique of initiation into the CCR in Goa, used by the GST, is the Life in the Spirit seminars/retreats, which can be regarded as a formal course of initiation. Life in the Spirit seminars are the safe, acceptable, middle-class induction techniques used in the Catholic movement, and are gradual and orderly (McGuire 1974). Once a person joins the prayer group and gets some understanding of scripture and other teachings, he/she participates in the Life in the Spirit Seminar, which is for 5–6 days. The GST conducts on an average one initiation retreat (Life in the Spirit Seminar) every month.

The talks during this retreat, given by laypeople chosen by the GST, usually begin with the Charismatic Christ, then move to the Charismatic Renewal, where a general description of the Charismatic Renewal is given right from the Pentecost event till the time it began in the Catholic Church in 1967 and also cover other important topics such as healing, baptism in the Holy Spirit, Charisma or ministry gifts,

---

[11] Interview with a member and former leader of the CCR prayer group of Mapusa on 3 August 2007.

the Charismatic Virgin Mary, and so on (Iragui 1977). People are also asked to make a general confession. Since the Charismatic movement has no rule of life or written constitution which all the members are obliged to abide by, membership in the CCR is voluntary and they can leave whenever they wish to: full commitment is achieved through Life in the Spirit seminars and retreats that assist the members to gain more knowledge about the CCR and its ideology.

An Overview of Neo-Pentecostalism in Goa Today

Any sociological description of neo-Pentecostals in Goa has to deal with two immediate problems. One is defining who a neo-Pentecostal is, while the other is getting reliable and accurate statistics about their numbers, given that there are hardly any written records. Moreover, even if there are any records, they are not easily available to 'outsiders', given the highly competitive religious economy of Goa. As clarified in the previous chapter, this work defines 'neo-Pentecostals' as including all the 'non-denominational' and independent Pentecostal–Charismatic groups and sects that came up since the 1970s and the Charismatics within the mainline Protestant Churches. They are also known as Born-Again Christians or Believers. Therefore, Classical Pentecostal denominations such as AG, IPC, and so on, and sects such as Jehovah's Witnesses are excluded from the category of neo-Pentecostals. Historically, neo-Pentecostalism in Goa is a recent phenomenon, with most of the groups originating after 1970.

IPC Pastor C.M. Saji, in his research on the Church-planting techniques used by different neo-Pentecostal Churches in Goa during his Master's in divinity studies, estimates that there are nearly 120 Churches in Goa comprising around 6,000–7,500 neo-Pentecostals or Believers, with about 90 known pastors (see Figure 2.2 for details of the main neo-Pentecostal groups). These statistics more or less match with those found in the *Transform Goa Update*, a prayer bulletin released at the All Goa Church Meet at Nuvem on 6 April 2007, which mentioned that at that time there were 115 Churches in 74 villages of Goa. At an All Panjim Church Meet on 21 March 2008, the assembled Believers were informed that by the end of 2007 there were 143 Churches in 102 villages of Goa. This means that in around eight months they were

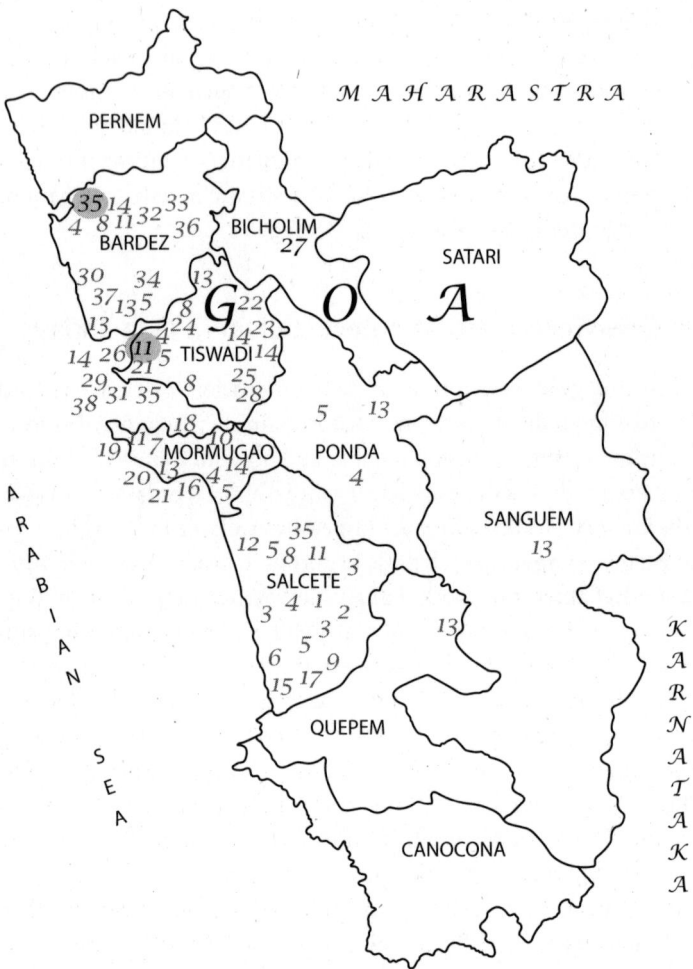

Figure 2.2   Distribution of New Christian Groups in Goa

Disclaimer: This map is not to scale and is provided for illustrative purposes only.

Notes: The 11 and 35, marked within circles, are the Churches where ethnographic fieldwork was carried out.

Symbol	Name of the Group (Number of Churches)
1	Samaritan Church (1)
2	Rhema Bible Fellowship (1)
3	Corner stone (3)
4	New Life Fellowship (5)

5	Indian Pentecostal Church (6)
6	Xubha Varthaman (1)
7	Word for the World (1)
8	Bethel House of Worship (4)
9	The Pentecostal Mission (1)
10	Evangelical Church (1)
11	New Frontiers International (4)
12	Eternal Life Fellowship (1)
13	Believer's Church, India (7)
14	Assemblies of God (5)
15	Christian Fellowship (1)
16	Laymen's Evangelical Fellowship (1)
17	Paraclithos Fellowship (1)
18	Goa Faith Community (1)
19	The Divine Delivery Ministry (1)
20	Good Shepherd Community Church (1)
21	Baptist Church (2)
22	Grace Fellowship (2)
23	His Family Worship Centre (1)
24	New India Church of God (1)
25	Bethesda Church (1)
26	Emmanuel Fellowship (1)
27	Susanthesh Prayer Assembly (1)
28	Emmanuel Church (1)
29	Hindustani Covenant Church (1)
30	Covenant Blessing Church (1)
31	Shilo Prayer Fellowship (1)
32	Greater Grace fellowship (1)
33	Jesus Christ the Corner Stone (1)
34	Zion Pentecostal Church (1)
35	World Revival Ministries (3)
36	Gilgal Fellowship (1)
37	Full Gospel Church of Calangute (1)

Source: Prepared by the author based on data collected during fieldwork.

able to plant 28 New Churches. These statistics need to be treated with caution as they cannot be verified.

From the around 120 neo-Pentecostal congregations in Goa, I used purposive sampling to choose two neo-Pentecostal groups for detailed ethnographic study, namely the WRM at Siolim and the ROLC at Panaji.

The criteria for selecting them were: the group should be representative of the neo-Pentecostal movement, should have at least 100 members of which a majority should be Goans, should have a pastor who is open to my interviewing his members, and should be affiliated to some foreign mission board (since I am interested in the import of globalized Charismatic Christianity into Goa). WRM, though an independent indigenous group, is affiliated to New Covenant Family of Ministries, which is based in the USA. There are around 500 members in three Churches at Siolim, Panaji, and Margao. The pastor conducts the services at Siolim and Margao, while a member of his congregation trained by him and his wife Joan conduct the services in Panaji.[12] The Church at Siolim is more than 200 strong and its members are mainly from a rural background. ROLC, which belongs to the NFI from UK is urban-based, having more than 100 members from different parts of Tiswadi taluka.

Place: Siolim

Siolim, a village adjoining the town of Mapusa, is spread out over a large area, with a total population of 10,936 (Census of India 2011). The literacy rate of 80.8 per cent and the sex ratio of 1,098 females per 1,000 males are much higher than that of Merces and Mapusa, indicating better human development in Siolim. This is seen in the long list of people of Siolim, who have excelled in different fields—music, sports administration, and also in priestly vocations. Hindus are the majority community at 65.8 per cent of the total population, while Christians are a sizeable minority at 30.5 per cent. There are two Catholic Churches in Siolim: St Anthony of Lisbon (1907) at Marna

---

[12] One of the criteria for selecting a neo-Pentecostal group was that the pastor should be open to my interviewing his members. Initially Pastor Domnic was quite friendly, allowing me to interview him and attend the Sunday prayer meetings. He even hosted a lunch for me at his house. However, after 2–3 months of participant observation when I requested permission to distribute a questionnaire among the members of his congregation and conduct a few interviews, he refused, thus disrupting my work. Thus, my data on neo-Pentecostalism, which was to be based on interviews and questionnaires from two groups, is now drawn mainly from the ROLC. The data from WRM is drawn mainly from participant observation and informal conversations.

and Our Lady of Consolation of the Persecuted (1971) at Sodiem (*Archdiocese of Goa and Daman Directory* 2006: 216). Besides WRM, there is another neo-Pentecostal Church belonging to the New Life Fellowship.[13] Siolim hosts the famous festival of Guddem Zagor, a manifestation of the cultural amity that exists between the two communities, who celebrate the Zagor jointly.[14] In the past, fishing, toddy-tapping, and distilling palm feni were the main professions. Today the people have shifted to small-scale industries, tourism, and business ventures with the village having many banks, hospitals, schools, shops, and restaurants. Additionally, many villagers have gone to the Gulf and other countries in search of greener pastures.

The capital city of Panaji in Tiswadi taluka is located on the southern left bank of the river Mandovi. Panaji, which succeeded the city of Goa (now Old Goa) as the capital of Goa in 1843, has a total population of 70,991 with a religious composition similar to Siolim—Hindus constitute 64.1 per cent of the total population, while Christians are 26.5 per cent. It has a Catholic Church founded by the Dominicans before 1541 and dedicated to Our Lady of Immaculate Conception (*Archdiocese of Goa and Daman Directory* 2006: 158). This small but crowded and bustling city has nine neo-Pentecostal Churches, including the ROLC. The major Classical Pentecostal denominations also have Churches here. Besides, there are well-known temples such as the Mahalakshmi temple (1817) and the Maruti temple (1933).

People

Getting reliable and accurate information about the socio-economic profile of the neo-Pentecostals was a difficult task. Often for strategic

---

[13] Taken from a list compiled by Pastor C.M. Saji.

[14] The word Zagor comes from the word *zargan* which means night vigil. It is a nocturnal vigil of the deity in honour of the village protector (Rakhno), locally known as Zagorio, for the protection of the village from every evil. The Zagor is a night-long dance–drama, which has no continuous plot or narrative and is performed in Siolim village on the first Monday after Christmas. Only males perform all the dances and women are not allowed on the stage in the Siolim Zagor, which is unique since both Hindus and Catholics jointly participate and organize the celebrations, the most notable manifestation of syncretic popular religiosity in Goa.

reasons, sects may feel called upon to exaggerate their size at moments when growth enhances a claim or to exaggerate their diminutiveness at moments when smallness seems to substantiate the theological and ethical correctness of a group's concern (Marty 1960: 129). The pastors of both the WRM and ROLC refused to allow the administering of a questionnaire to their members to elicit information about their socio-economic profile. As a result, the profile of the neo-Pentecostals that is described below is gathered from participant observation, informal conversations, and interviews.

The congregation at WRM, Siolim, that is around 200 strong, includes people from different villages in Bardez taluka, situated around Mapusa town. Most of them are married adults and are Hindus coming from poor or lower middle class families, and from lower castes. Around one-fourth of the congregation are from a Catholic background. Several of the Catholics have dual membership—they attend the Sunday services of the WRM and also continue to belong to the Catholic Church. Paul Parathazham (1996), who did a study on neo-Pentecostals in India, found that 41 per cent of the neo-Pentecostals in his sample, drawn from 328 neo-Pentecostal Churches, were previously members of the Catholic Church, while 31 per cent were formerly members of other Christian denominations such as the Church of South India (CSI) or Church of North India (CNI). Parathazham's study also shows that 26 per cent of those who left the Catholic Church were formerly actively involved in Catholic Charismatic groups. Around 10–15 per cent of the congregation are from the middle or upper-middle classes, well-educated with at least a college degree, and holding good jobs. Since the majority of the congregation are Goans, their services, which are on Friday (2.30–5.00 pm) and on Sunday (9.30 am–12.30 pm), are in English and Konkani. They also have a service in Panaji for migrants from Karnataka and North India, conducted in Hindi and Kannada. According to the pastor, the psycho-social background of the congregation reveals that many of them are people coming from broken families or single-parent households with deep emotional and psychological scars.

The congregation of NFI at Panaji comprises around 100 people, though an average of around 80 people attend the Sunday services. Around two-thirds of the congregation are Goans, while 25 per cent are settlers from other parts of India and around 10 per cent are foreigners from UK, Korea, Nigeria, and Germany. Due to this ethnic and linguistic mixture, the lingua franca in all their prayer meetings is English. The NFI congregation has a preponderance of women and married people, with more than 60 per cent being female worshippers. Around 30 per cent are youngsters and children (below the age of 30). A majority of the worshippers (more than 60 per cent) are in the age group of 30–50 years.

The profile of the neo-Pentecostals shows variations from Church to Church. Some Churches have mainly the migrant population and so their services are in Hindi or other vernacular languages. Other Churches deal mainly with locals and have their services in English or Konkani. The majority of the neo-Pentecostal groups are in the towns and cities, as can be seen in Figure 2.2. While there is a lot of diversity among the neo-Pentecostals, we can draw up a broad profile of the typical neo-Pentecostal in Goa. A majority of the neo-Pentecostals are adults in the age group of 30–60 years. Interestingly, only one in every five neo-Pentecostals is a youngster (below 30 years), in spite of the fact that their mode of worship with strong emphasis on the Western type of music and dancing should appeal to the younger generation. A majority of the Goan neo-Pentecostals were formerly Catholics. Neo-Pentecostalism in Goa is predominantly middle-class, with nearly two-thirds of their members belonging to the middle class. Close to one-fourth of them belong to the poor class and over 5 per cent can be classified as rich.

Sociology of Organization of Neo-Pentecostals in Goa

Any discussion about the nature and organization of new religious movements has to deal with the debate over what constitutes a sect/cult or denomination. Ernst Troeltsch and Max Weber, while theorizing about Church–sect typology described a sect as essentially a society established by contract as opposed to the institutional and 'natural' or organic ecclesiastical body (Eister 1967).[15] Sects over a period of time, due to the quieting of religious fervour and also due to various political factors, tend to take on the character of Churches as they establish

[15] For a critique of the Church–sect typology of Weber and Troeltsch, see Allan W. Eister (1967).

themselves in society. Most of the theories regarding the Church–sect typology have been built on Richard Niebuhr's theory by modifying his deprivation model to include other variables. In his work *The Social Sources of Denominationalism* (1960) he modified the Church–sect model of Weber and Troeltsch by introducing the concept of denomination. He stressed on genesis—when one is born into the Church, a natural social grouping—and entry—when one has to join the sect. The latter is the outlet for self-determination against the grain of religious or secular society. Niebuhr held that sects may have started as dissenting movements against the existing religious institutions but as the sect begins to develop economically, it becomes less dissent-oriented and more established in the mainstream as a respectable denomination. This gives rise to the need for another schism and the development of a new sect. This dialectical pattern in Niebuhr's model was built on the premise of the economic deprivation of its followers (Miller 1996). Niebuhr's model does not hold for the neo-Pentecostals in Goa since few of them come from economically deprived classes. Regarding entry into the sect, all the neo-Pentecostal groups stress that only when a person is mature enough to decide whether he/she wants to become a member, that person becomes a member. One does not become a neo-Pentecostal by birth. The children of the neo-Pentecostals have to choose whether they want to become a member of that Church once they cross 18 years.

Marty (1960) builds on Niebuhr's deprivation model by emphasizing the role of context rather than differences in content to distinguish between sects, cults, and denominations. The more isolated, intransigent, and withdrawn, and the less exposed and eroded a group has been, no matter what its size or influence, the less it has come to be regarded as a normative religious expression in America or elsewhere. Such groups belong to the category of sects and cults (1960: 128). Sects, by asserting their witness of the divine, organize themselves either in physical spatial contradistinction to or at least in psychological distinction to other competing groups, especially the typical or mainstream denominations (1960: 129). Ellsworth Faris' notion that the contemporary significance of sects is their isolation in a modern world (in Marty 1960: 131) and Stark and Bainbridge's Church–sect typology (1985) based on the criterion of 'state of tension' with the surrounding sociocultural environment are similar to Marty's ideas. A Church is thus characterized as a religious group that accepts the social environment in which it exists, while a sect is a religious group that rejects the social environment in which it exists (Miller 1996; 101).

The WRM was started by a man who had earlier been part of the CCR. He left the Catholic Church and started his own independent group. This group bears several of the above-mentioned characteristics of a sect. There is a lot of tension between the group and the local Catholic community, including physical fights. The state of tension with the surrounding environment found in Stark and Bainbridge's Church–sect typology is noticed in the tense relations that WRM has with the Catholic Church, the print media (who they feel are hand-in-glove with the Catholics), and the local village administration (especially the Sarpanch or the head of the Panchayat). He contrasts the 'hypocrisy' in the Catholic Church, whose traditions and practices are not in accordance with what God wants for his Church, where they stress on the relationship of individual members with God and are strict on not compromising on the Christian way of life taken from the Bible.

On the whole, the WRM is isolated from other neo-Pentecostal Churches as the pastor of the WRM is not very involved with the All Goa Pastor's Association and hardly attends any common programmes. Besides, other pastors are not invited to give teachings at the WRM's Sunday services, since the pastor is afraid that his congregation may get confused by other teachings. This isolation of the WRM fits with Faris' notion that the contemporary significance of sects is their isolation in a modern world.

During their Sunday prayer meetings, they recreate a different world with their loud music, singing, dancing and shouting, emotionally charged preaching, and bursts of praying in tongues. In this process of recreation, the worshippers are psychologically insulated from the real world outside.

Through their testimonies and teachings, the neo-Pentecostals are kept in constant tension with their social environment and also set themselves against too much organization and planting deep roots in a place. Their testimonies are often about people who have rejected lucrative job offers in the world and have decided to serve the Church full-time. Their pastors teach them that there are so many evils such as killings, divorces, sexual aberrations, and the like in the world, which urgently need Renewal. A pastor's prayer for every neo-Pentecostal in Goa was: 'Lord, restore the fire, do not just restore them to Church membership.'[16] Though the neo-Pentecostal groups that I studied exhibited several characteristics of sects, the self-identity of the neo-Pentecostals is that they believe they are the 'true' Church who have the only truth, while other groups that do door-to-door evangelization are sects and cults. Some of them also label the Catholic Church as a cult.

Recreation of the Concept of New Testament Church

Any organization has some degree of specialized division of labour, which generates a hierarchy of authority and a system of rules to achieve clearly defined and specific goals. While the global neo-Pentecostal movement is a loose conglomerate with no specific, clearly defined goals binding the entire movement, the organization of the specific neo-Pentecostal Churches is greatly influenced by their self-identification with the NTC. The neo-Pentecostals, through their teachings and practices, and the use of sacred symbols and ritualistic observances, tend to recreate the world of the early biblical Christians, found in the New Testament of the Bible. The NTC was a Church in the making without any well-defined structures or organization. Many passages in the Bible speak about the expected second coming of Christ in the immediate future, and so they were busy preaching the gospel and converting people to Christianity rather than establishing an institutional Church with permanent structures of governance. Therefore, all the organizational structures of the early Church were transitory in nature.

The neo-Pentecostal Churches try to recreate the NTC and, hence, do not plan large and permanent organizational structures. Since things are rapidly changing, often the precepts that the neo-Pentecostals hold as important on a particular day may be changed or replaced by some other teaching the next day. In many of the independent neo-Pentecostal Churches started by individual Charismatic personalities, there are no fixed liturgies or well-defined procedures and most of their

---

[16] Sermon by pastor of the ROLC during a Sunday Praise and Worship.

structures are fluid. Also, in most of them membership is constantly fluctuating with the influx of new members being balanced with the outflow of old members leaving for various reasons. This also adds to the transitory nature of the organization of neo-Pentecostalism.

Symbolism of the Sunday Prayer Meeting

The weekly prayer meeting, normally held on Sunday mornings, can be regarded as the symbol in recreating the world of the NTC. They normally meet in a hall, either in a hotel or a theatre, or at a member's house depending upon the number of worshippers. The weekly prayer meeting tries to recreate the community of the New Testament Christians who would meet behind closed doors in the houses of the disciples. Usually, the general structure and order of the neo-Pentecostal prayer meeting is as follows:

1. Praise and worship
   a. singing songs
   b. sharing testimonies
   c. reading scriptural passages
   d. prophesying
2. Announcements
   a. announcing forthcoming events
   b. introducing and welcoming newcomers
   c. collecting tithes (offerings that are one-tenth of one's total income)
   d. praying for those celebrating birthdays and anniversaries that week
3. Talks or teachings, usually based on the Bible (children are usually taken separately for Sunday school)
4. Concluding prayer/words by pastor
5. People chat and mingle, usually over coffee and snacks

In the prayer meeting of the WRM, members take the Bible pledge soon after the praise and worship to emphasize the importance of the biblical imagination. Normally, they have the breaking of the bread or communion ritual to recreate the biblical scene of the Last Supper once a month. The importance of the Sunday service as the key liturgical ceremony and the foundation of symbols in the recreation of the NTC is seen in the fact that most of the neo-Pentecostal groups have a serving team, which looks after the planning and organization of the service. In the ROLC, of nearly 100 members who attend the Sunday services, around 25 are in the serving team. On a Sunday morning, some members of the serving team reach the venue of the meeting by 7 am to get the hall ready for the first service, which begins at 8.30 am. The members of the serving team of the WRM, to emphasize the importance of serving, have a formal dress code—the women are in dark blue skirts with light pink blouses and dark blue vests and the men are in light pink full-sleeved shirts and dark blue vests.

The Sunday service recreates a world far removed from the world outside, with people packed in a hall swaying to amplified music blasting from huge speakers, which can be likened to a rock concert. Here, the worshippers can forget the world outside with all its worries and problems and freely dance, jump up and down, clap, sing, swing their arms, and cry or laugh aloud, without any inhibition. Music, a very important component of their Sunday service, has a therapeutic impact on the worshippers. The sophisticated music systems used in their meetings consisting of mixers, big speakers, electric guitars, expensive keyboards, drum sets, and the like transport them into the world of the NTC.

Leadership Structure among Neo-Pentecostals

Among neo-Pentecostals such as the CCR, leadership is not based on rational–legal authority but is charismatic. The pastor is the key authority figure in the local Church. Different neo-Pentecostal groups have different criteria for choosing their pastors. From among the NFI Churches, a pastor is chosen after observing for some time whether the person has the qualities mentioned in 1 Timothy 3:2–7,[17] namely, the person should be above reproach, the husband of one wife, temperate, sensible, dignified, hospitable, an apt teacher, not a drunkard, not violent but gentle, not quarrelsome, and no lover of money. He must manage his own household well, keeping his children submissive and

---

[17] All biblical references are taken from the Holy Bible, Revised Standard Version, Catholic edition.

respectful in every way, and must not be a recent convert. Additionally, he must be well-thought of by outsiders. There is no formal training or academic qualifications required to become a pastor, but the person chosen to become pastor gets some training in the Bible and psychology.[18] The jurisdiction of the pastor extends to every member of his congregation and in case of any dispute involving his members he arbitrates, but if the pastor himself is involved in the dispute then the pastor of the main Church of NFI, which is in Gogol, Margao, steps in to arbitrate.

To assist the pastor in looking after the congregation, there is a group of elders. In the WRM, which is an indigenous group founded by Pastor Domnic, there is no structure of elders since he is the sole charismatic authority. In the NFI, they hold that for good governance in the Church, God needs to raise many elders. One person can lead at the most a Church of 90 people. Once the number exceeds that, they need to have another structure of leadership, namely a group of elders. The qualities required of a bishop/elder are similar to those of a pastor taken from 1 Timothy 3:2–7. The NFI Church teaches that the leadership role in the Church is for men alone. It is not essential that elders should be preachers. A person could be helping only in one section such as accounts or administration and still be an elder. Usually, a person should have completed at least three years after he became a Christian before he can be considered for eldership. The three years are required to gauge a person and his walk with God.

While the neo-Pentecostals hold that elders are chosen by the Holy Spirit, which is the legitimization of their charismatic authority, it is actually the pastor who chooses the elders. Governing is the main work of the eldership team. The team of elders are like shepherds, entrusted with the work of governing and ruling the Church and keeping stability and unity among members in the Church. Besides the elders, there are prayer cell coordinators who are appointed by the pastor. Their duty is to animate the prayer cells, which meet once a week in different houses. None of the above structures of leadership require any formal training or technical qualifications. The only

---

[18] A more detailed analysis of the office of the pastor in the light of priesthood and marriage follows in Chapter 6.

prerequisite demanded of a leader is that he should know God and listen to his voice. In other words, a leader is one who shares in the charisma of the ultimate leader of the group, namely Jesus Christ. Thus, like the leadership in the CCR, the neo-Pentecostal leaders are charismatic people, whose charisma is routinized into a legally and rationally defined office.

Membership Recruitment Patterns of Neo-Pentecostals

Most of the Catholic Charismatics that I interviewed pointed to the financial help and material support given to the new converts as the main reason for their enrolment. For them, it was very obvious that these neo-Pentecostal Churches, heavily financed by foreign mission boards, offered lots of money to the poor migrants and Goan Hindus to join them. In a study on conversions within the Kerala Muslim community, Dale concludes that the conversion process was largely a steady and prosaic one that resulted from the interaction between a dynamic, egalitarian Islamic mercantile society and an exceptionally conservative version of Hindu caste society (in Robinson and Clarke 2003: 54–74). He makes an important point that some students of Indo-Muslim history, unaware of the size, economic significance, and wide distribution of early Muslim trading settlements, felt it necessary to offer a catastrophic explanation for the large Muslim population, which they felt was possible only due to 'forced' conversions (Robinson and Clarke 2003). In this section, I would like to situate the growth of the Pentecostal–Charismatic movement and their membership recruitment patterns in the context of a broader discussion on conversions with reference to the fieldwork data.

Membership recruitment among neo-Pentecostals begins with sustained, aggressive evangelism. This aggressive and enthusiastic evangelism stems from the vision of the NFI, which is to save the lost. This mission of saving the lost is realized through both public and private evangelism. Examples of public evangelistic events are Crusades, biblical dramas, prayer walks, gospel musical shows, and programmes on radio and television. A drama called 'Heaven's Gates and Hell's Flames' was staged in Panaji in April 2008 by several neo-Pentecostal groups. The drama portrayed Heaven as a place to cherish, something every human being should aspire to go to, while hell was shown as a fearful and frightening place, which every person should abhor. At the end, the main presenter appealed to the audience that those who wanted to give their hearts to Jesus should come forward near the stage, where several counsellors met them and took their names and addresses. The NFI pastor told me that a few families joined his Church due to that recruitment drive.

Equally effective is the private evangelistic technique of one-to-one evangelization such as door-to-door distribution of religious tracts and house visits practised extensively by most neo-Pentecostal Churches in Goa. A Catholic woman, who used to attend Charismatic meetings in Dubai and would get a lot of joy and peace from them, was unable to get what she wanted when she moved to Goa. At that time, the pastor of the ROLC had just moved to her neighbourhood and he and his wife would go around distributing tracts about giving one's life to Jesus and joining their Church. This woman who was searching for a substitute for her Dubai Charismatic meetings read the tract and decided to go for the meetings at the ROLC. Another example of the efficacy of house visits is the example of a woman who had just started attending the Sunday services of the ROLC. Since she was just recovering from an illness, she did not go one Sunday. Immediately the pastor visited her place to enquire and pray for her. That touched her a lot and convinced her that this was the Church for her.

The neo-Pentecostals in Goa are ready to go to any extent and expend any amount of time and energy to woo new converts. The pastor of the NFI Church, while explaining how he became a neo-Pentecostal, said that his mother was dying of kidney failure. His family, which was Catholic, had heard that there were some Christians who would pray and heal people. After exhausting every possible means, they called these Christians to come and pray. They phoned them at around 9 pm, and were surprised to see an English man and some Goans with him (of NFI) at their doorstep by 10 pm. Their willingness and commitment to drive more than 10 km and come into their village at that late hour impressed the pastor and his brothers who later joined their group. The main reason given by the pastor for joining the NFI was the curing of his mother, which he attributed to their prayers. The above incident brings us to another important factor contributing to people joining the Pentecostal–Charismatic movement, namely the phenomenon of Pentecostal supernatural healings and miracles. Choi in his study of new religious movements in Korea found that the most common motivation for attending the Full Gospel Church was to get healed (1986: 142).

Most of those whom I interviewed were attracted by private evangelism practised by family members, relatives, and acquaintances. This approach of using micro-social networks of kinship relations and personal contacts appears more effective in the growth of the neo-Pentecostal movement in Goa, just as in the case of the CCR. Every neo-Pentecostal is expected to be a missionary in his/her family, neighbourhood, and workplace. The research studies of Stark and Bainbridge, Max Heirich, and Chambers suggest that interpersonal relationships, affective bonds, and informal social networks of individual adherents are an essential element of recruitment in typical Charismatic congregations (Hunt, Walter, and Hamilton 1997: 144). Parathazham (1996: 4) also found that the majority of the neo-Pentecostals in India were introduced to the movement through their friends or family members. The importance of personal contacts and networks of social relationships in the recruitment of members in the neo-Pentecostal movement is illustrated in the case of a Hindu woman, who married a Goan Catholic. Being brought up in Mumbai she was exposed to all kinds of religions in her childhood. In a bid to find a solution to her marital problems, which began soon after her wedding, and the fear of darkness that was constantly affecting her, she involved herself vigorously in Hindu rituals and customs, but to no avail. At that time, one of her friends had come from Potta and on her advice, she tried Catholic prayers, novenas, and rosaries, but her fears remained. Then, another friend challenged her to read the Bible and keep a fast. When she did that, she felt as if some oppressive burden was being lifted from her. One night she went with that friend to a Crusade and since then her faith in Christ began strengthening and she became a neo-Pentecostal and joined the ROLC.

Sometimes, bonds of kinship also lead to the acceptance of the new faith by kin or affines of neo-Pentecostals. A member of the ROLC was, before his conversion, a Catholic. In 1989, he married a Catholic woman only to discover after marriage that she secretly was a Born-Again Christian. His parents, who were also Catholics, were not at all happy, but since her background was good, they decided not to throw her out. Slowly under her influence, as she shared the

Bible with them, both he and his parents became neo-Pentecostals. Dube, in a study on conversion to a popular Hindu religious group called Mahima Dharma in Orissa, mentions that in several cases Mahima Dharmi daughters-in-law succeeded in influencing their husbands and parents-in-law to become *bhakta*s or devotees (in Robinson and Clarke 2003: 236).

Another illustration of the influence of family members on conversion to neo-Pentecostalism is seen in the case of Terrence (name changed), a Hindu from Tamil Nadu. His mother, whom he considers a brave woman and visionary, wanted her children to be out of that place due to the languid pace of life and conservative nature of the society in that hilly area. Therefore, she sent his younger brother to a Christian orphanage, where he not only got educated, but also became a Pentecostal without the knowledge of his family members. Once, when he came home, he brought along with him a Christian missionary from his orphanage. His mother was touched by the missionary's teachings and decided to become a Christian. She also requested the missionary to take Terrence out of that place. Therefore, he was brought to Bangalore to a Pentecostal pastor's house, where he learnt all the teachings on sin, eternal life, and salvation and thus became a neo-Pentecostal.

Once the initial contact has been made with the potential member, he/she is invited to attend the Sunday services and the prayer cell meetings. Both these structures, through the ecstatic mode of worship, loud music, and ritualistic practices such as testimonies, prophecies, and glossolalia, are geared towards attracting, recruiting, and socializing the neophytes. The intense group interaction and the participative nature of the Sunday services give a sense of fellowship and belongingness to the new members, providing them with the much-needed support system to increase their commitment levels. Similar to the role of the Life in the Spirit seminars adopted by the CCR as an induction technique, the NFI groups use the Encounter with God programme to familiarize the new converts with the basic foundations of faith.[19] The aim

---

[19] The Encounter with God programme is a specific induction technique used by NFI, generally lasts for 1–2 days, and is intended to convey their main teachings to neophytes in order to help them become committed members of the Church.

of the programme is to give, in a nutshell, the main teachings of the ROLC so that those who want to become committed members, that is, take water baptism, can make an informed decision. This fits in with Harper's model of conversion, which proposed that full commitment is achieved through the gaining of more knowledge about the group and its ideology.

The above cases of conversion to neo-Pentecostalism reveal that there is no single predominant factor that explains all the conversions. While in the case of many it was the strong evangelization drive, both public and private, that led them to join the movement, for others it was through family members or other acquaintances that they were attracted and recruited. Some were attracted by the high level of commitment and the power of healings present among the neo-Pentecostals. In the case of other converts, a crisis event in their lives acted like a trigger, pushing them eventually towards a change of religion. Some of them were attracted by the ecstatic style of praise and worship and the warmth and fellowship they experienced from the neo-Pentecostals. In most cases, it was not one single causal factor or event that led to a change of religion, but a combination of factors, often mundane and set in the context of everyday life, that opened up new possibilities for the convert and eventually led to a change of religious identity, often without the person even realizing the magnitude of the change.

Unlike mass conversions where some major social or political events trigger conversion, individual trajectories of conversions are never so dramatic and do not follow a linear cause–effect path. From my field data, it can be argued sociologically that a person does not convert for purely rational reasons. In most cases, rationalization is a post-conversion reflection on the part of the convert when confronted with the question, 'Why did you convert?' In the above analysis of conversion to neo-Pentecostalism, I have tried to follow Dale's advice that it is necessary to populate theories of conversion with individuals and place them in a specific locale rather than a general context (in Robinson and Clarke 2003: 72). Otherwise there is a tendency to end up with general and rather vague theories of conversion that posit force, financial benefits, miracles, and healings, or a crisis event as the casual factor for the change of religion, which in reality is only a partial explanation for the phenomenon of conversion.

Economy of the Religious Organization

Like the CCR, the neo-Pentecostal Churches in Goa are voluntary organizations with no fixed sources of income. According to Weber, in an
organization based on charismatic authority there is no systematically
organized economic support for the organization. Salazar, in his study
of the fundamentalist evangelical movement in the Philippines, reports
that some groups such as the Bread of Life Ministries assert that they
do not receive donations from other Churches but depend entirely on
tithing (Fuss 1998: 499). Both the neo-Pentecostal Churches in Goa
that I studied claimed that they do not regularly receive any funds from
abroad but get all their finances from tithes and donations. From my
fieldwork, I have noticed that the practice of giving tithes is given lot
of importance in the Sunday services of the neo-Pentecostal Churches.
The pastors spend a lot of time speaking on tithes and urging their
faithful to give tithes generously. The pastor of the WRM is very brazen
in asking his congregation to give tithes. He openly asks his congregation for ₹1,000,000, which can be met if ten people give ₹100,000
each. He frightens his faithful with quotations from the Bible such as
Malachi 3:6–12, which says that people have robbed God by not giving their tithes and offerings and they have no right over that money,
since it belongs to God. If they do not give tithes, they are allowing the
Devil to attack their family and children and are inviting a curse from
God. Other pastors are more subtle in their approach to persuade their
faithful to give tithes. A pastor at a large gathering of neo-Pentecostals
informed the people about the total money spent on that day's meeting
and used biblical quotations such as 'he who sows sparingly will also
reap sparingly … God loves a cheerful giver' (2 Corinthians 9:6–12) to
urge the people to give generously.

A technique used often by the pastors to inspire and urge the people
to give tithes generously is recounting the testimonies of people who
have donated generously to the Church and have been blessed by God.
The pastor of the New India Church of God at Panaji shared with his
congregation that a woman, a former member, who is now in England
recently sent a cheque of ₹60,000 for the Church. She told the pastor that she appreciated what she had learnt there. The pastor used
this example to convey to the people the message: 'God blesses you
not according to the size of your purse but according to the size of

your heart'.[20] Using the image of a ₹60,000 heart, he drove home the point that they can have the smallest purse and the biggest heart.

Another pastor compared giving tithes to investing in God's bank. While banks in the world have different offers of returns—10 per cent or 12 per cent—God's offer is 100 per cent or even more than 100 per cent. The effect of all these teachings and other techniques used by the pastor on the congregation is felt in the Sunday collections of the NFI Church. On an average, their Sunday collection is always above ₹5,000. For the drama 'Heaven's Gates and Hell's Flames' organized by the NFI Church in April 2008 in collaboration with some other Born-Again Churches, the Church collection reached nearly ₹100,000. Being a city-based Church with a predominantly urban, middle-class, white-collared working crowd, their Sunday collections are much higher than rural neo-Pentecostal Churches. Many of the people in the NFI Church come by car for the Sunday services, whereas the pastor of the WRM has to arrange a bus to transport his people from Mapusa to Siolim since many of them do not have a vehicle of their own. All the people of the NFI Church that I interviewed said that they give one-tenth of their income to the Church for the welfare of the pastor and other expenses. Besides fulfilling the function of sustaining the Church and its activities financially, tithing reiterates the sense of importance of each individual and the sense of contributing to the well-being of the spiritual family, that is, the Church. Through their donations to the Sunday collection, members are made aware of their important contribution to the building up of the true Church of God modelled on the biblical Church.

Both the neo-Pentecostal Churches in Goa are connected to Western evangelical groups—the ROLC to NFI, UK, and the WRM to the New Covenant Family of Ministries, USA—who spend a lot of money to plant Churches in different parts of the world. For example, NFI spent £3,436,547 in 2005 of which 50 per cent was spent on apostolic ministry and Church-planting. There is no empirical data on the finances of the New Covenant Family of Ministries. The ROLC is managed completely by professionals. The pastor of the ROLC works full-time

---

[20] Sermon by pastor of the New India Church of God during a Sunday service.

for the Church and depends on the monthly remuneration from the Church to maintain his family, including his wife and two daughters. The pastor's wife mentioned to me that since she found it difficult to run the house, she had to supplement her husband's meagre income by baking and selling cakes. All the Church accounts are handled by one of the members who has a doctorate in commerce. The Church has two trusts, which are looked after by a chartered accountant. The Church also has an advocate, whom the pastor consults for legal advice, and computer professionals, who look after the Church news bulletin. The Church office with its two full-time staffers, both members of the Church, is situated on the third floor of an apartment building within the city limits of Panaji. The above-mentioned professional staff and office premises entail large expenses besides the expenses of the various religious programmes and events organized by the Church as part of evangelism. Therefore, it is difficult to accept as credible their claims that they do not regularly receive funds from abroad but manage with tithes and local donations.

It is true that ROLC has a group of committed members who voluntarily offer their services for organizing any Church-related programmes. This group of highly committed and motivated individual members who contribute free labour help in cost-cutting for the ROLC. On the other hand, the WRM is much more secretive about sharing information and no empirical data is available on their finances. The founding pastor and his wife have a social trust, which reaches out to abused women. They have an ambulance, which provides free service for the entire village of Sodiem.[21] The venue of the weekly prayer meeting is the former residence of the pastor, where a large Church has been built. Nearly 15 young men and women are working full-time under the pastor and all of them are looked after by the organization. The pastor has a large well-furnished residence and also has a lot of land. A rough estimate of the assets of the WRM in 2007 would amount to nearly ₹10,000,000. All the worshippers who come for the prayer meetings are provided free transport from the nearest town of Mapusa and also given snacks and refreshments.

---

[21] For more details about all the social work done by the WRM, see http://www.fivepillarscc.org/socialservices.php?hd=8 (accessed on 13 September 2019).

Just as in the case of the ROLC, the WRM and most neo-Pentecostal Churches in Goa, too, are very secretive about their finances. However, given that these groups are rather diminutive in size and they spend a lot of money on organizing different religious programmes, especially connected with evangelism, they would require ample financial resources. Thus, the common belief that they receive substantial foreign funding appears true. The amount and nature of receiving foreign funds vary from group to group. Many of them have registered social trusts that are involved in various types of social development work such as running shelters for street children, homes for the aged, and providing health care services such as looking after HIV patients. While most of the neo-Pentecostal Churches in Goa receive funding from abroad and have formed trusts for their various works, they do not possess well-defined and systematically organized economic structures to run their Churches, which are voluntary organizations dependent on the largess of sponsors and benefactors.

* * *

While the previous chapter was a journey through the pages of history of the Pentecostal–Charismatic movement, this chapter has focussed on the present-day Pentecostal–Charismatic movement in Goa. Using purposive sampling, I have chosen two Catholic Charismatic prayer groups and two neo-Pentecostal Churches for a more detailed study. Based on a questionnaire administered to a sample of the Catholic Charismatics in Goa, the following profile emerged of a typical Charismatic: a middle-aged (above 40 years), married Goan woman, who is educated up till high school, is involved in the domestic domain (household work), is not earning, and belongs to the lower middle class. On the other hand, there are a lot of variations between the two neo-Pentecostal Churches studied. A majority of the neo-Pentecostals in Goa are Goan adults (between 30 and 60 years), mostly residing in the urban centres of Goa. Unlike the CCR, which has hardly any migrants, the neo-Pentecostal sects have a sizeable number of migrants from the neighbouring states and also a few from abroad.

The main goal of the CCR is the spiritual and personal transformation of the individual Christian and this requires spontaneity, orality of tradition, and minimum of structures. The CCR is neither a hierarchical nor a highly structured organization and the model of the umbrella body or web-like network describes the decentralized CCR organization the best. The basic building blocks of the web-like network of the CCR are the parish-based prayer groups that come under the jurisdiction of the local pastor. The neo-Pentecostal Churches of the ROLC and WRM can be both characterized as sects based on the models of Niebuhr and others. Both these sects identify themselves as the true biblical Church and recreate the world of the NTC through the symbol of the weekly prayer services.

The leadership model both in the CCR and among neo-Pentecostals echoes aspects of Weber's model of charismatic authority. Both the leaders of the CCR and the neo-Pentecostal Churches share in the charisma of the divine leader of the movement, namely Jesus Christ. Members are recruited to the neo-Pentecostal sects through public and private evangelism, healings, crisis events, networks of kinship relations, and personal contacts, and socialized through Sunday services, prayer cell meetings, and the Encounter with God programme. Among the Catholic Charismatics a crisis event, recruitment by friends and relatives, and charismatic retreats—such as the Potta retreat and Life in the Spirit seminar—play an important role in the recruitment of new members and the strengthening of that commitment. In the broader discussion on conversions to neo-Pentecostalism, several cases were examined and it was found that no single causal factor but a combination of leading factors, often mundane and set in the context of everyday life, led to people joining the neo-Pentecostal Churches. The examination of the economy of neo-Pentecostal groups in Goa revealed that most of them received foreign funds through registered trusts involved in various developmental works.

3 The New Testament Church and the Emergence of Religious Identities

Since Pentecostalism is now being studied by various external disciplines such as sociology, theology, anthropology, economics, and political science, one has a broader understanding of what it means to be a 'Pentecostal'. Thus, no single definition for the term 'Pentecostal' is possible anymore and we must think of Pentecostal–Charismatic movements with multiple definitions. Therefore, instead of foisting a standardized definition on the neo-Pentecostal Churches within the purview of my study, I allowed a local-level definition and identity to emerge from the answers of the individual Believers I had interviewed. Most of the neo-Pentecostals I interviewed identify their Church with the idea of the New Testemant or biblical Church and identify themselves as *Bible-believing Christians*. Since most of the neo-Pentecostal Churches in Goa are less than 40 years old, they assume the garb of the early biblical Churches to show a continuum between present-day neo-Pentecostalism and the nearly 2,000-year-old NTC. The members of the NFI quote from the Book of Revelation in the Bible, which speaks about seven independent Churches such as the Church in Ephesus, Church in Smyrna, and so on, and equate their congregation in Panaji to such independent biblical Churches. They identify their Church not as a denomination of the Catholic Church or coming from some Protestant movement, but as an NTC based on the Bible and animated by the Pentecost event, similar to the above-mentioned seven independent Churches.

In the process of identity formation for any individual, group, or section of society, the first step is identifying the other(s) and showing that they are distinct from the individual, group, or section of society. The NTC, which was a Jewish sect trying to assert its own separate identity after the death of Jesus, first tried to separate itself from the Jewish community on the one hand and the Roman state religion on the other. Second, to attract converts from the Jewish community, the nascent Church had to show some continuity with Judaism (Matthew's gospel is a good example of this) and at the same time maintain its 'newness' and superiority over the old Jewish faith (Pauline theology is an attempt to do this). The neo-Pentecostal movement in Goa, which identifies itself with the NTC, has also tried to carve out a separate religious space, which is distinct from other religious traditions in Goa. This marking of sharp and distinct boundaries with Catholicism and Hinduism, the two major religions in Goa, is carried out at different levels and at different loci. This chapter will describe the process of identity formation of the neo-Pentecostal movement both at the corporate and the individual levels, with the recreation of the NTC or biblical Church as the guiding marker.

Marking of Boundaries with the Catholic Community

As stated earlier, the NTC emerged from the Jewish community with all its early members and leaders, including its founder, Jesus Christ, being Jews. So, initially, the main tussles and conflicts were between the Christians and the Jews[1] as the nascent Christian community tried to separate itself from the parent Jewish community by selectively borrowing certain Jewish religious beliefs, practices, and symbols, as well as critiquing and rejecting others. Thus, the biblical Church at the first council of Jerusalem[2] rejected the practice of circumcision—the key external marker of Jewish identity inscribed on the body of the individual Believer.

Similarly, the neo-Pentecostals in Goa, whose founding leaders and early members were mainly from the Catholic community, have carved

---

[1] The Book of Acts in the Bible cites several instances of conflicts between the Christians and Jews.

[2] Acts 15.

their own separate identity by critiquing and rejecting many religious beliefs, practices, and symbols of their parent Catholic community. The neo-Pentecostals have had several conflicts with the Catholic community in Goa, which is described in detail in Chapter 6. The main contrast between neo-Pentecostalism and Catholicism, according to the neo-Pentecostals, is based on the idea of the NTC. The neo-Pentecostals argue that the Catholic Church has lost the original vision of the NTC and has compromised biblical values, while they have remained loyal to the vision and values of the New Testament.

The neo-Pentecostals, therefore, re-interpret the history of Catholicism as a history of greed for power of and manipulations by the Roman Empire and various other Christian kings over a long period of time, underlining how the Church has misused power during the Inquisition and other events in history. They argue that the Holy Spirit, which came down upon the NTC at Pentecost, is no longer working in the Catholic Church, which worships only Father, Son, and Mother Mary and so Catholics, just as the Hindus and Muslims, are still searching for the true and real God. So they redefine Catholicism as a man-made religion—'it is not god's wisdom, but man's wisdom,' said the pastor of WRM.

Popular Marian Devotion and Usage of Images

The two very important external markers of separation between the neo-Pentecostals and the Catholics, which are cited by many of the common folk, are popular devotion to Mary and usage of statues and images. Both these Catholic traditions are rejected by the neo-Pentecostals. These are not part of their idea of the NTC and so are strictly forbidden practices. Thus, litanies at wayside shrines; celebration of the feasts of saints and other parish feasts with their characteristic processions, fireworks, and fairs; innumerable wayside crosses and chapels; and larger Churches and Cathedrals seen all over Goa are characteristic of the Catholics and serve as external markers of distinction between them and the neo-Pentecostals. According to the neo-Pentecostals, popular Marian devotion is taboo since it portrays Mary, a human being, as God.

The neo-Pentecostals opine that Catholics are people who do not know how to pray, since for them to pray means reciting the rosary (intercessions to Mary). The neo-Pentecostals cite different examples to illustrate the inefficacy of prayers to Mary, which they regard as empty rituals. An example they give is that of a Catholic worshipper who tried to cast away a demon from a sick woman by placing a rosary on her and commanding the demon to come out in the name of the rosary. The end result was that the rosary fell on the ground and the sick woman did not get healed. The neo-Pentecostals term the Catholic tradition of using images, statues, amulets, and so on in their religious observances as idolatry. They cite from the Mosaic Law to show that idolatry is against biblical tradition.[3] Thus, a complaint heard from several Catholics is that the Believers visit Catholic houses and advise them to remove all images and statues from their houses. They also accuse the neo-Pentecostal pastors of making the new converts walk on rosaries or crosses to prove that they have apostatized their Catholic faith, since venerating and respecting rosaries and crosses is seen as a key external marker of Catholic identity.

Rejection of Catholic Practices and Traditions

The neo-Pentecostals reject several Catholic doctrines and traditions such as the necessity of good works of mercy and charity for salvation, celebration of Christmas on 25 December, feasts of different saints and the three kings, prayers and masses for the dead, and so on, all of which they claim are not in accordance with the values of the biblical Church. They say that Christmas is linked to a pagan Roman festival offering worship to the sun god, which was celebrated on 25 December, while the exact date of Christmas is unknown. They believe that a person after death is transported to a fantastic place in the presence of God, to be with Jesus forever. Therefore, there is no need to pray for the dead. Individual neo-Pentecostals criticize several observances and traditions practised by the Catholics, interpreting them as demonic and against the word of God.

The pastor of WRM said that he made a study of the crosses installed in different villages in Goa, wherein he found that people offer blood sacrifices at these crosses and many Catholic families have been affected because of this. A member of the ROLC gave the example of

---

[3] Deuteronomy 5:8–9, from the Bible.

Catholics in a village in Goa, who make a pilgrimage every year to Hindu temples and offer oil, coconut, and livestock to the Hindu gods. The point that the neo-Pentecostal groups are trying to make is that the Catholic Church has accommodated a lot of human traditions and cultural practices to permeate into their ritual observances, unlike the Born-Again Christians who only follow practices and traditions that are in accordance with their understanding of the Bible.

The neo-Pentecostals are especially critical of the religious professionals of the Catholic Church. The Catholic clergy is accused of promoting traditions and practices that are not in accordance with the NTC model. They cite the example of the festival of Zagor held in Siolim village where the Catholics and Hindus together worship the Zagorio, which is a demonic spirit.[4] They claim that this tradition was started by the local Catholic priest. The Catholic priests are also accused of not having adequate knowledge of the Bible. The neo-Pentecostals especially attack the Catholic position on the necessity of celibacy for priesthood and label the Catholic clergy as womanizers, drunkards, and not faithfully following their vows. They say that there is lot of hypocrisy and covering up with respect to the Catholic priests, whose faults are condoned on the pretext that they are also human.

Neo-Pentecostalism is assumed to be governed by grace in contrast to Catholicism, which is governed by rules and regulations. The neo-Pentecostals encourage Catholics to join their Churches since they argue that their faith is at a higher level compared to Catholicism. This idea is influenced by the letters of St Paul in the Bible wherein he labels the Jewish religion as legalistic (following the letter of the law) in comparison to Christianity, which is the religion of love (following the spirit of the law). They also reject the Catholic doctrine of transubstantiation[5] and the Catholic practice of infant baptism, which are both not in accordance with the standards of the biblical Church. They believe that neither the bread nor the wine becomes the body or

---

[4] Abreu (2007).

[5] Transubstantiation, according to Catholic theology, means essential change. This doctrine teaches that at the time of consecration in the mass, the substance of bread and wine, by the power of God, changes into the substance of Jesus' body and blood, while the empirical realities of bread and wine as phenomena remain.

blood of Christ respectively. The pastor of the ROLC, while giving a teaching on the Lord's Supper, ridiculed the Catholic position, saying that when the bread (host) falls down from the hands of the officiating priest, they may think Jesus tripped and fell.

The neo-Pentecostals are very careful in maintaining boundaries with the Catholic community, especially when it comes to participating in Catholic religious ceremonies. The pastor of the ROLC was once asked by his close Catholic friend to share the word of God during his wedding mass, but he refused, giving the reason that he did not want to interfere with the authority of the Catholic priest since that would cause problems. However, when the friend insisted that he at least sing in the choir during the mass, the pastor agreed with the condition that he would sing songs directed only to Jesus Christ and not to Mary. At the All Goa Church Meet held at Nuvem on Good Friday, 6 April 2007, and attended by more than 1,500 Born-Again Christians, a pastor said that while other religious people in Goa were mourning (implying the Catholics), they were singing and praising God. He justified their joyful behaviour by saying, 'Our God is a living god, he is the risen Lord and therefore we are not sad.'[6] This emphasis on Christ as the all-powerful risen Lord, while downplaying the human aspect of Christ, is an implicit critique of the popular Catholic tradition centred around the passion and death of Christ. Most villages in Goa celebrate the crucifixion (*pask* in Konkani) with a procession on Palm Sunday and a dramatic re-enactment of the passion of the Lord on Good Friday.

Marking of Boundaries with Other Religious Traditions

While the primary process of boundary marking for the neo-Pentecostals in Goa has been with the Catholic community, they have also drawn sharp boundaries with other religious traditions as well as other Christian traditions. A neo-Pentecostal family which moved from Bombay to Goa in 1993 were told by their pastor in Bombay that they could go to any spirit-filled or Pentecostal Church in Goa. They began going to a Pentecostal Church close by for fellowship, but soon realized

---

[6] Pastor at All Goa Church Meet, Nuvem, on 6 April 2007.

they were not comfortable there as there were many rules and regulations. So they stopped going anywhere for a year, and only when they found a neo-Pentecostal Church did they resume their Sunday worship. This shows that even among the Born-Again Christians there are different self-identities, which are in competition with one another. This will be taken up in more detail in the section titled: 'Assuming the Identity of the New Testament Church'.

When it comes to other non-Christian religions, the neo-Pentecostals have rather extremist positions. They draw their position from the New Testament model, where St Paul strongly condemns the existing pagan practices of the Greek and Roman religions. According to them, Satan's plan is to use different religions to take mankind away from God. Most of them subscribe to the view that the non-Christian religions are leading people away from heaven and into hell. The neo-Pentecostals clearly distinguish between the worldly persons (gentiles), who do not have the mind of Christ, and themselves, who have put on the mind of Christ. They use the biblical imagery of the weeds and the wheat to distinguish between the gentiles and themselves. Hollenweger (1972: 485) opines that the 'tribal religion' of Pentecostalism needs clear and tangible 'tribal marks' in order to make abundantly clear who belongs to one's own 'tribe', the Church, and who belongs to the 'hostile tribes', the world.

They draw clear-cut boundaries with other religious scriptures, pointing out that only the Bible is the word of God. Some of them even go to the extent of saying that all other scriptures are Satanic. Just like they do with the Catholics, the neo-Pentecostals cite negative examples of Hindus and Muslims, whose lives do not match with their scriptures to prove their point that other religious traditions and scriptures are taking people away from God. A woman when asked about her views on other religious scriptures narrated a joke about Bill Clinton, who after his death is given a choice by God to go to heaven or to hell. Clinton decides to check out hell where he sees glamorous and glittery bikini-clad women, while in heaven he sees everyone praying in white robes in silence. So he tells Jesus that he wishes to go to hell. After some time Jesus goes to see what has happened to Clinton. When he sees Jesus, he says, 'Please save me from here. I am burning in this fire.' Jesus tells him, 'But I gave you a choice. You wanted to go to hell.' Clinton replies, 'When I went to hell I saw bikini-clad women, which was actually only a screen saver.' The woman concluded by saying that other religious scriptures are like screen savers.

Since many of the neo-Pentecostals flock to babas and gurus, the pastors sharply attack these New Age gurus labelling them imposters and alleging that they take teachings from the Bible and change and twist them. The pastors strongly urge their Believers to read their Bible instead of seeking advice from these gurus and babas. For the neo-Pentecostals, practices such as yoga, meditation, Art of Living, and so on are taboo, since they believe that these practices are not just cultural but are rooted in religious traditions.

Neo-Pentecostalism as a new religious movement in Goa strives to carve out a separate religious space for itself, distinct from Hinduism, Catholicism, and other religions existing in Goa. They do that by showing that the others (pagans and gentiles) are stagnant and worship dead or false Gods, while their faith is characterized by dynamism, growth, revival, and commitment. The neo-Pentecostals believe that they are advancing the kingdom of God by assuming the values, symbols, and practices of their model of the NTC. They believe that as New Testament Christians they are the chosen ones certain of being saved and this gives them power over the pagans. Their God is a mighty God who will deal with their enemies and so, though they are few in numbers, their faith in Christ will give them victory over all their enemies.

Assuming the Identity of the New Testament Church

Dualistic Spiritual World View

The neo-Pentecostals have appropriated the world of symbols of the early Church that was characterized by a dualistic spiritual world view. They believe that they are in the world but not of the world. They are in enemy territory. But once they leave their mortal body, the enemy (Satan/Lucifer) can do nothing to them. An important aspect of this dualistic spiritual world view is the emphasis that things of the spirit are more important than worldly material things. At a neo-Pentecostal prayer meeting, the pastor asked the congregation to applaud the SSC students who were present all day at the prayer meeting in the midst of their board exams. The pastor's gesture brought home the point that the students, by trusting in divine intervention to help them in their exams, had taken a big step of faith.

They live in the spiritual world of the NTC, where the good spirits are engaged in a continuous spiritual warfare with the principalities and powers of darkness that are holding people in bondage. They use the name of Jesus, which is a powerful weapon for them to battle the evil forces, to break the bondage of the Devil over their families, their businesses, and their health and claim victory. This spiritual outlook makes them believe that all their day-to-day activities and all life events are the workings of the divine and so they offer spiritual solutions to social, economic, and political problems. They see God as one who is actively involved in the day-to-day activities of people, who is acting powerfully and doing amazing things in people's lives.

Thus, often in their prayer meetings the pastor and his team of elders pray over people who are suffering from different problems and afflictions. Many times, those prayed over fall to the ground or break out into loud weeping and wailing. They believe that day-to-day difficulties and problems such as broken marriages, quarrels, sicknesses, and different types of addictions are due to the tricks of the enemy, the Evil One. In this spiritual warfare between God and the Devil, the Devil troubles only the godly people, working overtime to steal from God. Therefore, the neo-Pentecostals have to be very active and alert in their lives to avoid becoming the victims of the Evil One. So, when they are in financial difficulties, or experiencing sicknesses or marital problems they are advised spiritual solutions such as turning to God more vigorously, fasting for several days, or forgiving someone in their family. They also undertake prayer walks, which is walking around a particular area or house to break down all the strongholds of the enemy. Their belief is that evil spirits have built strongholds in different areas, which can only be broken down through prayer—by commanding the evil spirits to leave in the name of Jesus.

The following example illustrates how they have recourse to the supernatural and see the working of the spirits in their day-to-day activities. A neo-Pentecostal woman wanted to buy a scooter but did not have enough money. She prayed to God to give her a scooter for six months, by which time she would have enough money to buy one. A neo-Pentecostal family gave her a Kinetic scooter to use until they came back, as they were going abroad for around six months. However, when the six months were coming to an end she realized she still did not have the money to buy a new scooter, so she again prayed to God since she needed a scooter. Now, it so happened that the owners did not come back and so she could use it for the whole year. Finally, when they came back they did not need it and so it was gifted to her. She interprets this as God answering her prayers and she calls her house a house of blessings.

Along with the dualistic spiritual world view of the NTC, the neo-Pentecostals also imbibe the language of those times. The biblical language was characterized by allusions to visions, conversations with spirits, appearance of angels, hearing of voices from heaven, and so forth. For example, when Peter was arrested by King Herod, the angel of the Lord appeared to Peter and led him out of prison[7] or when Saul was going to Damascus to persecute the Christians he saw a light and heard a voice which claimed to be that of Jesus.[8] Individual neo-Pentecostals tend to describe their daily experiences using the language of visions, supernatural presences, and voices. A woman who has done her PhD in geology and was teaching in the prestigious National Institute of Oceanography in Goa has heard voices several times in her life. Once she asked God why she should praise him so much and when she was sleeping, she heard a voice saying, 'I deserve to be praised.' Another time she had stopped worshipping God and while sweeping the house she heard a voice saying, 'Where are my praises?' The above description fits very well with the language of the early Church as is seen by the following account of the encounter between Philip and the Ethiopian eunuch, taken from Acts 8:26–9.

> But an angel of the Lord said to Philip, 'Rise and go toward the south to the road that goes down from Jerusalem to Gaza.' ... And behold, an Ethiopian, a eunuch, a minister of Canda'ce the queen of the Ethiopians ... seated in his chariot, he was reading the prophet Isaiah. And the Spirit said to Philip, 'Go up and join this chariot.'

A neo-Pentecostal, who works in the automobile industry, had two dreams about his marriage. Though he was to get married soon, he did not have any money with him. In his first dream, he saw that he was going and checking the bank ATM and to his surprise, a big amount of

---

[7] Acts 12:1–11.
[8] Acts 9:1–7.

money was deposited in his account. What he saw in his dream actually happened. He was in his pastor's house when he got a call from someone who owed him money. When he checked at the ATM, he found ₹100,000 in his account. In his second dream, the exact date of his wedding—4 June—was revealed to him. He found it amazing since that too happened exactly as he dreamt. He was able to get married in an open-air wedding hall on that day, even though Goa usually gets rains around that time of the year. Thus, the neo-Pentecostals, like the early biblical Christians, interpret their life histories and their everyday events as actively directed by God through a series of visions, dreams, and divine voices.

A dualistic spiritual world view with complete reliance on the divine and emphasis on strong faith has prompted some of the neo-Pentecostal pastors to admonish their followers that taking tablets and going to the doctor will not cure them till they put on the mind of Christ, who is the divine healer, and submit to his will. This type of teaching leads some neo-Pentecostals to refuse to see a doctor or take medication when they are ill. Before any important event, they come together and pray, so that the forces of evil do not disrupt that event. Thus, when the NFI organized a drama titled 'Heaven's Gates, Hell's Flames' in April 2008, the pastor and all the members of the congregation prayed fervently during the previous Sunday service that through the drama God would do great things for the city of Panaji and the people of Goa and that God would hold back the forces of darkness against that event. In addition, when the assembly elections in Goa drew near and they had to decide whom to vote for, at an All Goa Church Meet held at Nuvem on 6 April 2007, all the neo-Pentecostals in Goa prayed together to God as a community for the salvation of their MLAs and other candidates. They also prayed that candidates, who were scheming wicked plans against Christians, should not come to power. They believe that when they pray together like this, what comes out of their mouths is important and has an impact on correcting reality and directing destinies.

The neo-Pentecostal philosophy drawn from the NTC is that all the powers in the world—whether social, economic, or political—come under the authority of their God. The early Christians did not fear the mighty Roman Empire and readily accepted persecution under different Roman emperors since they believed that their lord Jesus Christ was mightier than all the worldly powers and the worldly kings, who could

only destroy their earthly bodies but not harm their immortal and inde-
structible souls. Thus, the neo-Pentecostal pastor in his Sunday sermon
urges the faithful not to be bothered, even if the Hindutva forces rule
over this land, since they will not be able to harm the Christians unless
their God allows them to do so.

On 7 September 2008, thousands of Born-Again Christians in their
respective Churches all over India prayed for the persecuted Christians
in Orissa.[9] The following was the prayer of one of their pastors, 'We
bind the powers of darkness over Orissa in the name of Jesus, and we
speak to you—*get out* [said very loudly] of that place in Jesus' name.' He
did not pray for the suffering of the persecuted Christians in Orissa to
be alleviated, but for the success of the spiritual war in Orissa. Thus, for
the neo-Pentecostals, the political sphere, like any other sphere, is under
the authority of God. A pastor gave the example of Seoul, a former
communist city, which is now 80–85 per cent Christian, as an example
of societies that have changed. Another pastor described every prayer
programme that they organize in Goa as the ammunition needed to
demolish the walls of Goa (erected by the Evil One) so that they can
walk in and take the land for Christ.

The neo-Pentecostals believe that there is a demonic power, an evil
spirit behind the materiality of idols (bronze or stone statues or paper
pictures). Therefore, when a person offers sacrifices to an idol he gets
exposed to another kind of spirit, which is evil. A pastor giving a talk on
idolatry and witchcraft gave the example of a man who was possessed
by demonic forces because he used to offer chickens to St George. While
St George may have been a good man, once someone makes an idol of
him, a demon takes over and gladly accepts your offerings and worship.
The consequences of living in idolatry or witchcraft, which they liken
to living under a curse or living in a mirage, are strife in the family, constant sickness, constant breakdown of relationships, financial difficulty,

---

[9] In the last week of August 2008, the Dalit Christians in Kandhamal district
of Orissa experienced the fury of the worst-ever communal rage in Orissa—
Churches were set on fire; Christian institutions, orphanages, and hamlets were
destroyed; pastors were attacked; one nun was burnt alive; and another was
gang-raped. The ethnic divide between the *adivasis* (tribals) and Dalits was
conveniently converted by right-wing militant Hindu groups into a Hindu–
Christian communal confrontation.

and other everyday problems. To replace the curse with blessings every person is urged to give up idolatry and witchcraft and make Jesus the Lord and Master of their lives.

The neo-Pentecostals also believe that misery comes from the Devil, while joy comes from the Lord. Therefore, they are called to be joyful Christians, since the Devil does not like joyful Christians. According to a woman from the ROLC, when she, in times of trouble, decided to put on the Lord's songs and jump and dance, she was able to break the strongholds of the Evil One. A pastor told his congregation that Christians can laugh on Good Friday since the Devil has been defeated on the cross. This concept of being joyful or Easter Christians drawn from the model of the early Christian community is an important marker of neo-Pentecostal identity in contrast to the Catholics who are portrayed as Good Friday Christians. This identity as joyful Christians is connected with the preaching of the prosperity gospel, which emphasizes the right of every Born-Again Christian to the blessings of the Abrahamic covenant, to have prosperity, wealth, good health, and blessings in married life. It emphasizes on the image of Jesus as the living God who is mighty and powerful, while downplaying the human-suffering aspect of Jesus. The prosperity gospel is emphasized in the preachings during the Sunday services of the WRM, which promises that all the desires of the people will be fulfilled this year. People will get jobs, enter into new businesses, buy new houses, or settle property matters. People are urged to dream about a good house or a car, winning a lottery, acquiring a good-looking spouse, and are taught that those who wait on the Lord and pray to him will get victory in the Lord and will do well in life. A technique used in the Sunday services that is based on the prosperity gospel is to ask the worshippers to turn to their neighbour and say, 'I am going to be rich.' Given the socio-economic profile of Pentecostal–Charismatic Christianity in Goa—most of them are involved in the domestic sphere, are not earning much, and belong mainly to the lower and middle classes—the prosperity gospel that promises them jobs, houses, wealth, and so on, is very appealing to them.

Mission: To Save the Lost

The vision of the NFI Church in Panaji is to 'Save the lost, worship God, impact the community and make disciples'. The most important component of their vision is saving the lost, which stems from their dualistic spiritual world view, wherein they distinguish between the 'saved', the Born-Again Christians who know the truth, and the 'lost', those of other faiths. The NFI Church attempts to save the lost through friendship evangelism, prayer cells, supporting and promoting missions, and Church plants.[10] The importance of this mission of preaching the good news and bringing souls to Christ is emphasized again and again by the pastor and other preachers at their Sunday prayer meetings. The members of the ROLC are reminded that as Born-Again Christians their passion is not land or property or wealth or a big bank balance, but to put everything that they have, their sweat and blood, to bring souls to Jesus Christ.

A distinct characteristic of the neo-Pentecostals is dreaming big dreams with respect to their mission, which may appear far away from reality, but which they believe will be fulfilled by God soon. The pastor of the NFI Church in Vasco, once while preaching during a Sunday service, prayed that people such as Bal Thackeray and L.K. Advani[11] come to the Lord. He asked the congregation, 'Can you imagine L.K. Advani raising his hands and praising the Lord among 5,000 Christians at Tilak Maidan, Mumbai?' To this the people reacted vociferously by clapping and saying amen. This characteristic of dreaming big dreams is linked with the phenomenon of reverse mission, another characteristic of Born-Again Christians. Reverse mission, the south going north or the east going west, is understood by them as how, in the past, missionaries

---

[10] New Frontiers International, which is part of the house church movement in the UK, believes that the most effective way of evangelizing a new area is to plant a Church. Their understanding is that the gospel not only needs to be proclaimed but also needs to be demonstrated in tangible ways, and the best way is through Christians living out the gospel together in a locality. In concrete terms a Church plant, also known as a 'house church', consists of a few Christian families having their prayer meetings in people's houses.

[11] L.K. Advani is a leader of the BJP, a right-wing, national political party, while Bal Thackeray is the founding leader of the Shiv Sena. The Shiv Sena, which began as a party espousing the 'sons of the soil' over outsiders policy in the state of Maharashtra, later expanded its mandate to include all Hindus and, therefore, became an ally of the BJP, which also espouses the cause of Hindu nationalism.

came from every nation to India, but now they strongly believe the time has come when God will take them to far-off places such as Africa or Europe to preach the gospel. Even though they are numerically very small in Goa and India, their belief in a mighty and powerful God leads them to expect big things from God. This belief that their religious faith will reconstitute and expand reality leads them to assume the identity of a global missionary is a very distinct identity of neo-Pentecostalism. The mission of the neo-Pentecostals and all Born-Again Christians to aggressively and urgently evangelize and proselytize people in all corners of the world has been strongly emphasized in many of their common state-level and regional meetings and conferences.

The missionary thrust of the neo-Pentecostals is seen in the preaching of a pastor at the 'All Goa Church Meet' at Nuvem on 6 April 2007, who said that the purpose for which they had gathered there in such large numbers was to evangelize every nook and corner of Goa. He stated that God is a God of mission and his mission is to seek and save those who are lost. He compared the Born-Again Christians in Goa to Jonah who did not want to do the work of God and wanted to run away from God's plan (Book of Jonah from the Bible). Both, according to him, were reluctant missionaries. In his fiery preaching, he chastised the people—'woe to you'—for not opening their mouths and proclaiming Jesus outside the Church and called on them to decide that very day to become a missionary to their family, neighbour, village, taluka, and the land of Goa. He exhorted the 5,000 Born-Again Christians in Goa to preach Christ to the 1.5 million people in Goa in these words, 'Are you ready to open your mouths for the 1.5 million people in Goa? God has given thousands and thousands of occasions for us but we've been afraid, reluctant to come out from our comfort zones.' They are constantly reminded that God is moving them from being comfortable Christians, from 'bless me, my family, my business' to saving 1.5 million people in Goa. Their spiritual mission of saving the lost in Goa and capturing Goa for Christ, which combines religious and nationalist goals, has political overtones.[12]

At a national-level conference organized by the NFI at Borivali, Mumbai, in October 2008, the main theme that kept coming up in all

---

[12] The political agenda of the neo-Pentecostals is taken up in Chapter 7.

the sessions was 'go and scatter' to the many unreached areas in India.[13]
At the same time, the NFI Churches are family-oriented and there is a
tension between managing their families and going out on mission. A
lot of give and take is involved in balancing family responsibilities with
the demands of mission. One of the speakers in the Borivali conference
referred to this when he said that their Church, which is at present
95 per cent family and 5 per cent army needs to change to 100 per cent
family and 100 per cent army. This is a reflection of the ground reality
where many of the Born-Again Christians are reluctant to leave their
families and go to far-off places to evangelize the lost.

To provide legitimacy to their mission of saving the lost, they show
how it is in conformity with the pattern of mission of the NTC by referring to chosen biblical texts such as Matthew 28:19–20: 'Go and make
disciples of all nations, baptizing them in the name of the Father and
of the Son and of the Holy Spirit.' A careful analysis of this text reveals
that it is a triadic formulation of Christian baptism—verse 19: baptize
them 'in the name of the Father, and of the Son and of the Holy Spirit'.
Christian baptism was initially administered in the early Church in the
'name of Jesus'. 'And Peter said to them, "Repent and be baptized every
one of you in the name of Jesus Christ"' (Acts 2:38). 'But they had
only been baptized in the name of the Lord Jesus' (Acts 8:16). Biblical
evidence strongly suggests that Matthew 28:19 was a later expansion of
the simpler and earlier baptismal formula 'in the name of Jesus' (Dunn
1977: 155–6). In their attempt to legitimize the activities of evangelization, proselytization, and numerical expansion as their mission, the
neo-Pentecostals interpret Matthew 28:19–20 as the great commission
from the Lord Jesus Christ, the mission mandate, which is binding on
all Christians and overlook or reinterpret other mission texts such as:

1. The Spirit of the Lord is upon me, because he has anointed me to
   preach good news to the poor. He has sent me to proclaim release
   to the captives and recovering of sight to the blind, to set at liberty
   those who are oppressed, to proclaim the acceptable year of the
   Lord' (Luke 4:16–19).
2. 'Jesus said to them again, "Peace be with you. As the Father has sent
   me, even so I send you. … Receive the Holy Spirit. If you forgive the

---

[13] Unreached areas are those areas that have no presence of Christianity.

sins of any, they are forgiven; if you retain the sins of any, they are retained"' (John 20:21–23).
3. 'And Jesus said to them, "Go into all the world and preach the gospel to the whole creation"' (Mark 16:15).
4. 'A new commandment I give to you, that you love one another. By this all men will know that you are my disciples, if you have love for one another' (John 13:34–35).

The above texts emphasize that mission means preaching the good news and spreading justice, love, and forgiveness, not merely baptizing and proselytizing, which is emphasized a lot by the neo-Pentecostals. Their missionary venture, more than spreading the love of God and preaching the gospel, is directly concerned with numerical expansion.

The Transform Goa programme with its news bulletin 'Transform Goa Update' jointly looked after by the Born-Again Christian Churches in Goa sets clear-cut goals for the expansion of their Churches. While 'whole heart, whole life, whole Goa' is the long-term vision for Goa, the short-term goal is that every village of Goa will have a house church by 2010. A pastor at the All Panjim Church Meet held on 21 March 2008, where several Born-Again Churches came together, said that in 2007 they had a total of 143 Churches planted in 102 villages of Goa, while their target is 202 Churches in 161 villages by the end of 2008. The main future target of Transform Goa is that by 2010 each of the 400-odd villages and towns of Goa have a house church. To achieve this target the neo-Pentecostals map the territory of Goa into reached (where there is a house church) and unreached areas (see Figure 3.1). Thus, the mission of saving the lost implies a strong drive towards proselytizing and planting New Churches in unreached areas with time-bound, clear-cut goals and targets.

Another characteristic of the mission of neo-Pentecostals is the urgency of evangelization. This urgency to proselytize draws from the pressing need felt by early Christians to evangelize, which was due to the apocalyptic understanding among them that the second coming of Christ would take place soon. The belief that they are living in the End Times is the driving motivation for all Born-Again Christians to urgently proselytize and spread the gospel of Christ to the ends of the earth so that everyone in the world is prepared for the imminent last judgement. A pastor preaching at a drama organized by the ROLC in

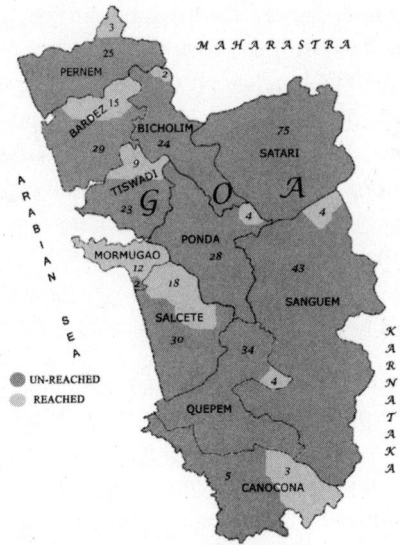

Figure 3.1   Neo-Pentecostal Mapping in Goa
Disclaimer: This map is not to scale and is provided for illustrative purposes only.
Note: The numbers depict the number of villages reached or unreached in that area.
Source: Transform Goa Update, Prayer Bulletin, April–June 2007.

Panaji in April 2008 told the audience, 'Tonight is the time to give your lives to Jesus. You may never get a second chance.' Additionally, the reality of being a small and demographically and politically insignificant minority community in Goa is a big motivating factor to woo members of other religious communities to join them in order to swell their numbers.

The neo-Pentecostals are constantly reminded about their mission of proselytizing and expanding through the innovative use of expressions, metaphors, and songs. In their Sunday prayer meetings, cell meetings, and other programmes, expressions and metaphors such as 'expanding Church', 'Church on the ove', 'a going people', 'Christians like rabbits always multiplying', 'no family planning for the Church', and 'God is building his Church' are used to emphasize the importance of the mission of expansion. In the NFI Church, they often sing the song 'Goa will bow down and worship the Lord' (they substitute Goa with Panaji, India, the nations, every tribe, and every language).

At a Sunday prayer service the pastor told the congregation that when he got trained to become a pastor, about 15 years ago, there were hardly around 50 NFI Churches all over the world, whereas in 2008 there were nearly 700 Churches. As he gave these figures, he exclaimed in an excited voice, 'Wow! What an expansion. God is building his Church.'[14] Thus, proselytization and numerical expansion are very important aspects of the neo-Pentecostal missionary identity and are, therefore, emphasized at every forum.

A Persecuted and Besieged Community

One of the characteristics of sects is their isolation from the modern world. The more isolated, intransigent, and withdrawn a group is, the less it is regarded as a normative religious expression and the more it belongs to the category of sects and new religions. This characteristic of being 'isolated' is linked with the image of 'the persecuted community', which was characteristic of the biblical Church. Early Christianity, due to its stringent criticism of the Hebrew socio-religious norms and practices and the fact that most of the early Christian converts were drawn from Judaism, posed a serious threat to the Jewish religious leaders. At the same time, the emerging Christian sect posed a political threat to the Roman Empire as early Christians refused to worship the Roman Emperor. Thus, early Christians were besieged by hostile forces on all sides—attacked by the Jews on one side and the Romans on the other.

The neo-Pentecostals in Goa identify with the biblical image of a persecuted or besieged community as they claim to be under threat from the right-wing forces of the majority Hindu community on the one hand and the large and powerful Catholic community on the other. These religious contestations and conflicts will be taken up in Chapter 6. Neo-Pentecostals believe that when there is persecution there is more growth in the Church and God advances his kingdom. They cite the example of the NTC, which was attacked on all sides but grew rapidly. They also give the example of Orissa, where hundreds of Christians were killed but another 10,000 people were ready to go and plant Churches there. They interpret such situations not as a consequence of their direct and rather aggressive attempts to proselytize,

[14] Pastor at the Sunday service for the ROLC, Panaji, on 2 November 2008.

but as an invitation and opportunity to make even greater and bolder efforts at evangelization.

They also believe that God will not leave or forsake his people during times of persecution but strengthen those who are persecuted. They say that God does not hate persecution but he hates lukewarm Christians, who sit in their chairs and do nothing about God. They also believe in divine retribution and assert that those who stand in the way of the children of God will have to face the wrath of God. The wife of the pastor of the NFI Church while speaking about natural calamities gave the example of the Gujarat earthquake that followed the burning of Churches and the genocide of Muslims there, and the severe floods in Orissa that took place soon after the killing of Christians there. She said if the people of God are troubled, then the vengeance of God will not be far away. The concept of divine retribution is the spiritual tonic used by the neo-Pentecostals to cope with persecution in a non-vengeful and non-violent manner, knowing that their God will take care of the persecutors.

Intra-group Solidarity and Fellowship

Perhaps the most distinct identifying marker of the Born-Again Christians in Goa is strong intra-group solidarity and fellowship. They pride themselves on the aspect of close relationships and fellowship with one another and point disparagingly at the lack of it in other religions. The first-century Christian community was a small, insecure, and nascent group still finding its moorings in the Jewish society. The twin threats from the Jewish and Roman authorities necessitated strong intra-group solidarity. The Christian community found in the Book of Acts was a closely knit group, living in communes, sharing their resources. The neo-Pentecostals in Goa imitate this New Testament model of solidarity and fellowship among the Christians, leaving out the idea of living in communes.

The main venue of fellowship for the neo-Pentecostals is the Sunday prayer meeting. Worshippers make it a point to stay back after the service is over to engage in fellowship with one another. Since the number of worshippers is small—most Churches have about 50–100 people—they are familiar with one another at a personal level. The people I interviewed find that among each of the 100-odd worshippers of the NFI Church there is fellowship. The 17-year-old drummer who gets up early every Sunday morning and leaves home by 7 am to help in the arrangements for the Sunday service finds there is a lot of bonding and there are many close relationships within the worship team (those who play the musical instruments during the praise and worship). The people within this active serving group find the Sunday services very satisfying and even if they go out somewhere they make sure they are back before Sunday, so as not to miss the service.

During the Sunday services, they have a fixed slot for welcoming newcomers and also those coming after a long time. The importance given to fellowship is seen in the division of labour for the Sunday service in the NFI Church's serving team. Two people are assigned to 'visitor's care' and two others are assigned to 'welcome'. While the job of the first two people is to look after newcomers, the latter two have to be at the door to open it and greet the people as they enter the hall. One member of the Serving Team is also assigned to 'celebrations' and their job description is to look after the birthday celebrations. This involves wishing those who are celebrating their birthdays or anniversaries at the Sunday services with a greeting card and a birthday/anniversary song. Apart from the pastor, the elders of the Church also periodically visit the homes of their members scattered in different areas to boost their spirits. Thus, the NFI Church has well-defined structures in place to initiate and sustain solidarity and fellowship among their members. For many members who are alienated from their family and are socially boycotted by their Catholic and Hindu neighbours since they are Born-Again Christians, the Church community takes on the role of the family.

Unlike the NFI Church where there are specific people assigned to welcome and build fellowship, in the WRM it is the pastor who does everything. He makes those who are coming for the first time or those who could not come the previous Sunday to stand up, asks for their name and place, and introduces each one of them to the congregation. He has a warm and personal style of introducing each new person using the words: 'Welcome in the name of Jesus.' The task of praying for those celebrating their birthdays is also done by the pastor. At the end of the meeting, he calls up to the stage those celebrating birthdays or wedding anniversaries and prays for them. He asks the entire congregation to stretch their hands forward and join him in praying for them.

During the week, they interact in the prayer cell meetings, where the group dynamics are much more intense. The prayer cells normally comprise 3–4 families that gather once a week in one of their houses. The intra-group solidarity and fellowship of the neo-Pentecostals is consciously built up and sustained through various group-building techniques. On the cover page of the monthly newsletter of the NFI Church's *The Panjim Times*, they usually have words of welcome. While the April 2008 issue had the words, 'Welcome to the River of Life Church for a refreshing morning in the presence of the living God. ... A special welcome to our visitors. We are glad to have you with us', the May issue had a note from the pastor saying, 'A warm welcome to each one of you. We trust you will have a great time as we worship the Lord together.'

Another technique of building fellowship and familiarity among the members of the congregation is asking them to go across to their neighbours and share or ask something. Sometimes they are asked to just say 'God is with you', but often they are told to pray for their neighbours. When they have to pray for some particular needs, they often get into small groups of around 4–6 people and pray. They also celebrate occasions such as 'Mother's Day' or 'Father's Day' during their Sunday prayer meetings. This type of increased interaction helps the members who come from varied backgrounds to become familiar with one another and build relationships. It also gives them a sense of identity, equality, and belonging to one community irrespective of their social, cultural, or economic status.

Besides the interaction in their prayer meetings and other Church-organized programmes, of which there are quite a few, they also come together for birthday celebrations, picnics, and other social functions. I was present for one such celebration, which was on the occasion of the ROLC pastor's birthday. In spite of it raining quite heavily that evening, nearly 20 people were present for the celebration, which was an informal family get-together with a lot of fellowship and bonhomie among them. The birthday dinner was cooked by several female members of the Church, besides the pastor's wife who prepared a cake and also cooked one or two dishes.

Global and Local Dimensions of Neo-Pentecostalism in Goa

Neo-Pentecostalism in Goa, just as all over the world, operates at two levels—the global and the local. On the one hand, their identification with the NTC, with a mission mandate to go out to the ends of the earth and bring in disciples, gives them a global, corporate identity transcending regional and national boundaries. They consider that though the Born-Again Churches have different names, belong to different denominations, and have doctrinal differences, they are all part of one universal body of Christ with Jesus as the head. All these Churches, according to them, are based on the Book of Acts—engaging in fellowship, sharing with one another, and reading the word of God and practising it. On the other hand, the concept of the local Church is central to their autonomous ecclesiastical identity. Every local Church has its own emphasis and is autonomous in its functioning. This balancing act between the global identity as the universal Church of Christ and the local identity as an independent Born-Again Church gives the movement its distinct Pentecostal–Charismatic identity.

The corporate identity of the neo-Pentecostals as the universal body of Christ is formed and nurtured by regional and national programmes. The ROLC had sent several members for a national conference organized by the NFI at Borivali, Mumbai, in October 2008, in which the following themes were discussed: leadership, prophecy, culture, and family on a mission. Those who had gone for the conference shared their experiences with the other members of the Church, giving a global picture of the NFI Churches spread all over the world that are working for the same mission. In 2007, all the Born-Again Churches of Goa met on Good Friday for a day of prayer and fasting. That meeting, which saw nearly 1,500 Born-Again Christians gather together along with 32 pastors, boosted the corporate image of the Christian Church of Goa.

The corporate identity of the Born-Again Christians in Goa has taken concrete shape in the form of a registered organization called United Goa Pastors and Leaders Association. This association, which began around 1994 and was registered in 2002, contains pastors from different Christian Churches in Goa and heads of para-Church organizations[15] such as Operation Mobilisation, YMCA, and others. They have a steering committee comprising three members, who are elected every year.

---

[15] Para-Church organizations are organizations parallel to or resembling the Church organizations, which supplement the Church.

The pastors meet once a month and normally around 40–50 of them attend these meetings, which is less than half of the total number of Pentecostal and independent Charismatic pastors in Goa.

Their meetings, which are more spiritual in nature, focus on prayer and sharing the word of God, while avoiding any discussions on doctrine or issues pertaining to particular groups. They also discuss current events and any common programmes but any decisions they arrive at are not binding on any of the member Churches. The pastor of the WRM told me he has hardly attended any of the meetings of the pastors association. Thus, in spite of several attempts to foster the corporate identity of the Christian Church of Goa, it appears to be more in the realm of the imaginary—since they are all worshipping the same Christ, so they belong to the one Church with Christ as the head—rather than in any concrete form.

Niebuhr's theory (1960) states that sects may have been formed as dissenting movements against the existing religious institutions on a doctrinal basis or to regain the orientation of the first-century Church as they understood it. However, as a sect begins to develop economically, it becomes less dissent-oriented and more established in the mainstream as a respectable denomination. In the 1980s and 1990s, when the neo-Pentecostals emerged and spread in Goa, they started out both as dissenting movements against the mainline Catholic Church and as attempts to assume the original, genuine identity of the first-century Church as understood by them. Initially, they were underground concealed movements that exhibited a high level of tension within the surrounding sociocultural environment. Gradually, as they grew numerically and financially, they have gotten more established in the mainstream and today they lay claim to the status of a respectable Church. While the WRM still has a tense relationship with the local Catholic community in Siolim, the ROLC has improved its equation with the Catholic community and has expanded and rationalized its organization with professionals handling Church affairs. As the neo-Pentecostals get integrated into mainstream Christianity in Goa, they now look down on the numerous diminutive Christian groups struggling to establish themselves through door-to door evangelization and label them as cults. These groups have no place in the neo-Pentecostal understanding of the global NTC. They are regarded as belonging to the Antichrist and not following the right gospel, but preaching their own 'man-made' doctrine.

As we have seen so far, the corporate identity of the universal Church of Christ is rather vague and more in the realm of the imagination. This is seen in the fact that most of the members when interviewed did not know much about the worldwide Pentecostal–Charismatic movement and even about the foreign organization to which their local Church belonged. The more tangible reality for them in their day-to-day lives is the local Church, which serves as an extended family for its members with the pastor and his wife as the spiritual parents. It provides support, fellowship, close relationships, and bonding for its members. Thus, at the level of individual Believers, the local identity of their independent neo-Pentecostal Church is more tangible and visible than the global identity of the universal Church of Christ.

Negotiation of Identities by Individual Neo-Pentecostals

At the institutional level, the local dimension of the identity of neo-Pentecostalism as an extended family offering support and fellowship to its members as well as the global dimension of neo-Pentecostalism as the universal body of Jesus Christ based on the principles of the NTC feed into one another, fostering a distinct identity for the movement. This local–global identity of neo-Pentecostalism attracts people from across cultures and has enabled the spread of the movement to all parts of the world. How do individual neo-Pentecostals understand and negotiate this institutional identity in their day-to-day lives and what are the self-identities that emerge from these negotiations? What role do social factors such as caste, class, gender, and linguistic and regional background play in these day-to-day negotiations?

To answer these questions I look at the life history of a neo-Pentecostal belonging to the ROLC. Pedro (name changed) was born in a Catholic family of fisherfolk in Siridao village. Among the Catholics, all the castes and sub-castes that were not part of the two upper castes of Bamonn and Chardo were grouped under the caste of Sudir or Shudras. The fisherfolk (*harvi*) were looked down upon because of their occupation and were located at the lower end of the Shudras. Most of them were uneducated and lived in fishing villages near the coast. Both he and his wife, who also comes from a fishing family, are not very educated.

Pedro's father was a traditional fisherman (*ramponkar*). After the departure of the Portuguese in 1961, massive public funding was earmarked for developmental projects and as a result, industry, mining, tourism, and mechanized fishing started to develop and expand. Pedro's father took advantage of this and shifted from traditional fishing to using a mechanized trawler. They were one of the first to enter into mechanized fishing and had even acquired big engines from the government for the trawlers. They became one of the well-known fishing families and were famous for their good catch. Access to material wealth led to occupational mobility and enabled such groups occupying the lower levels of the social ladder to challenge the traditional social hierarchy. They had money, they had everything, but there was no peace in the family. Disputes broke out between the brothers and that forced Pedro to leave his house and come to his in-laws' place in Goa Velha.

After that followed a tough period since he did not have a job and coming from a trawler-owning family, he felt ashamed to go and work on the jetty. To support his family he was forced to go to Saudi Arabia. Out-migration from Goa had begun to some extent in the mid- and late nineteenth century and picked up in the first few decades of the twentieth century. This process of mostly Christian men going out to work on ships or in the Gulf accelerated after 1960. So, along with Pedro there were many other Goans working in Saudi Arabia. One such man introduced Pedro to the Bible and told him about Jesus. That was the turning point in Pedro's life. Earlier, he used to hardly attend mass and was not really interested in religion, but now he was reading the Bible and praying regularly.

After his contract expired in Saudi Arabia, he came back to Goa and was again jobless. But now he was a different person: he was on fire for the Lord and left the Catholic Church. He explains that God made him change from Catholic to Born-Again Christian. He joined a small Bible group, and after some time left it and joined the NFI Church in Margao. After being in that Church for 10 years, he became a member of the NFI Church in Panaji. After leaving the Catholic Church, he had to deal first with his wife and children and also with the local Catholic community. His wife and children eventually joined his Church but he was socially boycotted from the predominantly Catholic village. According to the 2011 Census, 68 per cent of the population in Goa Velha are

Christians, of which almost all are Catholics. Pedro feels assuming this new identity of a Born-Again Christian has helped him handle any type of situation.

Though after returning from Saudi Arabia he was jobless, God directed him to the fishing business and he started as a small-time fish trader with a small pickup van. He kept on praying to God who, he says, has been good to him. Today he stays in a fairly big house, which is well-furnished with marble flooring, a television, a computer and all other modern gadgets. He has a flourishing fish business, now run by his married son, with several workers and three pickup vans, besides a large cold storage facility next to his house to preserve the fish. He believes all this prosperity is because of his identity as a Born-Again Christian who has followed God's will. The previous misery and tough times he faced as a Catholic were because he was blind and not able to see the kingdom of God. Thus, in the process of negotiating one's identity as a Born-Again Christian in the midst of a predominantly Catholic environment, the individual neo-Pentecostal has to deal with issues such as social boycott, schism in the family, economic difficulties, demands from the new religion, and the like.

Identity and the Catholic Charismatic Renewal

When Pentecostalism erupted in the historic Churches, including the Catholic Church, many questions were raised about the identity of the new movement. Was it just some temporary spiritual phenomenon that would die out soon or was it some powerful revolutionary movement, which would soon change the way we practise religion? The rapid growth of the CCR in the USA, from its humble beginnings at Duquesne University in 1967, and its simultaneous advancement in different parts of the world dispelled the above-mentioned doubts about the movement. Pentecostalism within the Catholic Church has spread in just three decades to almost every corner of the Christian world, numbering around 119 million Catholic Charismatics in 2000. Very few parts of the Christian world have not been touched by this movement. However, questions about its identity still persist.

Right from the beginning, the CCR was guided and shaped by high-ranking Church officials such as Cardinal Leon J. Suenens of Belgium, who was appointed as its first episcopal advisor. This ensured that the CCR got identified as an 'indigenous' Catholic movement and did not acquire a separate and distinct identity. This was in stark contrast to the emergence of the Classical Pentecostal movement, which led to schisms within the older Methodist and Holiness denominations. With the help of several well-known Catholic theologians and writers, the CCR has tried to carve an identity distinct from the Pentecostal movement. Thus, most of the Catholic Charismatics I interviewed in Goa would distance themselves from the Pentecostal movement and assert that the Charismatic Renewal is an indigenous movement, which has emerged from the Catholic Church.

Yet the question that arises from the analysis of the field data is whether the CCR should be viewed as the 'Pentecostalization' of the Catholic Church or the 'Catholicization' of the Pentecostal–Charismatic movement. Another question that emerges from the data is whether the CCR has emerged as a dissenting movement within the Catholic Church, as a critique and a challenge to the Church hierarchy and its beliefs, rituals, and practices? How have the individual Catholic Charismatics in Goa balanced their Charismatic identity with their Catholic identity and how have they marked their boundaries with Pentecostals and neo-Pentecostals? These and other questions concerning the corporate identity of the CCR and the self-identities of individual Catholic Charismatics in Goa will be dealt with in the following section.

'Catholicization' of the Pentecostal–Charismatic Movement: Similarities and Differences between Neo-Pentecostalism and the Catholic Charismatic Renewal

When dealing with the identity of the neo-Pentecostals it was noticed that the recreation of the NTC and the resultant dualistic spiritual world view was the guiding principle for all their beliefs and ritual observances. In comparison, the recreation of the NTC does not play such an important role in forming the identity of the CCR. On the other hand, the presence of the ecstatic style of worship, the importance given to visions, prophecies, miracles and healings, the stress on intra-group solidarity and fellowship, the dualistic spiritual world view, the primacy of the word of God, and other such ideas and practices prevalent in the CCR today exhibit the influence of the Pentecostal system of meanings on the Renewal. While the advent of the Charismatic Renewal in the Catholic Church is described as the 'Pentecostalization' of the Church by some scholars of Pentecostalism, my study of the CCR in Goa suggests it is more a 'Catholicization' of the Pentecostal–Charismatic movement. This implies that the Catholic theological system of meanings has interrogated and interpreted Pentecostal spirituality and theology within the categories of Catholic orthodoxy and accepted only those beliefs and practices that were not in direct conflict with their own theological tradition.

The careful sifting of the theological underpinnings of Pentecostalism through the sieve of Catholic theology by several well-known Catholic theologians such as Donald Gelpi, Francis Sullivan, Stanislaus Lyonnet, Kilian McDonnell, and others has helped the CCR develop its own unique style and identity. For example, the founding leaders of the Pentecostal movement such as Seymour and Parham put forth the doctrine of the baptism of the spirit as distinct from the 'second blessing', with speaking in tongues as its distinguishing characteristic and only biblical proof. The CCR rejected this baptism of the spirit doctrine right from the beginning and while they accepted the practice of speaking in tongues, they downplayed its importance. Thus the CCR can be regarded as a mediating ground for Pentecostal beliefs and practices to be sifted through Catholic teachings and beliefs, from which something new has emerged, having both similarities and differences with the Pentecostal–Charismatic movement.

Hollenweger (1986) wrote that the worldwide growth of Pentecostalism was not due to any particular Pentecostal doctrine, but because of its black roots. This black Pentecostal theology included orality of liturgy and inclusion of dreams and visions into personal and public forms of worship. It also included maximum participation at the levels of prayer and decision-making. The ecstatic style of Charismatic praise and worship found in all the CCR prayer groups in Goa, with a lot of body movements, uninhibited expression of emotions, and loud singing with even louder music accompanied by sudden bursts of praying in tongues is very similar to the Pentecostal style of praise and worship. This is quite different from the typical liturgical service of the Catholic Church, which stresses on decorum, solemnity, and sobriety. During the prayer meetings of the CCR, people share their testimonies and prophecies and quote from the scriptures. 'Glossolalia' (praying or praising or singing in tongues) is found in all the Charismatic prayer groups in Goa. What strikes any observer about the praise and worship of the Charismatic prayer group of Mapusa is how middle-aged and also younger women clap, wave their hands, dance, jump, smile at each other, and make actions like little children when singing action songs. Since Charismatic prayer is spontaneous, having no fixed liturgy, these middle-class, urban Catholic women are able to let their hair down, something which would be considered taboo in the traditional Church's liturgical worship.

At the same time both the Catholic Charismatics and the neo-Pentecostals observe that the CCR praise and worship is not as noisy as the neo-Pentecostal prayer meetings, which resemble rock concerts with high decibel levels. The Catholic background of silent, meditative type of prayer is seen especially during worship, when the songs are very slow, the music is rather subdued, and the Charismatics are on their knees. There are moments when the leader asks the entire congregation to kneel down, close their eyes, and pray in silence.

On the other hand, the neo-Pentecostal prayer meetings are marked by a conspicuous absence of silence. Even during the period of worship, when they sing slow songs and the mood becomes quieter and more reflective there will always be some music playing in the background or the leader speaking in a soft tone, but never total silence. The neo-Pentecostals are much more uninhibited, boisterous, and loud compared to the Catholic Charismatics.

Another important difference in the styles of prayer between the Catholic Charismatics and the neo-Pentecostals is the introduction of Marian devotion in the prayer meetings of the former. While the CCR prayer meetings have a Christocentric focus, most of the prayer groups in Goa also recite the rosary in the meeting. Other Catholic elements of worship such as mass, confession, and adoration to the Blessed Sacrament have become part of each CCR retreat or seminar. Thus, the CCR worship has acquired its own distinct style, differing in many ways from the neo-Pentecostal style.

One of the main characteristics of the neo-Pentecostal identity is the appropriation of the world of symbols of the biblical Church with a dualistic spiritual world view. This world view of the first-century Church is also found in the CCR, but in a more limited manner.

According to Charles Whitehead, former president of ICCRS, the distinguishing characteristic of the CCR is their understanding of the primacy of the role of the Holy Spirit in the Church, which has not changed since the first century.[16] Today, Christians experience the outpouring, power, and gifts of the Holy Spirit in the same way the first Christians experienced them and Whitehead wishes this experience of the Holy Spirit become the norm for the Church.

The Catholic Charismatics, like the neo-Pentecostals, believe that the Devil is very active among them and people are being held under the curse of the Evil One. Several of their talks deal with topics concerning the Devil and how to engage in spiritual warfare. Connected to the dualistic spiritual world view is the concept that joy, happiness, and prosperity comes from the Holy Spirit and misery, pain, and suffering comes from the Evil One. Catholic Charismatics believe that the early Christians who experienced Pentecost were joyful people and so the Catholic Charismatics are urged to be joyful Christians. Like neo-Pentecostalism, the CCR claims to have converted the mournful Good Friday Catholics into joyful Easter Sunday Catholics. The CCR is likened to meeting God in a picnic, a very informal, friendly manner, while the Catholic Church is seen to have too much decorum and reverence.

The neo-Pentecostal concept of joyful Christians leads them to emphasize on the prosperity gospel[17] and on the concept of Jesus Christ as the living and mighty God, whereas, due to the influence of the teachings of the Catholic Church, the CCR does not emphasize the prosperity gospel and lays stress on both the human and divine aspects of Jesus without downplaying the image of the suffering Christ. The neo-Pentecostals draw sharp and clear-cut boundaries with people of other religious traditions (pagans/gentiles), whom they term as the lost or the unsaved. They believe that only those who have faith in Jesus Christ will be saved and are convinced that they are among the

---

[16] *Shalom*, February 2007: 7.

[17] Prosperity gospel is an ambiguous term with a variety of meanings depending on the context in which it is used. Here I understand prosperity gospel as claiming that the blessing of the Abrahamic covenant promised to a particular people is extended to all through the atonement of Christ. As a Born-Again Christian, one is the possessor of blessings and faith and is personally empowered (Coleman 2000: 27–8).

chosen elect. On the other hand, the Catholic Charismatics do not make sharp distinctions with people of other faith. Their understanding of salvation is more inclusive and they believe that Christ came to save everyone. Anyone who has lived a good life according to the will of God will be saved. They opine that Pentecostals and other Christians are doing good work and will be saved.

The dualistic spiritual world view of the neo-Pentecostals makes them regard their scripture as the word of God and condemn other religious scriptures as the work/word of the Devil. The Catholic Charismatics in general respect other religious scriptures and do not condemn them. One of them said that while other scriptures give a way of life, the Bible gives *the* way of life. However, some individual Charismatics reject inter-religious dialogue, holding the view that other scriptures are not divine but human and consider practices such as yoga and Indian forms of meditation taboo. For the most part, however, the Catholic Charismatics do not fully embrace a sharply dualistic spiritual world view.

Like the neo-Pentecostals, a strong emphasis on building solidarity and fellowship within the Charismatic prayer group is found in both the Mapusa and Merces prayer groups. The Mapusa group follows the practice of praying for those celebrating birthdays and anniversaries. This is a common practice in many of the neo-Pentecostal sects. In the Merces prayer group, which is an all-women group, the solidarity and fellowship is noticed in the sharing of responsibilities within the group. As a group, they visit hospitals, pray at the houses of sick people and dead people, or just go to visit people. They have different techniques of improving fellowship and showing concern for one another. When a member of the group dies, they all gather together and pray for the dead member. Also, if anyone fails to attend their prayer meetings, they go and visit her to find out why she did not turn up. If a person from a particular ward fails to attend a meeting, then some people from that ward visit her. The leader of the Merces group shared that when she was sick and hospitalized, every day the group members were present in the hospital and took care of everything. Women who would never make prayers at the prayer meetings came to the hospital and prayed for her.

A characteristic of neo-Pentecostals is the reduced cognitive dissonance that is a consequence of the intensive, emotional, group dynamics found in their praise and worship (Salazar in Fuss 1998: 500). This makes them speak in one voice and reduces self-criticisms and differing views. On the other hand, one finds a variety of differing and critical views among the Catholic Charismatics. While some argue that if the group is a Charismatic group it should manifest the gifts of the spirit and wonders and signs should follow, others are against the idea of healings and prophecies taking centre-stage in the Renewal. Still others criticize the emphasis of the CCR on spiritual conversion of people while neglecting the social dimension. Some of them are also self-critical, pointing out that Charismatics tend to have spiritual pride and a holier-than-thou attitude. Some of them candidly admitted that the Charismatic movement is going through a period of stagnation at present.

While there are similarities and differences between the CCR members and the neo-Pentecostals, the many differences mentioned above point to the Catholic influence on the CCR. The distinct Catholic teachings are imparted through regular leadership-formation training, meant for prayer group leaders, core group members, sector and zonal leaders, and apostolate leaders. Besides the teachings of the Church, the stress on typical Catholic practices such as regular confession and Eucharist, having a spiritual director, and time for silent personal prayer give the Catholic Charismatics a unique identity distinct from the neo-Pentecostals.

Catholic Charismatic Revival: A Protest Movement in the Church

The CCR has always been looked at as a spiritual Renewal movement with a distinct lay spirituality. In the process of bringing reform in the belief system and liturgical worship of the Catholic Church, the CCR has brought about a critique of the mass reproduction of religious experience found in the mainline religions. By pointing out shortcomings in the abstract and rigid liturgical worship of the Church, the Renewal has made a pitch for a more experiential, evocative, non-liturgical, and individual-centred form of worship. Most of the Catholic Charismatics I interviewed preferred the spontaneous praise and worship of the Renewal over the dry liturgical worship of the Church. According to them, an experience of God or an experience of conversion is absent in from the Eucharist. They contrast the big crowds that come and sit for hours at Charismatic retreats and outreach programmes with people who get bored sitting for an hour during the Sunday mass. A male member of the CCR gave the example of a working woman who was being battered by her alcoholic husband. If she went for the Sunday mass and listened to the priest and got bored, she may not want to go there again, but at the Charismatic meeting during the time of worship many people feel the anointing of God. That feeling of God will be the pull factor for her to come again and again. So he advised her to attend the prayer meeting to find solace from her family problems.

The distinctly non-clerical nature of the Charismatic movement has encouraged more participation of the laity in different Church activities. The Renewal has produced people who have been empowered by the Holy Spirit and who have been trained in scriptures, spirituality, and leadership. The presence of an empowered and well-trained laity has emerged as a possible threat to the religious professionals of the Catholic Church. Most of the Charismatics whom I interviewed were critical of the role of the priests in the Church. On the other hand, most of the diocesan clergy in Goa are averse to the Charismatic Renewal and are very reluctant to support it. A diocesan priest who is the spiritual advisor of the GST and who has been in the Renewal for the last 30 years finds that priests have not promoted the Renewal positively and instead have kept it at a distance. A common criticism of Charismatics by the clergy is that they consider themselves as spiritually elite and have a holier-than-thou attitude. McDonnell (1987: 54) also finds that priests are often not open to the Renewal. The various reasons for this apathetic, often hostile attitude are that some identify the Renewal with emotionalism; others identify it with a conservative, fundamentalist, or simplistic theology; while still others see the Renewal as marginal and unconcerned with the real issues in the Church and world. The tension between the Mapusa Charismatic prayer group and the local pastor is seen in the fact that he does not allow them to use the Church for their prayer meetings and does not announce about their prayer meetings during mass. If the Charismatics do not attend the parish council meetings the local pastor questions their loyalty to the Church with comments such as, 'These Charismatics give more importance to their association than to the Church.' Such criticism puts pressure on the Charismatics and they are not sure what to do—whether to give more importance to the prayer group or to the parish.

The Charismatic movement has always been accused by its critics in the Catholic Church of accelerating the exodus of Catholics from the Church to the neo-Pentecostal sects. Paul Parathazham's study on neo-Pentecostals in India (1996: 4) shows that 26 per cent of those who left the Catholic Church were earlier actively involved in the CCR. However, most of the Charismatics whom I interviewed were of the opinion that the CCR has stemmed the flow of Catholics leaving the Church. According to Parathazham (1996: 8), the three most frequently mentioned pull factors for people to join neo-Pentecostal Churches are 'God-experience', 'centrality of the bible', and 'fellowship experience.' The Charismatics I interviewed argue that all the key points offered by the Born-Again sects such as God experience, word of God, and fellowship are present in the CCR. Therefore, the main reason for Catholics leaving the Church has been removed by the CCR and in the process it has exposed the inadequacy of the pastoral strategy of the Catholic Church. In big parishes of 5,000 or more people, the parish priest has his hands full with many funerals, baptisms, masses, and lots of administrative work. In such a situation he is not able to focus on pastoral work such as family visits, family counselling, and so on, which alienates the flock and leads them to leave the Church. The CCR by offering spiritual food to the faithful provides an implicit critique of the pastoral work of the clergy.

Negotiation of Identities by Individual Charismatics

For new members of the CCR the first appraisal of identity is through comparison with other Catholics who are not in the Renewal. In what way does being a 'Charismatic' Catholic make them different from or better than other Catholics? For many of them their identity as a pre-Charismatic was a troubled one. Most people who join the Renewal are those who need some help. They come to get some healing from their pain, physical or mental, or relief from some financial or family problems. Very few people who are completely hale and hearty come to the CCR. Some of them come from tough backgrounds such as belonging to a single-parent or below-poverty line family or having a family member who is an alcoholic. Some of them were too busy making money, often working late at night and even on Sundays. They once lived lives that were far away from God. Some were alcoholics or drug addicts. Others had family problems and illnesses. Though many were brought up in religious Catholic families, they were just nominal Catholics before joining the Renewal.

Entry into the Charismatic Renewal has brought about significant changes in their lives. While many of them were religious and Church-going before, they feel that being in the CCR is like being connected with the source and discovering Jesus and the Holy Spirit. Most of them have experienced dramatic shifts in their lives in terms of spirituality, commitment, prosperity, and overall satisfaction in life. They have got new houses that are much larger and better-furnished than the previous ones, their family problems and disputes have been resolved. They read the Bible and pray regularly in their homes. Their spouses or children have got good jobs. Thus, for an individual member of the CCR, their identity as a Catholic Charismatic implies significant, dramatic changes in their life from a troubled background and nominal practice of faith to a deep spiritual experience with increased spirituality, commitment, and prosperity.

An interesting illustration is that of a 60-year-old Hindu widow from Merces, whose motivation for joining was discussed in the previous chapter. This unlettered woman is not a baptized Catholic, does not go for mass, and yet belongs to the Merces Charismatic prayer group. She had an experience of Jesus that touched her heart and for the last three years she has been attending the prayer meetings regularly. She prays to Jesus and Mary and has experienced a lot of peace in her life and for her children. Since the time she joined the Renewal, her health has improved a lot. The major shift she finds in her religious identity is that now she has learned to pray first for the well-being of her neighbours' children and families and then pray for the well-being of her children and family as well as for all the people in her *wado* (street), both good and bad. Thus, entry into the CCR has expanded her concept of her neighbour and made her religious identity broader and more inclusive.

For the members of the CCR, another important and rather diffi-cult negotiation of identity is with the neo-Pentecostals, who strongly criticize the Catholics and point out many flaws and loopholes in their belief system. On the other hand, the Catholic Charismatics do not outright condemn them. They admit that they are people with good knowledge of the Bible, who have detailed explanations and proper teachings about the word of God and have lot of fellowship and unity.

They criticize the neo-Pentecostals for not giving any importance to Mother Mary and for their aggressive evangelism targeted at enticing the Catholics. They point out that first they need to improve their home and family situation and look at their own lives before trying to evangelize and change others. Almost all the Catholic Charismatics feel that the neo-Pentecostal sects attract people by offering money and material benefits. Many of them have relatives who have joined these sects.

In Goa, a safe distance has been maintained between the CCR and the neo-Pentecostal sects. There is no interaction between the two in social work or any other common endeavour, either at the organizational level or at an individual level. The Catholics are afraid that if they work together, the neo-Pentecostals will use the occasion to convert them. The fear is due to the fact that several Catholic Charismatics quietly attend neo-Pentecostal prayer meetings since they are attracted by the good music and their charismatic leaders.

The leader of the Merces prayer group, who told me that she had never attended any neo-Pentecostal meetings, distinguished between the Catholic Charismatics and the neo-Pentecostals in the following manner:

> Once the parish priest had sent us to visit one of the 'Believers' regarding the Small Christian Community. I did not find anything regarding Mother Mary in his house. When we questioned the family members, they said for them first was Jesus Christ and then Mary. ... They don't go for mass. They will come for the funeral mass if someone dies from the ward, but they do not take communion. ... Now we have our baptism, they have one more baptism it seems. They don't receive communion on the wedding day and their wedding is not in our Church but in their own Church.[18]

* * *

The recreation of the NTC, as the neo-Pentecostals define it, is the basic analytical principle, the guiding motif that informs the corporate identity of the neo-Pentecostal movement and the construction of individual identities built around their everyday life practices. The

[18] Interview with the leader of the CCR prayer group of Merces on 21 September 2007.

process of identity formation for the neo-Pentecostals involves marking of clear-cut boundaries with Catholicism and Hinduism, the two dominant religious traditions in Goa. The neo-Pentecostals, many of whom are former Catholics, distance themselves from the Catholic community and from Catholic beliefs, practices, and symbols by a discourse that elevates neo-Pentecostalism to the status of a true biblical Church, while downgrading the Catholic Church. Neo-Pentecostals reconstruct the identity of Catholicism as a man-made religion, which has strayed over the centuries from the original vision and values of the New Testament. They have a strong extremist position concerning other religions, which they regard as part of Satan's plan to take people to hell. The social interaction of the neo-Pentecostals is restricted to their own community.

Assuming the identity of the NTC involves appropriating the dualistic spiritual world view of the early Church, this dualistic and spiritual outlook to life makes them see everything in life in the form of paired opposites—spiritual vs material, good spirits vs powers of darkness, prosperity and blessings vs poverty and curses. This world view guides them to seek spiritual solutions to the problems of everyday life. It also guides them to define their mission as saving the lost, the lost being Catholics, Hindus, Muslims, and all others who are not Born-Again Christians. The identity of the neo-Pentecostals is closely linked with their understanding of their mission—urgent, aggressive proselytization, and numerical expansion—as seen in expressions such as 'expanding Church', 'Church on the move', and 'a going people', which are used to describe their Church. In order to legitimize their understanding of their mission as coming from the biblical Church, the neo-Pentecostals selectively refer to and interpret certain biblical texts that they call the mission mandate, while overlooking or reinterpreting other biblical mission texts.

The identity of the neo-Pentecostals in Goa is characterized by a degree of isolation and persecution, distinct characteristics of sects. The identity of being a persecuted and besieged community is interpreted positively, as a sign of Church growth. Intra-group solidarity and fellowship follows from their identity of a persecuted community, nurtured in the Sunday prayer meetings and the weekly prayer cell meetings. The balance between its universal identity as the worldwide Church of Christ and its local identity as an autonomous Church gives a distinct identity to the neo-Pentecostal movement in Goa. Neo-Pentecostalism, which was initially an underground, concealed movement, exhibiting a high levels of tension within the surrounding religio-cultural environment, has grown numerically and financially and today claims to be part of mainstream religion in Goa. While negotiating one's identity as a Born-Again Christian in a different religious background, the individual member is forced to tackle issues such as rupture of kinship ties, social and cultural boycott, financial problems, and strict demands of the new religion.

While the CCR has tried to carve out its own style and identity, distinct from Pentecostalism, there are several similarities and differences between the CCR and neo-Pentecostalism. With the process of sifting Pentecostal beliefs and practices through the sieve of Catholic tradition, which can be called the 'Catholicization' of the Pentecostal–Charismatic movement, the CCR has evolved into a unique, indigenous, Catholic movement, different from both Pentecostalism and traditional Catholicism. The CCR's ecstatic style of worship with an emphasis on the individual Believer and a strong intra-group solidarity and fellowship has led to them critiquing the mass reproduction of religious experience found in the Catholic Church. The presence of empowered and well-trained ordinary Catholic Charismatics, many of whom are critical of the role of priests in the Church, has emerged as a threat to the religious professionals of the Catholic Church. The relationship between the Church clergy and the Charismatics is characterized by some unease and tension, with most of the diocesan clergy in Goa being averse to supporting the Charismatic Renewal. While negotiating his or her identity as a Catholic Charismatic, the individual member of the CCR avoids social intercourse with the neo-Pentecostals due to the fear of being converted.

The NTC motif with its resultant dualistic spiritual world view, which informs and shapes to differing degrees and in different ways the identities of the neo-Pentecostals and the Catholic Charismatics, leads to the formation of a distinct Charismatic world of symbols. An exploration of the world of symbols of the Charismatic movement, including both neo-Pentecostalism and CCR, is taken up in the next chapter.

4 A Semiotic Exploration of the World of Charismatic Christianity

A religious system offers a special and distinct message, which evokes awe and surprise in its believers. Every religious system has a distinct and unique system of meanings with its own range of sacred symbols that synthesizes the adherents' ethos and opens them up to a new world in which to live, with new ways of being and notions of a better life. Thus, making sense of the religious symbols and discourses that the Pentecostal variant of Christianity holds as authoritative and truthful at a given period of time is necessary to understand the world view and ethos of its adherents. Geertz (1973: 90), in looking at religion as a cultural system, defines religion as 'a system of 'symbols' which acts to establish powerful, pervasive, and long-lasting moods and motivations in men by formulating conceptions of a general order of existence and clothing these conceptions with such an aura of factuality that the moods and motivations seem uniquely realistic'. He defines symbol as any object, act, event, quality, or relation that serves as a vehicle for a conception—the conception being the symbol's 'meaning'. According to him, cultural patterns, that is, systems or complexes of symbols, have an intrinsic double aspect: they give meaning, that is, an objective conceptual form, to social and psychological reality both by shaping themselves to it and by shaping it to themselves.

Geertz's ideas have to be understood in the light of Talal Asad's criticism. Asad (1993) suggests that religious symbols cannot be understood independent of their historical relations with non-religious symbols, in which work and power are crucial. He argues that religious symbols are intimately linked to social life and so change with it, and that they usually support the dominant political power, though they occasionally oppose it. It is not mere religious symbols that implant true Christian dispositions, but power—ranging all the way from laws (imperial and ecclesiastical) and other sanctions (hellfire, death, salvation, good repute, peace) to the disciplinary activities of social institutions (family, school, city, Church) and the disciplining of human bodies (fasting, prayer, obedience, penance). What he argues is that the authoritative status of representations/discourses (their identity and truthfulness) is dependent on the appropriate production of other kinds of practice and discourse. The two are intrinsically linked. In the light of Geertz's conception of symbols providing a model of and for the world of the Believers and Asad's corrections about the important role of power in deciding which representations or discourses are accepted as authoritative, this chapter will analyse the religious symbols and discourses of the Charismatics and how they are used in their ritualistic observances.

Bourdieu's work *The Logic of Practice* (1990) is about resolving the dichotomy between objective knowledge and subjectivity of the researcher. In his attempt to understand more completely one's objective and subjective relation to the object, he defines terms such as habitus, space, and capital. The idea of habitus is very important to understand the world of symbols of the CCR and neo-Pentecostalism in Gòa. Bourdieu (1990: 56) defines habitus as 'the generative principle, the cognitive and motivating structures that generate social practices by reproducing the regularities immanent in the social conditions in which the habitus was constituted while adjusting them to the social conditions in which the habitus is implemented'. The habitus, a set of unconscious rules or guidelines, interpretive schemas, and cultural dispositions guide individuals to evaluate, organize, categorize, think and act, and strategize and negotiate structures and practices. The habitus itself is a product of the specific social and structural conditions and the position of the individual in society, though this relationship between agency and structure is not determining. Habitus, which are 'practical hypotheses based on past experience, give disproportionate weight to early experiences' (1990: 54). The specificities of each individual's habitus are influenced by his/her relationship to, membership of, and status within a range of different social fields that include academia, religion, the economy, and politics. Bourdieu's concept of the field, which is a system of social positions structured internally in terms of power relations, plays an important role in shaping the habitus.

Concept of Sacred and Profane

The habitus of the individual Charismatics generate cultural practices and ritual observances wherein certain objects or events or activities are termed as either sacred or profane, or as ambiguous. The conception of sacred and profane symbols for the Catholic Charismatics differs from the other Catholics due to the dialectic link between habitus and institutions. In addition, neo-Pentecostals who draw inspiration from the Pentecost event of the early Church have different conceptions of what constitutes as being sacred and profane. According to Bourdieu (1990: 57), the habitus, which is constituted in the course of an individual history, facilitates agents to partake of the history objectified in institutions and thus 'makes it possible to inhabit institutions, to appropriate them practically, and so to keep them in activity'. The habitus enables the institutions to attain full realization, that is, the Church made flesh (Bourdieu 1990). While analysing the concepts of the sacred and the profane in the CCR and neo-Pentecostalism, it is necessary to study the influence of the habitus, constituted in individual histories of members, on the institutions of the CCR and neo-Pentecostalism and unravel those 'authoritative representations/discourses' (Asad 1993), which have fashioned these conceptions and study the role of power in determining their authoritative status.

Often in discussions regarding the concepts of the sacred and the profane, we come across the idea of 'holy'. While the concepts 'sacred' and 'holy' are similar and are at times used interchangeably, there are subtle differences between the two. 'Holiness', or the quality of being holy, is generally used in relation to living beings, especially persons and relationships, while sacredness is mostly used in relation to objects, things, space, places, or time (events). Thus, a saintly person may be considered holy, but not sacred. Holy is linked to the verb 'to hallow', which means to make holy or sacred, to sanctify, to consecrate, or to venerate, while the adjective form 'hallowed', as used in the 'Our Father' prayer, means holy, consecrated, sacred, or sanctified.

On the other hand, something that is dedicatedly used in or set apart
for the service or worship of a deity, or that which inspires awe or reverence among Believers, is regarded as sacred. This quality or property
is normally ascribed to objects (a sacred artefact such as an amulet
or a totem that brings protection against evil and danger), or places
(sacred ground), or time (holy hour). Durkheim (1976: 37) considered the dichotomy between the sacred and the profane to be the key
characteristic of religion, which he defined as: 'A religion is a unified
system of beliefs and practices relative to sacred things, that is to say,
things set apart and forbidden—beliefs and practices which unite into
one single moral community called a Church, all those who adhere to
them' (Durkheim 1995: 44). According to Durkheim, at the heart of
every religion, whether simple or complex, stands one common characteristic: a classification of all the things, real and ideal, of which people
think, into two classes or opposed groups, generally designated by the
words 'profane' and 'sacred'. By sacred he meant all phenomena and,
thus, anything could be sacred. Therefore, Durkheim's idea of sacred
also included the idea of holy. Sacredness is not a quality inherent
in certain objects. Objects are made sacred by groups of people who
set them apart and keep them bounded by specific actions. Human
beings acting collectively make and remake this quality of sacredness,
which must be added to the object again and again by collective human
doing. For Durkheim, the sacred represented the interests of the group
or community.

The profane, according to Durkheim, cannot be understood except
in relation to the sacred. Durkheim does not define the profane except
as that which threatens, undermines, or abolishes the sacred, and
destroys its essential attributes. Thus, sacred and profane have always
and everywhere been conceived by the human mind as two distinct
classes, radically opposed to one another. During his fieldwork among
the Australian tribes, he found that the act of eating and all secular
occupations such as hunting, fishing, and war were suspended when
the great religious ceremonies took place. Therefore, all work that met
the secular needs of life became part of profane activity.

For the continuation and growth of any voluntary movement, it is
necessary to recruit a large number of committed volunteers who are
able and willing to render a large amount of 'free service' to the entire
group. Since the group cannot remunerate the volunteers economically

or socially, it formulates a discourse that elevates the leader and the others on the serving team to be a chosen group of the elect.[1] In lieu of financial, social, or political remuneration, which is not always possible, their 'service to the group/Church' is set apart from other work and given the status of a 'sacred' activity. Only those who are divinely called and who show themselves to be responsible, trustworthy, and close to God are deemed worthy enough to be on the serving team of the group. Service to the Church is necessary for a person to be given more responsibilities in the Church. A member of the ROLC, while speaking about his experience of serving the Church, said:

> When I joined the Church, I began to serve, like setting up the chairs, arranging the mike, and cleaning the toilets, besides preparing food and serving people who were sick. Those in the pastoral role recognised that this gentleman is serving hard. They choose people who have passion and serve hard to give responsibilities. Slowly, in my case they told me to look after the prayer cell.[2]

The individual neo-Pentecostals believe that this is the natural order for leadership roles in the Church—first serve the community and then become an elder or pastor. This matches Geertz's (1973) idea of religion as a system of symbols that formulate conceptions of a general order of existence and clothe them with such an aura of factuality that they appear uniquely realistic.

The discourse on service to the Church draws from biblical models of service, such as Jesus washing the feet of his disciples, and at the same time attaches the sure promise of eternal salvation, besides an enhanced status among the members of the group as rewards for the service rendered. The first service of the ROLC begins at 8.30 am every Sunday and so the serving team has to reach the venue quite early in order to keep everything ready before 8.30 am. While the people assigned to serve have to make sacrifices such as coming earlier than the others and leaving last, they also have the privilege of access to equipment, facilities, and contacts, and being part of the inner decision-making group—the

---

[1] Group of the elect comprises Believers who are chosen by God to be saved. Since the neo-Pentecostals follow the Protestant theological position of salvation only through faith, only those who profess their faith in Christ can be among the group of the elect.

[2] Interview with a member of the ROLC on 23 December 2006.

core group or the team of elders. Often during the service, the pastor would commend the serving team for getting everything ready on time and ask the congregation to give them a good round of applause. Once, the pastor made a special mention of a couple on the serving team who did a good job welcoming people at the door and made them stand up while everyone applauded them. This practice of public acknowledgement of the serving team enhances the discourse on the importance of service to the Church. As Asad (1993) mentions, the authoritative status of representations/discourses depends on the appropriate production of other kinds of practices. The goals of this discourse are to identify what type of work can be considered as 'service to the Church', to motivate people to work and serve, and to elevate mundane chores such as sweeping, cleaning the hall, arranging the chairs, arranging the mikes, and preparing tea and coffee to the level of sacred activity. These chores when done in one's house or work place would be reduced to the level of profane activity.

For the Catholic Charismatics, this discourse of eternal reward for those who do community service fits in well with their theological position of salvation through faith and good work, unlike the neo-Pentecostals, who follow the Protestant position of salvation only through faith. The latter try to wriggle out of this dilemma by arguing that once a person is certain of salvation he will lead a life of service in gratitude for the free gift of God. Thus, those who serve the Church are the selected ones within the group of the elect.

Sacred and Profane Space

One of the most influential thinkers on religion and territory or space is Mircea Eliade, who argued that religious difference was a result of diverse instantiations of the sacred that erupted into the seen world in 'hierophanies', thereby creating the 'sacred space' (McAlister 2005: 250). Most of the current scholars of religion such as J.Z. Smith, David Chidester, Sam Gill, and Karen McCarthy Brown criticize Eliade's theory of the sacred space, which posited a universally existing, natural dualism between the sacred and the profane space, as ultimately resting on a Western theological template. These current scholars instead begin with a premise from philosopher Henri Lefebvre, whose book *The Production of Space* (1991) parses out any given local space in a tripartite synthesis of physical, mental, and social spaces that operate simultaneously. Thus, space is always a part of material culture, always social, and always produced, and there can never be any neutral or merely physical space (Lefebvre 1991). These scholars also state that 'place', 'space', and 'territory' are all 'second-order categories',[3] that is, they create the terms they attempt to describe (McAlister 2005: 250–2). Therefore, it is no surprise that neo-Pentecostals deny that there is any period or moment, which they call as sacred time or any specific place that they term as sacred space. For them, sacredness is derived from the activity performed at a particular place and in a particular time.

This is in contrast to the Catholic position, which holds a spatial distinction of the sacred and the profane and identifies the physical and social space of the Church universally as 'sacred'. This sacred character is theologically explained by the belief of the Catholics that the real presence of God is found in the consecrated host kept in the tabernacle.[4] The sacredness of the Church space is reflected in the reverence and decorum shown by the worshippers when they are within the physical confines of the Church. The Church cannot be used for profane activities such as parties, dances, or games. More than the physical structure of the Church, it is the restriction and control of social behaviour within the Church premises that produce the sacred Church space. As referred to earlier, Lefebvre argues that space is always social and always produced. Stirrat (1992: 64) identifies the use of space and controls over behaviour within spatially defined limits to highlight the distinction between the sacred and the profane found at a Catholic pilgrimage centre in Sri Lanka. He notes how the pilgrims were aware of the rule-bound nature of the sacred and the expectation that they should act with decorum within the boundaries of the Church land. This expectation was not experienced outside. Besides the physical space, the Catholics also regarded the social space of the Church or shrine as sacred, and

---

[3] Space comprises a synthesis of physical, mental, and social spaces. Place implies only the physical aspect of space, while territory involves the idea of ownership, jurisdiction, and boundary.

[4] Tabernacle in this particular context refers to a particular place in the Church, normally close to the altar, where the host that is consecrated during mass is kept. There will always be a light burning to indicate the holy presence of the Lord.

contrasted the sense of oneness in the Church with the divisions of normal society (Stirrat 1992: 66). Visvanathan (1999: 36–8) points out that for Syrian Christians a place, whether a Church or a house, is a mnemonic expressing the continuity and linearity of historical time.

On the other hand, the Pentecostal Christians, who value sacred time more than historical time, argue that every moment and every land in the world is holy since it is charged by God's presence and activity. They, thus, map the universe into Christian-reached and unreached (demonic) territories. This global-mapping is not only of 'people groups' but also of territories (McAlister 2005: 252). Territories can be ruled by 'principalities' or 'powers' invested with theological, spiritual significance. Unlike the Catholic Charismatics who hold the territorial confines of the Church as sacred, the neo-Pentecostals spiritually map the entire universe into swathes of sacred and demonic territories—sacred where there has been successful Church planting and demonic where their ancient peoples had transacted pacts with un-Christian powers. On the basis of this distinction, McAlister describes an additional concept, namely the '10/40 window'. The phrase '10/40 window' became a prominent concept in evangelical Christian discourse. It maps a territory from 10 degree to 40 degree north, a rectangular 'window' between northern Africa and Eastern Asia where the Christian population is quite small and evangelization is deemed necessary. McAlister (2005: 253) also gives the example of the Haitian revolution in 1791 and the subsequent independence of Haiti, which the Pentecostals interpret as the enslaved religious leader, Boukman Dutty, making a 'pact with the devil' and dedicating Haiti to Satan. They hold this unholy alliance as having been responsible for Haiti's subsequent 200 years of misery. While theologically, the Catholic Charismatics regard the entire universe as sacred and charged with God's presence, they spatially distinguish between the sacred space of the Church (place set apart for worship) and the profane space of the everyday world outside. The neo-Pentecostals, on the other hand, stress on the idea of the entire uni verse being divided into Christian (reached) and demonic (unreached) territories, both of which are sacred spaces. Through conversion to Christianity, a territory and its people can detach itself from demonic entrenchment and become a righteous land standing before God.

The Pentecostals reject the 'place' concept of Church (they believe that the Church is not a particular building located at a particular place) and identify the Church with God's people. In the mainline historic Churches, including the Syrian Christian denominations, the Church expresses a holy, closed, and official space for the enactment of the liturgy (Visvanathan 1999: 222). God has promised, according to the scriptures, that where 2–3 people meet in his name there he will be. Thus, sacredness of the institution of the Church is shifted from its specific venue or location and attached to the divine activity of people meeting in God's name. Sacredness is attached not to a particular individual, but to the community of Believers. Therefore, individual praise and worship in one's own house or before channels such as 'Miracle net' or 'God' on TV is not considered 'proper' worship by their pastors. The ecclesiology of the neo-Pentecostals is based on their Christology. They believe that, according to the scriptures, Christ is the head and the Church is his body. Since the Church is the body of Christ, they, as different members of the body, have to be part of it. The members believe that they are all part of the body of Christ and so they come together on Sunday to praise and worship God and to experience fellowship together.

Sunday Prayer Meetings

The Sunday service where all the members of the Church come together to praise and worship God is a sacred activity and they make sure that they do not miss it. So even if they go out of Goa for work or vacation, they either make sure they are back by Sunday or they attend praise and worship in some Born-Again Church wherever they are. Most of the neo-Pentecostals organize their Sunday prayer meetings in a hall. These halls, either located in hotels or schools, are otherwise used for weddings, conferences, parties, and other 'profane' activities. The WRM meets in the old residence of the pastor, which was earlier a bar and restaurant. The neo-Pentecostals believe that when the people of God praise and worship God during the Sunday prayer meetings, God himself is present there and this transforms the place from profane to sacred. This resonates with Geertz's idea that religion as a system of symbols constitutes reality. At the same time, the socio-historical conditions and practical considerations of the need for a place of their own influence their conception of sacred space.

The NFI Church has been in existence in Panaji for the last 10 years, but they still do not have a place of their own. They are tired of shifting from place to place and having their Sunday prayer meetings in rented halls, which lead to problems such as uncertainty about getting a hall every week, difficulty in transporting the sound system and other amenities to and from the hall, and restrictions on decorating and arranging the hall in the manner they want for worship. The pastor and many of the members whom I interviewed are looking for a permanent place and believe that God will give them a place of their own somewhere in or close to Panaji itself, but the lack of finances is a major hurdle. Therefore, the issue of having their own place is very important for them and influences their concept of sacred space. The same problem applies to most of the neo-Pentecostal groups in Goa, who are very small in size and do not have the resources to have their own Church. So while the neo-Pentecostals criticize the 'place' concept of Church as being a Catholic idea and consider the entire universe as sacred, their strong desire to have their own Church building indicates the importance they give to place as a sacred space.

The neo-Pentecostals believe that the day or time when they have their prayer meeting is not important. Sunday is chosen for convenience—it is a holiday and all can attend the prayer meeting. What makes Sunday a sacred day is the fact that they have the sacred activity of praise and worship on that day. One of the neo-Pentecostals mentioned that Sunday has become a sacred day for him, a day dedicated to and set apart for God and so he does not work on Sundays and attends the prayer meeting. A college-going youth has told his friends that he will be free to go out with them only on Sunday evenings. His friends know that irrespective of whatever plans they make for Sunday morning, he will not come because he will be busy with Sunday worship. Another Believer, somewhere in his late 40s, who did his MBA from Mumbai University and is a business consultant, mentioned that every Saturday evening he goes for evangelization work to the village of Diwar. Therefore, on Saturday afternoon he switches off his mobile and stops doing any work to prepareation to go to Diwar. All his colleagues know that he will not be available on Saturday afternoons, as he will be busy with 'God's work'. The habitus is the dual capacity to produce objectively classifiable practices and works and to differentiate and appreciate these practices and products (Bourdieu 1984: 170). In other words, the habitus is an organizing structure that organizes practices and the perception of practices (Bourdieu 1984).

The Charismatic habitus influences individual neo-Pentecostals to organize their social practices and behaviour patterns on Sundays by imposing restrictions on certain activities and encouraging other actions. Thus, the habitus guides them to give precedence to attending the prayer meeting over work or leisure and recreational activities on Sundays.

Sacred Time and Mapping of Human History

During a prayer meeting on 31 December 2006, the pastor of WRM predicted that the year 2007 would be a special year, wherein all the things that the people desired would be fulfilled. Four months later on 1 April 2007 during the Sunday service, he told the same crowd that many testimonies were coming that year about people getting jobs and houses, starting new businesses, and settling property matters. 'Sacred time' plays an important role in the religious discourses of neo-Pentecostalism. A certain period of time, either an hour or a day or a year, acquires a sacred character either due to the fulfilment of some vision or prophecy, or due to the expectation that some sacred event devoted to God will occur. The exact day or year can keep on changing depending on the content of the discourse feeding into its sacredness. The same pastor, who predicted that 2007 would be a special year, said during the Sunday service on 28 October 2007 that they were soon moving into the greatest year to come, when the living Church would take off in Goa. The present moment or the immediate future—either today or the coming week or month or year—is often portrayed as the sacred time, when the prosperity gospel will be fulfilled and their lives will change for the better. The millennial expectation of the Second Coming of Christ plays an important role in their conception of sacred time, which leads them to evaluate specific historical situations in the light of what is to be at the time of the Last Judgement. The idea of the Apocalypse as the end of time leads the Syrian Christian perception of history and the events that constitute history to take on a moral tone (Visvanathan 1999: 36). This dependence of the neo-Pentecostal conception of the present moment as sacred time on the millennial discourse is similar to Asad's (1993) contention that the authoritative status of a discourse is dependent on the appropriate production of other kinds of discourses.

The neo-Pentecostals look at time as eternity with God, and so their historical lives on Earth are just a fraction of it and are a preparation for eternity. The historical period on Earth is divided into different ages. There is the biblical age, which is divided into the Old Testament, the time from the creation of Adam and Eve until Jesus' entry, and the New Testament, that is, Jesus' time. They give a lot of importance to the New Testament period and link their faith and Church to it. The Old Testament is only important as preparation for the entry of Jesus Christ into the human world. It provides proof of Jesus' genealogy. From Jesus' times, it is the Christian era and Christianity as a religion has been growing. Once the word of God spreads to the ends of the world and the world is completely evangelized, the Christian age will end. God the Father and Jesus will appear to all people and that will be the end of humanity.

They hope that God will come while they are still alive so that they can see his coming. They have vivid descriptions about his coming. God will come with his army, with Moses, Abraham, and all the prophets. All those who are dead will rise up. Our human mind cannot comprehend what it will look like at that time. Every eye will be able to see him and he will come as a king. Due to the influence of millennialism on their conception of sacred time, they consider the present time the end days. At present, many people are speaking about the Antichrist, which is considered to be one of the signs that the present times are the end days. In their mapping of human history, which is primarily based on Christological considerations, the New Testament period and the present age are given importance because of Christ's entry into history and his imminent second coming respectively, while the intervening period of human history that includes the growth of Christianity is overlooked and not given importance. Being very young movements with almost no history, they conveniently play down the importance of human history by stressing only on the New Testament period and the present End Times. In a simplistic and unhistorical manner, the neo-Pentecostals connect their Church to the New Testament age, in sharp contrast to the Syrian Christian community in Kerala, the oldest Christian community in India, where the level of historical consciousness is extremely high and the arrival of Thomas in Malabar is accepted by all Syrian Christians as the source and beginning of Syrian Christian identity (Visvanathan 1999).

Bourdieu (1990: 54), while describing the link between habitus and history, says, 'The *habitus*, a product of history, produces individual and collective practices—more history—in accordance with the schemes generated by history.' The unhistorical neo-Pentecostal practice of mapping history with emphasis only on the biblical age and the present End Times is generated by the Charismatic habitus that is produced and shaped by their specific historical encounter with the Catholics and other unsaved people of Goa who have long religious histories. On the other hand, the CCR tries to 'stand in the Catholic tradition which gave birth to the itinerant prophets of the ancient Church, the preaching apostolate of the mendicant orders in the Middle Ages, the exercises of St. Ignatius ... and other apostolic and spiritual movements' (McDonnell 1980: 19).[5] The CCR, while rejecting a simplistic and ahistorical return to an idealized NTC, recognizes the unique role of the New Testament communities (McDonnell 1980).

Most Sacred Time of Worship and Other Sacred Symbols

During the Sunday prayer meeting, the time of worship, which follows praise, is the most sacred time for the neo-Pentecostals. That is the time they sing slow and devotional songs, many of them going on their knees or raising their faces or hands upwards, often with eyes closed or clouded with tears, in a posture of worship to the Lord. While the neo-Pentecostal prayer meetings are louder and more boisterous than the CCR meetings, the time of worship is a relatively quieter time: the music is softer, the leader's tone is softer, and no one is found dancing, shouting, or clapping. The children are also restrained from running around or making noise. During that time most of the Believers' faces are found suffused with emotions of ecstasy. Thus, the Pentecostal style of worship incorporates and gives meaning to intense emotions and personal experiences in their ritual. This negates 'the dominant assumption in the study of ritual in modern anthropology that "feelings", which are

[5] The relation of the CCR to the Catholic tradition and the NTC is found in the Malines Document I prepared in 1974 by Kilian McDonnell and an international team of theologians and pastoral leaders. This document states the official position of the CCR in theological and pastoral terms.

private and ineffable, are opposed to ritual, which is public and legible' (Asad 1993: 72). They believe that the time for worship is an intense moment where they remain still and experience the presence of God powerfully. This very sacred time is relived every week during their prayer meeting, reinforcing Geertz's idea that religion, which is a system of symbols, establishes pervasive and long-lasting moods and motivations in people (Geertz 1973). Actions such as clapping, dancing, and performing different actions, which in another context such as a party or a musical concert would not be termed sacred, acquire a sacred hue when performed in the context of the Sunday prayer meeting. Biblical texts that speak of praising God through different musical instruments and that describe King David dancing in honour of God form the discourse that transforms these profane actions into sacred ones.

For the neo-Pentecostals, any mundane activity such as sitting on the sofa, lying in bed, putting on a dress, or cooking in the kitchen becomes sacred and part of worship when combined with praying in tongues, reading the Bible, or just singing sacred songs. Their conception of sacred space is broader than that of the Catholic Charismatics, who make a clear and sharp distinction between sacred activities such as praying to God before the Blessed Sacrament and attending mass, which are normally restricted to the physical boundaries of the Church, and the mundane activities done in their day-to-day lives. The Charismatic movement has, to some extent, blurred the boundary between the physical sacred space of the Church and the space outside it, since Charismatic prayer meetings are now being held in the houses of laypeople. Additionally, the CCR, through its night vigils and Charismatic retreats held outside the Church premises, has extended the sacred space to areas beyond the physical territory of the Church. On the other hand, most Catholic Charismatic groups prefer to hold their prayer group meetings in the Church or in a chapel, where the Blessed Sacrament is present. In addition, many of them spend a lot of time praying in the Church before the Blessed Sacrament, indicating that for the Catholic Charismatics the Church is a special sacred space compared to the space outside the Church, which is the venue of mundane daily activities.

A very sacred symbol for both the Catholic Charismatics and the neo-Pentecostals that is used extensively in their sacred prayer meetings and services is the word of God, that is, the Holy Bible. The discourse on the recreation of the NTC and the resultant dualistic spiritual world view plays an important role in giving authoritative status to the symbol of the Bible in the lives of the Charismatics. Reading the Bible is one of the most sacred activities a Charismatic can undertake. It is not just a spiritual activity, but also an empowering and renewing activity, which can overcome demons and evil spirits, provide solutions for financial, family, and individual problems, and also cure illnesses. A housewife who was harassed continuously by her husband for becoming a neo-Pentecostal used to get up early and lock herself in the bathroom and read her Bible. Therefore, her closest times with God were in the bathroom, which became a sacred place for her due to this activity of reading the Bible and praying to God in there. This illustration is important, as it shows how any place is transformed into a sacred space by the neo-Pentecostals. This idea of the Bible as an important sacred symbol that shapes the everyday reality of the Believers and formulates conceptions of a general order of existence, will be taken up in more detail later in the section titled 'Orality of Tradition'.

The dualistic spiritual world view of the Charismatics lead them to make distinctions between various objects and activities as being either from God (good spirits) or from the Evil One (evil spirits). The CCR and many neo-Pentecostal groups distinguish between profane worldly music and sacred gospel music. While all the Charismatics are clear that sacred music comprises songs about God, there are no clear-cut criteria to distinguish between sacred and worldly music. For the neo-Pentecostals, sacred gospel music implies all songs directed towards Jesus Christ, God the Father, and the Holy Spirit. For the Catholic Charismatics, sacred music also includes songs directed to Mary and the saints. While Christianized *bhajans*[6] are regarded as part of sacred music by the Catholic Church and have entered mainstream Church liturgy, many Catholic Charismatics in Goa do not accept bhajans as sacred music.

Due to the cultural trappings of the Christian gospel, most of the music sung by the Charismatics is predominantly of the Western style,

---

[6] Indian style songs, normally sung during Hindu devotion, using Indian instruments.

with heavy use of the guitar, keyboard, and drums amplified through sophisticated music systems. The pastors and leaders of the CCR and neo-Pentecostal groups in Goa are trained in the Western style of music, which they associate with gospel or sacred music. The purpose of sacred or supernatural music is to draw people into deep worship and enable them to experience God, which will lead to healings, signs, and wonders. All other music that does not fall within under the category of sacred gospel music is profane worldly music. However, there are differing views among the Charismatics regarding which type of profane worldly music can be classified as satanic, evil music. To distinguish satanic music, they refer to a myth, which describes Lucifer as the archangel in charge of worshipping God. Once he was thrown out of heaven, he used his musical talent to glorify the Devil. Therefore, all types of worldly music that lead people to worship the Devil are satanic, according to that myth.

Several of the neo-Pentecostals that I interviewed said that rock music is satanic since it exposes the listener to drugs and alcohol. But the pastor of the ROLC, who is a good musician and likes the loud, noisy type of Western music, gave the example of a Pentecostal revival among the hippies in Argentina, in which worship was completely through rock music, since that was the only music they knew, to show that rock music is not demonic. An important point that arises from the pastor's example is that sacredness or profanity of any type of music is linked both with the cultural background of the one making the judgement and of the individual or group that composed and sang the song. While some hold that trance music is specifically demonic, gives evil thoughts, and corrupts the mind, others opine that the loud temple music or the loud chanting and proclamation from the mosques pollute the air by releasing demons. Some of the neo-Pentecostals believe that in order to categorize music as satanic, the background of the singer and the lyrics of the song are important. The song 'We are the World' is very popular and has a very powerful message but they believe that its singer, Michael Jackson, is a worshipper of Satan. They also claim that the song 'Hotel California', which has a very captivating and catchy tune, was written by the songwriter in an abandoned and haunted hotel in California. The lyrics of the song were inspired by the Devil and so they categorize this song as profane.

Sin Is Evil but Sacred

'Sin' is not just a sacred or profane activity. According to the Christian understanding of sin, it is not just an activity but rather the quality attached to an activity that classifies the activity either as sinful or good. The Christian understanding of sin is that it is a religious and ethical attitude (thought, word, and deed) that undermines one's relationship with the divine and draws the individual towards evil and the demonic. Sin in Christianity is always defined in relation to God. Both the Catholic Charismatics and the neo-Pentecostals place a lot of emphasis on sin and connect sin with God and his plan for salvation, Jesus Christ, the Devil, repentance, and human helplessness. All those who wish to become members of the CCR have to participate in the Life in the Spirit Seminar and undergo a general confession. Thus, membership, personal holiness, and conversion are linked with confessing one's sins, which is a part of disciplining the body.

The neo-Pentecostals, on the other hand, use a biblical discourse that identifies the human body as the temple of the Holy Spirit, to describe the symbol of sin. The human body, which is created by God, is holy and sacred. Each person on Earth is a pure and perfect plan of God. According to this discourse, Satan entered the scene and inscribed sin on this spotless body through the disobedience of Adam and Eve. This disobedience came about through the free choice given to humans by God. The notion of fear is also linked with sin. The neo-Pentecostal pastor teaches that the demonic spirit of fear entered into human history when Adam sinned. Fear causes one to do the exact opposite of what God wants them to do and thus fear causes one to sin. The discourse on sin also stresses that being sinners, human beings are unable to save themselves. The neo-Pentecostal pastor, while illustrating the impact of sin, gave the example of the most religious Church-going Christian. Even he would commit at least three sins a day. That would make it 90 sins a month and just over 1,000 sins a year. If we suppose the man died when he was 51 years, he would have committed 51,000 sins in his lifetime and would be condemned to hellfire.

The helplessness of people in the face of sin forced Jesus Christ to come and die on Earth in order to free people from their fear and take away their sins. Jesus through his sacrifice washed the human body with his blood and in the process erased the marks of sin left by the devil and once again inscribed holiness on the human body. The neo-Pentecostal discourse on sin contrasts the frightening implications of sin with the helplessness of human beings to free themselves of fear and sin in order to emphasize the 'free' gift of salvation. Yet this 'free' gift of salvation can be attained only by confessing one's sins to God and accepting Jesus as one's personal saviour. Thus, Charismatic theology portrays sin as evil and the antithesis of salvation, the good for which every Believer aspires.

However, sociologically, sin belongs to the realm of the sacred. Durkheim (1976: 37–9) classified all phenomena that is 'set apart' as sacred, not just the personal beings called Gods or spirits. For him, the profane world consisted broadly of all the secular activities of everyday life, while the sacred world consisted of all that is held apart. Veena Das (1976: 250) while applying Durkheim's concept of sacred and profane to Hindu ritual argues that he did not accept that the distinction between the sacred and the profane was equivalent to the distinction between good and bad. He divided the sacred itself into the 'good sacred' and the 'bad sacred', both of which retained the quality of 'sticking out' from the world of the non-sacred (Das 1976). Based on the above descriptions of the neo-Pentecostal and CCR notions—sin is connected to demonic spirits and Satan and is opposed to God and salvation, but at the same time is not placed in the realm of the profane everyday world either—sin would belong to the 'bad sacred'. Thus, sin is theologically evil but sociologically part of the 'bad sacred'.

Inscription of Moral Codes and Practices on the Christian Body

The discourse on the re-creation of the NTC and the resultant dualistic spiritual world view leads the Charismatics to label habits such as drinking, smoking, and taking drugs that are part of profane activities as evil habits. Similarly, practices such as fasting, praying, and doing penances, which are set apart from profane everyday activities, are classified as good practices. Restrictions on drinking are widespread both in the CCR and in neo-Pentecostalism. Teetotalism is the model for all neo-Pentecostals. These restrictions are enforced in some groups directly with a lot of pressure, including the threat of excommunication, and indirectly in others, using mainly psychological pressure. The New Testament discourse on the body being the temple of the Holy

Spirit and, thus, set apart to be 'holy, pure, blameless' and 'do the will of God' are linked to giving up evil habits such as drinking and drugs. Thus, both holiness and moral codes are inscribed on the physical body of the adherent through disciplining tools such as fasting, prayer, and penance and abstinence from alcohol, smoking, and drugs. This is what Asad (1993) meant when he said that true Christian dispositions are implanted through the disciplinary activities of human bodies such as fasting, prayer, obedience, and penance.

Some neo-Pentecostal groups that have strict codes of conduct do not allow their members to watch movies or television or to dance or listen to worldly music. Their discourse on fasting draws from biblical texts, which emphasize that certain types of demons go only through fasting and that Jesus fasted for 40 days in the wilderness. The practice of fasting gets divine legitimization through biblical texts and also through testimonies such as the following: 'During my student days when I was in Chennai, I was struggling to find God in my life. Then God spoke to me and asked me to undertake a 21-day fast. During my fast God appeared to me and asked me to remove the curse from my life. God put the words from Gal 3:13–14 in my mind and told me that Jesus had become a curse for me so that the blessings of Abraham could come down on me. From that day faith came into my heart and the curse was taken away from my life.'[7]

Thus, by shifting the physical body of the Believer from the realm of the profane to the sacred, emphasis is shifted from the physical and material aspects of the body to its spiritual and metaphysical dimensions. This shift in the physical body is achieved through disciplining tools such as fasting, prayer, and penance and abstinence from alcohol, smoking, and drugs. Since their body is the temple of the Holy Spirit, women and girls are urged to dress modestly and appropriately. They are told that the spirit of the Lord is watching over them and so they should be decent in their dressing. Many of the female Catholic Charismatics, who are involved in the Church bodies, chastise young women who come dressed inappropriately for mass. Thus, the discourse of the body being the temple of God together with notions

[7] Given during a talk on idolatry and witchcraft at Hotel Garden View, Panaji, on 28 June 2007.

about morality and ethics are enforced through such practices. As Asad (1993) argued, power gives authoritative status to religious symbols or representations.

'Hindu' Practices Are Taboo

Both the Catholic Charismatics and the neo-Pentecostals consider sacred practices such as yoga, Indian forms of meditation, pranic healing, star gazing, palmistry, and so forth as taboo and are forbidden from following these practices. While the repercussions for following such practices are considerable for the neo-Pentecostals—the sanction of hellfire and of disciplining the human body through prayer and penance in order to evict the evil spirits that enter because of such practices—the Catholics are not so stringent. The Catholic discourse on yoga as 'bad sacred' has to compete with the mainstream discourse in the Church on the importance of inter-religious dialogue and inculturation. It draws from the discourse on the recreation of the NTC and the resultant dualistic spiritual world view in order to portray yoga and Indian practices as taboo. When the CCR began in Goa in the 1970s, this was not a dominant view, as the early Charismatics were influenced by the position of Vatican II encouraging ecumenism and inter-religious dialogue. That is why in the early years of the Mapusa prayer group there were Americans coming and conducting healing sessions, some of whom were not Catholics.

It is only in the 1990s as the number of Hindu babas and gurus increased with their own brands of syncretic Hinduism and this got a lot of publicity through the media, did the Charismatics find that many of their members, especially those in urban areas, were flocking to these modern-age gurus to seek cures for different ailments. That is when voices within the CCR began branding 'Hindu' practices as a manifestation of self-power and even satanic. This discourse gained momentum with the entry of the neo-Pentecostal sects who were very stringent in their condemnation of other religious faiths as satanic. Radical elements within the CCR who were influenced by the views of these groups became more vocal. The gradual legitimization of this discourse within the CCR was largely due to the strong views expressed in the Divine Retreat Centre, Potta, against Catholics practising any kind of pagan worship. The message that practices such as yoga, pranic healing, palmistry, participating in Hindu worship during the popular Ganesh or Diwali festivals, and accepting *prasad*[8] at Hindu temples are taboo was repeatedly emphasized in the talks, sermons, and activities at Potta. Several of the Catholic Charismatics whom I interviewed were against yoga being practised in the Catholic schools in Goa. This view is based on the premise that yoga originates from Hindu mythology and yoga was practised by Hindu gods and goddesses. Therefore, if the Charismatics want peace of mind and tranquillity, they should go for the Charismatic prayer meetings or pray before the Blessed Sacrament in the Church rather than practise yoga.

Some Charismatics became critical of seminaries where Hindu bhajans were sung, Indian-style masses were celebrated by priests wearing saffron shawls, mass readings that were taken from other scriptures, and Hindu signs such as 'Om' were put on the tabernacle, all in the name of inculturation. This discourse, which regards inter-religious dialogue and inculturation with suspicion and rejects 'Hindu' practices such as yoga, is in conflict with the position of the Archdiocese of Goa, which has been promoting inter-religious dialogue.[9] With thousands of Catholics from Goa flocking to Potta from the 1990s, this view gained in popularity, though it had to compete with the discourse on inter-religious dialogue promoted by the hierarchy of the Catholic Church in Goa. Since the discourse, which regarded yoga and inter-religious dialogue as taboo, did not get the appropriate support from the Church, not many in the CCR subscribe to this view, validating Asad's statement that the authoritative status of representations or discourses is dependent on the appropriate production of other kinds of practices and discourses. Similarly, the neo-Pentecostals are moving from rejection of inter-faith engagement to a cautious dialogue, which has been prompted by the emergence of inter-faith issues from ecumenical dialogue with older Christian traditions such as the International Dialogue with Roman Catholics from 1972 onwards (Veli-Matti Karkkainen in Robeck and Yong 2014: 294–312). In the beginning, Pentecostal Churches in India

[8] A sweet offering offered by the Hindu priest and consumed by the devotees, who consider it as consecrated and holy.

[9] This role of the Church in promoting inter-religious dialogue has been discussed in detail in Chapter 2.

were ecumenical in nature, bringing together Anglicans, Baptists, Danish Lutherans, Methodists, and so on (Varghese 2015). However, with the passage of time, the ecumenical spirit faded away and the Pentecostals separated from the mainline Churches, avoided fellowship with other Christians, and tried to evangelize and convert them to the Pentecostal faith. Today, Pentecostal Churches do not favour ecumenism, which they fear would compromise and distort their faith and conviction. Some members of the CCR and many of the neo-Pentecostals share the view that practices such as yoga and other forms of Indian meditation are taboo and should be avoided, and are cautious and suspicious about ecumenical and inter-faith dialogue.

God of Love and God of Wrath

Both in the CCR and in neo-Pentecostalism, the worshippers have an anthropomorphic conception of God. Their idea of God is goodness personified. A female Believer, in one of the prayer cell meetings held at the pastor's house, said, 'It is good to know that our God has emotions and that our God even laughs.'[10] They believe that through the Charismatic movement they are imbibing the nature of God. For the Charismatics, God is predominantly male and a father figure, a resurrected living God, who is actively present among them. More important than the nature of God are his actions, since he is the creator, the provider of good, and the doer of good. Many of the Catholic Charismatics are certain that whatever they ask God, he will grant it to them, provided their intention in asking God is honourable, what they asked for is in according with his will, God thinks it will benefit the one asking, and the answer will come in God's own time.

The neo-Pentecostal God is a combination of the macho image of a strong, vengeful, maleficent God and the feminine portrait of a loving, jealous God who wants his people to come closer to him. This discourse of God as a punishing God, a judge whose wrath blazes on those who hurt his people, influences the views of the neo-Pentecostals regarding other religious traditions. Some of them whom I interviewed, including the pastor, said that some of the natural calamities that occurred

[10] Interview with St Inez on 24 July 2008.

in India were due to divine retribution. When the people of God are affected, God is also hurt and his vengeance will follow. The concept of God as a judge is not found among the average Catholic Charismatics, except among a few radical members. The idea of God as a judge among the neo-Pentecostals is shaped by the discourse of the neo-Pentecostal Church as the beleaguered and besieged early Christian community, which is embattled on all fronts, but draws comfort from a powerful God, who will protect his people from their enemies by striking terror in the hearts of their persecutors. This discourse gives rise to the idea of the exclusive Born-Again Christian Club, which includes the elect, who will be saved and excludes the gentiles, who are the lost.

This masculine symbol of God's wrath blazing down upon the enemies of the Christians is balanced with the feminine conceptualization of God as a real, warm, loving person directing and shaping their daily lives and talking to them daily. They believe that they need to take God's guidance in every area of their life. Some of the women even seek advice from God for the culturally defined feminine tasks such as what to cook or which dress to wear. Their idea of God is a strong masculine figure, who takes on the role of father, brother, husband, lover, or friend. This conception of a real, personal God intervening in their daily lives draws from the dualistic spiritual outlook of the NTC. The dual nature of God, both as father and mother who is good to his people and at the same time vanquishes their enemies, stems from the idea of a localized God. Their God is the God of the Born-Again Christians, who protects them and who is more powerful than the Gods of their enemies. The neo-Pentecostals regard the difficulties and problems they face in their day-to-day lives as manifestations of the Evil One. In order to combat the powers and forces of darkness in the world, they need the intervention of their God in their lives.

Pantheon of the Demonic

Normally, the word 'pantheon' is associated with Gods, but in the Sinhala Buddhist tradition, there is no great divide between Gods and demons (Stirrat 1992: 85). Demons can become Gods and Gods can become demons. In his study of a Catholic shrine in Sri Lanka, Stirrat shows that the Catholics unambiguously regard all the Gods of the Buddhist and Hindu pantheons as demons, besides the existing demons of the Catholic, Buddhist, and Hindu traditions (Stirrat 1992: 91). Mosse (quoted in Bayly 1989: 5, 6), while exploring the way in which Christianity has become embedded in the indigenous social and religious order of a Hindu–Christian village in South India, found that the sacred pantheon of the village has been formed out of a complex inter-penetration of Christian and Hindu cultural traditions.

Like the Catholics in Stirrat's work, the neo-Pentecostals see the entry of the demonic into the world through the lens of the Genesis account. The fall of the angel Satan is linked to rebellion in heaven and this fall is explicitly linked with the fall of human beings. Since they cooperated with Satan, they lost their dominion over the earth and came under the authority of Satan, leading to the entry of evil and suffering into the world. Satan sowed doubts about God's unconditional acceptance of humans and this led to the loss of peace and security for all mankind. According to neo-Pentecostals, all the demons are considered as being under the control of Satan who is frequently described as the 'boss' or leader of the demons. Immediately below Satan come the 'fallen angels', who accompanied Satan on his expulsion from heaven. Satan is regarded as a rejected being and a liar who tries to make people believe his lies rather than the truth of God's word. Besides linking evil and suffering in the world with the demonic, they also link moral transgressions such as sexual activity outside the marriage covenant with demonic spirits. A sexual union of a Born-Again Christian with someone outside the marriage bond results in the creation of an ungodly tie, which opens up the Believer to the transfer of demonic spirits from the person with whom there has been ungodly sexual activity. Satan, rather than God, is honoured, resulting in a curse rather than a blessing.

The neo-Pentecostals believe that activities such as occultism and witchcraft provide shelter to many demonic spirits. While all the Pentecostal–Charismatic Christians, due to their dualistic spiritual world view, believe in the presence and power of the Devil and his army of demonic spirits, they have differing views on whether the Gods of the Hindu and Muslim pantheons are demonic. The neo-Pentecostals are convinced that Hindu deities such as Krishna, Shiva, and others are demons, while only some radical elements among the Catholic Charismatics accept this. Thus, the pantheon of the demonic for the neo-Pentecostals and some Catholic Charismatics includes all the Hindu and Muslim Gods, besides the demons of the Christian, Hindu, and Muslim traditions. For them good and evil exist as two radical opposites, separated by an unbridgeable gulf, and there is no system through which power is delegated from relatively good to relatively evil beings. They do not accept that the Hindu and Muslim gods can change from the pantheon of the demonic and become part of the Christian pantheon of Gods.

Hierarchy of Gods

Neo-Pentecostalism and the CCR have a history of opposition to one another in Goa, with many Catholic Charismatics leaving the Church and starting their own independent groups. As a result, right from the beginning, the neo-Pentecostals directed all their prayers and practices towards Jesus Christ, with stress on the working of the Holy Spirit in reaction to the popular Catholic devotion to Mary. This was also in line with the Christocentric and pneumatic[11] stress found in the global Pentecostal movement. The tenets of faith of the New Covenant Family of Ministries, to which the WRM is connected, speak about the One True God and also the deity of Christ as the only begotten Son of God. While the NFI does not explicitly state their conception of divinity, their vision statement states that they promote Churches where the gifts of the spirit are worked out.

When Pentecostalism began in the Catholic Church, the emphasis was mainly on the Holy Spirit and, therefore, the well-known Christian sociologist Joseph Fichter titled his book *The Catholic Cult of the Paraclete* (1975).[12] Slowly, the writings of various theologians gave a more Catholic identity to the Renewal and the discourse changed from just a pneumatic emphasis to a Christocentric and a broader Trinitarian emphasis. Thus, the authoritative divine symbol in the CCR became Jesus Christ and its praise and worship is directed towards the Trinity—God the Father, Jesus, and the Holy Spirit. Hardly any songs are directed towards Mary, the mother of Jesus. This is in stark contrast

---

[11] Derived from a Greek word, meaning breath or spirit. Here it means related to the Holy Spirit.

[12] For a good review of Fichter (1975), see McDonnell (1975).

with popular Catholic religiosity such as the pantheon of Gods at a Catholic shrine in Sri Lanka, where the Virgin Mary is the key figure in the battle against evil (Stirrat 1992: 88). Most of the Catholic Charismatics I interviewed said that when they prayed to God, it was normally to Jesus. For some of them, prayer to God meant praying to the Father. Several of them, besides praying to Jesus and the Father, also prayed to the Holy Spirit, Mary, and different saints. Therefore, Jesus Christ occupies the pole position in the hierarchy of gods of the Catholic Charismatics. As the pastor of the ROLC said, 'We don't care if a million gods are worshipped, Jesus Christ is the lord. That means Jesus Christ is the Lord of our city, the Lord of all the Earth.' The position of the others in the hierarchy of gods is interchangeable, varying from individual to individual, group to group, and depending on situations and circumstances.

At the same time, Catholicization of the Pentecostal–Charismatic movement has led to the devotion of Mary creep into the Charismatic prayer groups in Goa. The habitus generating and shaping the practice of Marian devotion is drawn from popular Catholic devotional practices. This corresponds with Bourdieu's idea of habitus as organizing structures that are always constituted in practice (1990: 52, 53). In the 1980s and 1990s, several Catholic Charismatic members left the Church and started or entered neo-Pentecostal sects. This led to a lot of criticism from both priests and lay Catholics that the Charismatics were more Protestant than Catholic and their meetings were modelled more on the Pentecostal style of worship. In order to negate this criticism and prove their Catholic identity to their critics, rosaries and Hail Marys were accommodated in their prayer meetings. This competing discourse concerning the importance of Marian devotion has found a more dominant place in Charismatic prayer groups since most of the members are women who are able to identify better with Mary, as she is the only female figure in the divine hierarchy. Thus, praying to Mary through the recitation of the rosary or singing hymns in honour of her is juxtaposed with the emphasis on praying to Jesus, which has been the authoritative discourse in the CCR. Devotion to Mary is qualified by the idea that she is only an intercessor and not God. Thus, the divine hierarchy of the CCR adds Mary to the pantheon of God the Father, Jesus, and the Holy Spirit that is accepted by the neo-Pentecostal Churches.

Orality of Tradition

An important characteristic of all the ritualistic observances of the neo-Pentecostals is the combination of oral and written traditions. They combine the charismatic, ever-changing, dynamic inspiration from the Holy Spirit with the unchanging, eternal authority of the word of God. The Bible itself is regarded both as canon and charisma. Charisma and canon appear to be opposites, representing the dynamic and the static operating in religious communities. In any religious system, a canon is the result of a deliberate attempt to collect, arrange, and preserve the original message of the religious community and to protect it against all corruption (Stietencron 2001: 14). Canon transforms haphazard individual recollection into authoritative tradition or sacred scripture. In a world subject to perpetual change, the formation of a canon is a device to arrest time, or rather to pick out and separate from the change-inducing flow of time a selected set of elements that are considered essential and eternally valid and provide lasting orientation to the community (Stietencron 2001).

The Bible, when considered as the written word of God, is the canon for all the neo-Pentecostal religious practices, observances, and prescribed conduct for the community. Their faith life and even their everyday life are governed by the dictates of the Bible, which is, for them, the unchanging and ever-clear word of God. The canon of the Bible is permanent and not a word can be added or deleted from the Bible, which is the cornerstone, the bedrock of their faith. At the same time, the Charismatic movement emphasizes on change and innovation. It tries to bring in newness or Renewal in the already existing doctrines and practices of established Christianity. It tries to push its charismatic insights and innovative impulses against the natural resistance of the established historic Churches. In both the CCR and the neo-Pentecostal groups, religious ceremonies and practices are characterized by the belief in the interventionist model of the spirit, which continually renews their faith life. While the canon depicts the static dimension of religion, the charismatic aspect involves uncertainty, a jump in the dark.

As Francis Archer (1998) says, 'This is the difficult time we are going through, not alone, but with the Spirit ... who blows where he wills.' Through the charismatic working of the spirit, the written biblical tradition is being applied in innovative ways to present-day realities to suit particular strata of society. The written biblical canon, in the process of being interpreted through the inspiration of the Holy Spirit, takes on an oral nature. This process of balancing between the charismatic dimension and the canon of their scriptures, between the ever-changing, dynamic, oral nature on one hand and the eternal, static, written aspect of the Bible on the other, is characteristic of neo-Pentecostalism.

The socio-economic background of the adherents plays an important part in determining whether the oral or written aspect of the Bible is emphasized. In the CCR where most of the members are rural women who are not well-versed in reading and who are busy with household work, the emphasis is on the orality of the word, that is, the divine speaking to them and guiding them in their daily lives. Likewise, in many of the neo-Pentecostal sects, which cater mainly to the migrant labour force involved in manual work, most of whom are unable to read or write, the oral aspect of the scriptures with emphasis on the spoken word through preaching, teachings, and practices dominates the religious discourse.

Importance of the Oral Aspect of the Word of God

Particular words uttered by anointed or appointed religious professionals are believed to be efficacious in religious rituals and to bring about the desired result in the worshipper (Geertz's long-lasting moods and motivations). Besides the credentials of the one uttering the words, the context and place where they are uttered, the faith of the listeners, and the discourses supporting the power of the spoken word are also important ingredients in ensuring the perceived efficacy of the spoken words. In Christianity, the word of God is a very powerful religious symbol with multiple meanings. For the Charismatics, the Holy Bible is commonly understood as the word of God. The transformation of the written word of the Bible, nearly 2,000 years old, into the spoken word, which is alive and resonates today, is clearly seen in most of the Charismatic meetings and programmes. At the All Goa Church Meet held at Nuvem on 6 April 2007, a big board with the quotation 'Go and make disciples of all nations' (Matthew 28:18, 19) from the Bible was placed prominently next to the stage, which could be seen from all directions. The Pentecostal pastor, through his preaching, transformed this mission mandate, given by Jesus to the biblical Christians nearly two millennia back, into a message being given by Jesus today to the Church of Goa. The preacher admonished the audience that Goa was not saved so far because they had been reluctant to open their mouths and proclaim Christ to the 1.5 million people in Goa. They believe that the gospel spoken aloud is powerful and will lead to many conversions. As a Born-Again Christian, the adherent is a possessor of faith and learns to draw upon new-found power through specific acts such as 'positive confession' that draw divine influence into the world (Coleman 2000: 28). In positive confession, words spoken 'in faith' are regarded as objectifications of reality, establishing palpable connections between human will and the external world. It is derived from the idea that humans, made in God's image, can have divine dominion over creation by deploying language (Coleman 2000).

In the same meeting, another pastor spoke of the power and authority given to the Church in the name of Jesus. The phrase 'in the name of Jesus' is another powerful symbol for the neo-Pentecostals and is used as a weapon to battle the principalities and powers of the Evil One that hold people in bondage. They believe that 'in the name of Jesus' they are able to break every curse, cure illnesses, and command the demons to leave their bodies. The pastor described the scene from the Bible where the Israelites surrounded the walls of Jericho and through their prayers were able to demolish the walls and take the city (Joshua: Chapter 6). That incident, which has been part of the written biblical tradition for nearly 3,000 years, was re-enacted through the spoken word of the pastor. He prepared the people to believe that they were gathered there to demolish the walls of Goa. He made the people, numbering nearly 1,500, stand up and face in all four directions of north, south, east, and west and pray and prophesy that Goa will open its ears to the word of God and that the walls of Goa will be demolished as that of Jericho, so they can walk in and take the land. The word of God, enshrined in the canon of the written Bible, was transformed into a present-day scene that was very much alive and real for the Believers (Geertz's pervasive and long-lasting moods and motivations that seem uniquely realistic).

The Sunday prayer meeting is the main venue, where the written codified scriptures are transformed into real, oral scenes, which bring alive and imprint a moral for the people in the present. During these prayer meetings, one finds the main preacher or leader of the praise and worship enacting biblical scenes to make the word alive to the audience. The preachers also use several quotations from the Bible to substantiate the belief that the word of God is a powerful and efficacious symbol. For example, the pastor of the neo-Pentecostal group in Siolim often quotes from the prophet Isaiah (55:11), 'So shall my word be that goes forth from my mouth; it shall not return to me empty, but it shall accomplish that which I purpose.' The pastor told the people in a loud voice that as he spoke those words to them it would accomplish in them the work that was meant for them. They believe that the word of God spoken aloud every day transforms the lives of individuals. This resonates with Coleman's (2000) idea that humans can have divine dominion over creation through positive confession.

Thus, for a neo-Pentecostal, belief and confession go hand in hand and a person's faith grows stronger when he/she confesses it. To support this position, Romans 10:10 is quoted, 'For man believes with his heart and so is justified, and he confesses with his lips and so is saved.' One of the pastors emphasized the efficacy of the spoken word with the saying 'What you are is what you see, what you see is what you say, what you say is what you get', which is nothing but Coleman's positive confession. Often people at the Sunday services are made to read scriptural quotations aloud along with the preacher, since they believe that only when these things are spoken, will one see them happen. A member of the NFI Church, while preaching during the Sunday service, made all the people repeat after him quotes from the Bible such as, 'I am the salt of the earth, I am the light of the world, I am chosen and appointed by Christ' and so on. He then advised the people to recite these verses every morning and to expect a change in their lives soon. Similarly, for various problems—financial, marital, health, and so on—they have different biblical quotations, which they have memorized and which they believe will provide relief or solve their problems, or at least alleviate their sufferings. Through positive confession 'believers are supposedly enabled to assert sovereignty over multiple spheres of existence, ranging from their own bodies to broad geographical regions' (Coleman 2000: 28).

Another powerful symbol of the transformation of the written canon of the Bible into present oral tradition and which also canonizes religious codes of conduct is the ritualistic practice of testimony. The practices of visions, prophecies, and miracles also aid in this process.

Gerlach and Hine (1970) state that testifying to the experience serves to objectify a subjective change in identity and fixes it as a reality both to the convert and the group. Testimonies are an important part of the neo-Pentecostal prayer meetings. During these meetings, members of the congregation testify to personal conversion and the manner in which God brought happiness and success in their lives. Testimonies are also used in sermons and talks to emphasize some point being made. In most of the testimonies, mention is made of the role of spiritual practices, such as praying, fasting, or reading the Bible in finding solutions to their life problems. The normal pattern of a testimony is: the Believers describe the problem affecting their life, either physical, financial, spiritual, or family-related, either grave or simple. They then share how they took recourse to some spiritual means, how a miracle took place, and how they got relief from their problem due to divine intervention. Often the solution to the problem is directly from God without any human intercession. So their testimony is to publicly record their gratitude to God and also to the members of the congregation for their prayers.

Testimonies, visions, prophecies, and miracles are important since they enable the neo-Pentecostals to identify with the world of the biblical Christians. During a testimony at a Sunday service, the pastor of the WRM quoted from Acts 19:11–12 about how handkerchiefs and aprons touched by St Paul[13] were taken to the sick and their illnesses were cured. He then mentioned how his vest was put on a possessed boy in Siolim and the boy was healed. This was to emphasize the point that miracles happened not only in Paul's time but also occur today and, thus, link his Church with the NTC.

Testimonies, visions, signs, and wonders are regarded as an indicator or barometer of the faith of a person. They are a pointer to the working of God in the life of the individual Believer. For a new Believer, testifying to a God experience, prophesizing some future event revealed by God, or sharing about some miracle that took place in his/her life is a reiteration of the new identity and solidifies the position of the new convert in the group.

[13] St Paul is regarded as the apostle of Jesus Christ and the greatest missionary of the early Church, who travelled to various parts of Asia preaching about Christ.

The Canon of the Bible: Written Tradition

The Bible is the canon of the essential charismatic insights of different 'inspired' human authors from particular historical epochs. Nearly 2,000 years later, the spoken language has changed a lot, and social and economic structures and cultural mores and customs have undergone drastic changes. Additionally, different paradigms of thought have directed human intellectual attention to entirely different topics and so people today have difficulty in understanding and applying the original message of the Bible to resent times. Such unavoidable historicity is a major defect found in every canon and a dilemma that every religious scripture whether remembered or written down must face. It is in this dilemma that charisma plays a role. The original message has to be translated, transformed, and made meaningful for a changed society and in an altered situation. Thus, written text always involved the problem of interpretation and hermeneutics. The neo-Pentecostals believe that the Bible should be read literally, and a personal, experiential knowledge of the Bible is more important than an objective, scientific study of it. Every Believer is urged to read and study the Bible and ask the Holy Spirit for guidance to interpret it properly. Their interpretation of the Bible is guided by their conceptualization of the Bible as divine literature, as opposed to all other man-made literature, and as the most scientific and factual book. They leave the matter of interpretation to the individual and believe that the Holy Spirit, the best teacher of the Bible, synthesizes the different interpretations and presents a univocal message to all who read the Bible. Therefore, different neo-Pentecostal sects based on the sociocultural and theological background of their founder(s) and other socio-historical influences interpret the Bible differently and regard their commentary as canonical for their followers.

The ROLC regards the word of God as being the final authority, which cannot be questioned by any Believer. It is the eternal unchanging word of God that gives answers to all the problems in the world and guides the readers in all their day-to-day situations. In the WRM, all the members undertake a Bible pledge at every Sunday service. All of them hold their Bibles in their right hand while taking the pledge, which goes like this:

> This is my Bible, I believe what it says
> I believe it is God's eternal word,

I believe I will receive from the word today
And I will never be the same again.
In Jesus' name we pray. Amen.[14]

The pledge reflects a combination of the unchanging, eternal word, which is the written biblical canon and the charismatic aspect of the oral word that transforms people in the present. The neo-Pentecostals believe that the Bible is universal, eternal, and unchanging, and therefore not culturally bound. This idea of the transcendental and transcultural nature of the Bible is found in both the ROLC and the WRM.

The Bible also occupies a very important place in the lives of individual Charismatics. For most of them, the Bible has changed and transformed their lives. A woman from the ROLC who married late had hormonal problems during her delivery and this made her feel moody, upset, and suicidal. To counter these tendencies, she began reading the Bible and this helped her resist suicidal tendencies. Another woman from the ROLC who was pregnant went to all the good doctors in Goa and all of them warned her that the chances of the child being born normal were slim. On New Year's day when she, her husband, and others were praying, God gave them a word from the Bible that said, 'By faith Sarah herself received power to conceive even when she was past the age, since she considered him faithful who had promised' (Heb 11:11). She felt God confirming through the Bible what she had believed in her mind. Over the course of time, she delivered a normal baby girl. There are many such examples of how the neo-Pentecostals regard the Bible as a solution book, a guide for life, providing answers for every issue in the world.

Often the commentary itself becomes a canonical scripture in its own right. Thus, the process of canonizing involves interplay between charisma and canon and leads to a diversity of theologies and practices emerging within Pentecostalism, each claiming charismatic legitimization by linking their interpretation of the Bible to the one universal NTC. Most of the neo-Pentecostal Churches have regular Bible classes for their members, conducted mostly by their pastor or some other member of the congregation. According to Ignatius Fernandes (2007), the majority of the pastors in Goa do not have theological training.

---

[14] Sunday service of WRM Church, Siolim, on 1 April 2007.

Of the 20 pastors he interviewed, only four had a bachelor's degree in theology. Biblical experts or well-known evangelists from different parts of India or from outside India are invited to the different Churches to explain the word of God. The people also receive a lot of biblical knowledge through the preaching and teachings in Sunday services and the prayer cell meetings.

The Pentecostals run a few Bible Colleges in Goa. In 1999, Pastor Biju Thampy, the son of the founder of the New India Church of God in Kerala, started a Bible training centre at the Bethesda Bible College situated in Ponda, offering a three-year Bachelor of Theology programme. This college sends out around 30 young ministers every year to different parts of India to evangelize through the gospel of Jesus Christ. Another Bible training school offers two programmes, Diploma in Theology and Bachelor in Theology. Its aim is to equip youngsters for ministry in Goa and North India. There is no accredited Christian Bible college in Goa. The regular Bible classes for the neo-Pentecostals and the Bible colleges run by them show the importance they give to the Bible, both the written canon and the oral word.

* * *

In this chapter, the exploration into the Pentecostal–Charismatic world, which began in the previous chapter, has led us much deeper into the intersection of the fascinating world of symbols of Charismatic Christianity and the mundane day-to-day lives of the Charismatics. We have tried to make sense of the various religious symbols and their supporting discourses, which have shaped and legitimized the world view and ethos of the Charismatics. In this endeavour, we have drawn from the work of Geertz on religion as a cultural system of symbols that shapes and constitutes reality, seen in the light of Asad's criticisms concerning the role of power. We have also tried to make sense of Bourdieu's idea of habitus in understanding the world of symbols of the neo-Pentecostals and analysed the underlying Charismatic habitus that guides individual Believers to understand and respond to the social reality around them.

We have explored various conceptions of the sacred and profane, drawing from the works of Durkheim, Eliade, and others. The discourse on the recreation of the NTC and its dualistic spiritual world view leads the neo-Pentecostals to term certain symbols, spaces, and times as sacred and others as profane. Drawing from the biblical models of service and the practice of public acknowledgement of service to God, service to the Church is elevated to the level of sacred activity. The mapping of the universe into Christian-reached (sacred) and unreached (demonic) territories and the mapping of history with importance given to the New Testament period and the present End Times characterize neo-Pentecostalism. Unlike the Catholic Charismatics, who differentiate between the sacred space of the Church and the secular space outside, the concept of sacred space for neo-Pentecostals is broader.

The time spent in Sunday worship and the word of God, regarded as both canon and charisma, are very sacred in the world of symbols of neo-Pentecostalism, while yoga, Indian forms of meditation, 'worldly' music, ecumenical and inter-religious dialogue, and certain lifestyle habits are considered, taboo. Sociologically, these practices, including sin belong to the 'bad sacred' since the neo-Pentecostals connect them to demonic spirits. The Charismatic God is both loving and vengeful: the image of a God of wrath is juxtaposed with a loving, jealous God, while their pantheon of the demonic includes, besides Satan and his fallen angels, the Gods of the non-Christian pantheons. Jesus Christ occupies the pole position in the hierarchy of Gods in Charismatic Christianity, though devotion to Mary has crept into the CCR prayer groups as an answer to the criticism that they were more Protestant than Catholic in their practices.

5 Charismatic Life-Cycle Rituals and a Life Plan

Coleman (2000: 136) draws on the work of Csordas to emphasize the permeability of the boundaries between ritual events and the rest of existence. In tracing the creation of a Catholic Charismatic habitus, he thus refers to what he calls ritualization of life rather than to specific set-apart ritual events. In the previous chapter, I have attempted to show how religious activities and practices have contributed to the 'creation of a form of charismatic habitus, a form of embodied disposition' (Coleman 2000: 6). The process of understanding the constitution of this habitus has revealed that the Charismatic ideology, which creates disposition of faith, is articulated and manifested in the specific contexts of everyday life as well as in worship and religious discourses. This articulation of the Charismatic habitus that leads to Charismatic ideology, influencing the follower's social practices, space, and time, needs to be ethnographically explored in the practices of everyday life, especially the life-cycle rituals: 'events in which contact is established between man and the sacred' (Das 1976: 251). In this chapter, I argue that the rituals that mark the passage of time for the individual neo-Pentecostals do not literally follow the biological cycle. The neo-Pentecostal rituals also differ from the Hindu and Catholic life-cycle rituals due to the dispositions, motivations, and classifying and organizing principles generated by the Charismatic habitus. I analyse the life-cycle rituals of the neo-Pentecostals as 'cultural texts' (Geertz 1973) or 'ritual drama' (Newman 2001: 218–28), which may be read and interpreted to get a better understanding of the culture.

Das (1976: 248), while drawing from Durkheim's and Van Gennep's theories, argues that 'religion has to provide not only an all-encompassing sacred order that can transform the empirical tenuousness of institutions by placing them within a cosmic order, but it also has to devise ways and means by which the marginalities experienced by an individual can be dealt with, without any loss of meaning'. The life-cycle rituals that mark the transitions in the individual life-history of a Believer are placed in a broad sacred cosmic order by religion, thus providing stability and meaning to a social order threatened by different marginalities and profane individual interests.

Baptism

Notions in the Charismatic Habitus on Baptism

The Charismatic habitus, by generating ritual practices, brings the individual self in line with idealized and universally shared incarnations of faith, allowing followers to achieve a status of perfect health, happiness, and prosperity (Coleman 2000: 134). Through the rite of baptism, a neo-Pentecostal believes that God brings about a change in the individual self and all of one's ungodly ambitions, sinful past, and selfishness are buried in the waters of baptism. The Charismatic habitus makes the individual neo-Pentecostal regard the baptism rite as a funeral service, wherein one buries the old self and the new self is born again in God. Another notion connected to baptism is that it brings about the empowerment of the self by activating the Holy Spirit in their lives. Drawing from Turner, Newman (2001: 218–28) defines liminality as the threshold point in a process in which a participant in ritual drama is separated from normal time and normal social structure and undergoes a new experience through which he may perceive new truths, get a new status, assume a new role, and come to a greater understanding. The pastor of the ROLC gave the example of the baptism of a woman from his Church. They had to carry her into the water since she was hardly able to walk. When she came out after being baptized, she was able to walk up to the first floor of her house. She was amazed since she had never walked like that without someone's support and attributed the healing of her legs to God. Newman, while describing ritual dramas that are once-in-a-lifetime events, laden with symbolism and emotional meaning, says, 'Rite of passage has greatest meaning for the individual directly concerned, though everyone present may be influenced at some level (Newman 2001: 221).'

The symbolism of the rite of baptism is that it is a bridge-burning act wherein the new convert publicly declares his allegiance to the new faith and severs all ties with his old faith. Baptism is a public declaration to the world and to the Devil that one is a follower of Christ. Visvanathan (1999: 263) found that the Syrian Christian life-cycle rituals of birth, marriage, and death express the intrinsic correspondence between the life of Jesus and the life of every Christian. For most of the neo-Pentecostals who were Catholics before, the baptism rite effectively implies severing all family and kinship ties. On the other hand, baptism bonds the new convert to the community of Believers, who are referred to as the family of God. In the baptism I witnessed, after the ritual of immersion in water the newly baptized were warmly congratulated by all the other members with handshakes or hugs. Such notions expand the idea of community from being one that has abasis in biological ties, kinship, or lineage to one in which members have their spiritual unity in Christ and his gospel. The members of the community regard the neophytes as brothers and sisters, thus compensating for the new members' loss of kinship ties. A member of the ROLC mentioned that when he first joined the Church he was amazed by their love: 'When I would go to Church, Anna (an old woman) would come and give me a big hug. I had never seen that happen anywhere, people being so friendly.'[1] Robinson (1998), drawing on the work of Jack Goody, while analysing Goan Catholic life-cycle rituals, found that through such rites, which are celebrated publicly, the individual Catholic is made to feel at one with the community of Believers, who are referred to as his or her brothers and sisters in Christ. She adds that in attempting to make its members think of the Church—rather than of their lineage or kin—as the primary (spiritual) community to which they belong, the Church draws a distinction between kinship and blood relations on one side and membership of the Catholic community or 'family' ties (spiritual kinship) on the other.

Another important notion of the Charismatic habitus is that there are parallels between baptism is the circumcision of the Old Testament.

---

[1] Interview of ROLC member at his house on 25 September 2008.

In the Old Testament, the Jews were circumcised to physically identify that they were God's people, but today through water baptism
given by Jesus, the Charismatics are marked as God's people through
symbols. Thus, the rite of water baptism, like circumcision, is a ritual
marker of their membership in the new spiritual community of their
Church. It is a spiritual mark of identity inscribed on their body to
distinguish them from the others (whom they call pagans or gentiles).
Hollenweger (1972: 485) finds that the baptism of the spirit, with the
objectively ascertainable sign of speaking in tongues, serves as a 'tribal
mark' to distinguish between those who belong to one's own 'tribe',
the Church, and those who belong to the 'hostile tribes', the world. The
Catholic Charismatics would term baptism as the indelible seal of the
Holy Spirit. In the NFI Churches, water baptism is essential to become
a committed member of the Church. Only committed members are
eligible to take up any posts and responsibilities in the Church. Thus,
baptism is a vehicle to assume offices in the Church and enter the elite
group of elders who assist the pastor in running the Church. Catholic
life-cycle rituals differ from Hindu life-cycle rituals since they link the
Catholic with the beliefs and doctrines of the Church (Robinson 1998).
Neo-Pentecostal baptism, too, is linked to their teachings to give it
divine legitimization. Since the neo-Pentecostals believe that baptism
is not essential for salvation, the question arises: why get baptized? The
teaching of the ROLC runs like this: Jesus got water baptized (Matthew
3:13–17); Jesus lived his life on Earth as an example for all, therefore
they need to imitate all that he did and so get baptized. Baptism is,
thus, a command from God.

Adult Baptism

As seen earlier, among the neo-Pentecostals baptism is a bridge-
burning act, where the stress is on the deliberate choice of the individual to become a Christian. Therefore, they accept only adult water
baptism. The doctrine of adult baptism is based on a timescale that
does not follow the biological life cycle. The biological birth of a person is not as important an event as the spiritual birth (born again in
the spirit). For the neo-Pentecostals, life begins after one becomes a
Born-Again Christian, which is only through the baptism of the spirit.
While the Charismatics in historic Churches equate water baptism

with spirit baptism and independent Pentecostals generally separate the two, in both cases since they only accept adult baptism, life as a Born-Again Christian does not begin at birth. Infant baptism followed by the Catholic Charismatics recognizes the importance of biological birth, linking it with membership of the newborn in the Church community, and so gives membership to all children born of Catholic parents. On the other hand, the neo-Pentecostal water baptism does not recognize biological birth as a liminal event and membership is given only to a select few of the descendants of the neo-Pentecostals, who have repented and chosen to be baptized. In support of this position, they quote from the Bible that a person has to repent first and then be baptized. Since a newborn baby does not know what repentance is, it cannot be baptized. Repentance comes first, followed by baptism.

The ROLC does not have any minimum fixed age to be baptized. One of the members whom I interviewed received water baptism when he was 15 years old, while there are other members who have been baptized in their 50s and 60s. They accept the baptism of any other Church provided it is an adult baptism of immersion in the water. They reject the infant baptism of the Catholic Church, which, according to them, is a mere ritual. The majority of the neo-Pentecostals in India (77 per cent of the sample) were opposed to infant baptism (Parathazham 1996: 11). An important point of differentiation between Catholic and Hindu life-cycle rituals in Goa is that Catholic rites are raised from their primary location in the domestic domain and celebrated in the Church (Robinson 1998). The physical location of the rite of baptism differs between Catholics and Born-Again Christians. While the Catholics have the baptism rite in the Church, most of the neo-Pentecostals have it next to a stream or river or the sea. While the ROLC has it in the sea waters on Miramar beach, the WRM has a baptismal font in their Church. The presence of the baptismal font in the WRM Church reflects the Catholic influence on the pastor, who was a Catholic for many years before joining neo-Pentecostalism. In both cases, the ritual of baptism is shifted from the domestic domain to the spiritual, sacred domain. While the neo-Pentecostals emphasize on the full freedom of the individual to decide on Church membership, socializing into the faith begins at a very early age in the form of Sunday catechism classes. All school-going children have to attend the Sunday school where they are taught the basic doctrine of their Church by some designated members of the congregation, generally women in the case of the ROLC.

The Rite of Water Baptism

Each neo-Pentecostal Church has its own way of performing water baptism. As part of the preparation to receive water baptism, each catechumen has to attend a short foundation course. Even after attending the entire course, a person can decline to receive baptism. The catechesis consists of teachings on sin and other topics regarding the importance of receiving baptism. The teachings on baptism link the rite of baptism with the doctrines of the Church and contribute to building the Charismatic habitus. The following description of the baptism of some Believers of the NFI Church will explain the procedure of the rite. Five members of the NFI Church received baptism on the beach of Miramar, a popular tourist destination and the beach closest to the capital city of Panaji. This rite took place on 2 November 2008. Among the catechumens was a young Goan couple who were Catholics earlier, a Korean woman in her 30s, a young woman who was around 20 years old, and finally a Hindu woman in her late 20s. After the second service got over at the Church hall in Panaji, a crowd of nearly 30 people assembled at Miramar beach, which was only 2 km away. The pastor first prayed over the five catechumens and read a few portions of text from the Bible concerning baptism. He asked each one of them if they were getting baptized of their own accord or if they were being forced by someone.

The actual rite of baptism took place in sea water. Only the pastor and a member of the Church, who was assisting him, went into the sea along with the five catechumens. The water was above the knee level and the pastor, who was in his shorts was dressed appropriately for the occasion. All the others remained on the shore watching the rite and clicking photographs. The sand was burning hot, as it was around 1 pm. The pastor and his assistant held the catechumen, while the pastor laid his right hand on the person and said some prayers. They then dipped the person, head first, completely in the water either forwards or backwards. The catechumens who were in their Sunday best clothes were completely soaked. They immersed the catechumen only once unlike some other Born-Again Churches, who practice triple immersion. After finishing with all five, they came out on the sand where the rest of the people were standing. The congregation congratulated the newly baptized and the mood was one of joy and happiness. After that, the pastor asked the people to pray for them. He laid his hands on one of the baptized and the people also extended their hands and prayed for them. They also prophesied for the five new converts. The whole ceremony, which lasted for an hour, ended with a song 'I have decided to follow Jesus'.

Doctrine of the Charismatic Movement on Baptism in the Holy Spirit

When Catholic Pentecostalism, which soon after came to be known as the CCR, arrived on the Pentecostal scene in the USA, it led to a flurry of theological activity, as many churchmen were forced to make new assessments of their own understanding of the Pentecostal movement. During the 1970s itself, it became clear that since the Classical Pentecostals were either unwilling or unable to contribute to developing mainline Charismatic theology, scholars from the mainline Churches developed their own theology of the 'baptism in the Holy Spirit', which allowed Pentecostalism to flourish in the historic Churches without the 'cultural baggage' and rigid exclusivism espoused by many of the Pentecostal Churches (Synan 1997: 253). The new position, espoused by the Charismatics in mainline Churches, but accepted to varying degrees and with various modifications by the independent neo-Pentecostals, viewed the Pentecostal experience—'the decisive coming of the Spirit', according to McDonnell (1980: 27)—as an essential part of the 'rites of initiation', that is, baptism, confirmation, and the Eucharist. By receiving the Spirit in initiation, one becomes a member of Christ's body, is introduced into the people of God, and becomes a part of a worshipping community (McDonnell 1980).

Three broad schools of theological interpretation of the baptism in the Holy Spirit have emerged in the CCR in recent years (Alva 2014: 57). The first school links baptism in the Holy Spirit with the sacraments of initiation. They interpret the later experience of tongues and other gifts of the Spirit as a release or actualization of the latent energy and grace received during the sacraments of initiation. While it fits perfectly well within the Catholic doctrine, it portrays spirit baptism as an abnormal catch-up rendered necessary by deficiencies in the celebration of sacramental baptism. The second school understands spirit baptism as a new/fresh outpouring of the spirit, which fills the person with new graces and charismas for the common good of the Church. They find no link between the experience of spirit baptism in CCR and the sacraments of initiation. This school does not explain why there is a fresh outpouring of the Holy Spirit in the twentieth century. Moreover, a fresh outpouring of the Holy Spirit implies the inefficacy of the sacraments of initiation. The third school, like the previous one, finds no link between the experience of spirit baptism in the CCR and the sacraments of initiation. Peter Hocken, the main proponent of this interpretation, tries to reconcile the biblical usage of spirit baptism and the distinctiveness of the spirit baptism as experienced by Pentecostal–Charismatics today. He interprets it as preparation for eschatological judgement. While this theological interpretation does not explain the phenomenon of spirit baptism, it attempts to explain the timing of it, as a sign of the second coming of the Lord. In contrast to the above three theological interpretations of spirit baptism, the Classical Pentecostals view a separate *baptism in the Holy Spirit* subsequent to conversion and water baptism, with the necessary *initial evidence* and *biblical proof* of speaking in tongues. The Charismatics rejected the Classical Pentecostal position on the necessity of glossolalia. In adherence to the principle of 'one Lord, one faith, one baptism', they believed that a person could be baptized in the spirit as an infant at water baptism, while the gifts of the spirit could appear in one's later Christian experiences. They accepted that most Charismatics speak in tongues, not as initial evidence but as one of the authenticating gifts of the spirit.

On the other hand, the neo-Pentecostal groups in Goa differ in their interpretation of the rite of baptism. Unlike the Catholic Charismatics, the members of the ROLC do not accept that the Pentecostal experience is an essential part of the 'rites of initiation', since they do not accept the sacrament of confirmation and have a different understanding of the Eucharist. They distinguish between water baptism and spirit baptism, though they have no particular order for the two baptisms. Either water baptism and then spirit baptism may be performed on a new convert or vice versa. They teach that it is necessary to have both the baptisms, since both are equally important. One of the female Believers I interviewed compared receiving one baptism and not wanting to have the other to a woman loving a man and being happy to live with him but not wanting to marry him. Unlike water baptism, which is a public act and has a particular ritual, spirit baptism has no particular rite or place and can occur anywhere and anytime. Thus, the formation of a Charismatic habitus leads to the ritualization of life.

The most distinct external symbol, which has characterized Pentecostal movements all over the world and which has given it a distinct identity, is the practice of 'glossolalia'. The distinct contribution of the Pentecostal movement has been to single out 'glossolalia' as the only evidence of having received baptism in the spirit, making it part of 'normal' Christian worship rather than a curious by-product of religious enthusiasm. Like the Catholic Charismatics, the NFI does not accept the Classical Pentecostal position on the necessity of glossolalia as proof of being born again. The NFI pastor's wife while speaking of baptism in the spirit said:

> Spirit baptism is not practised in many Churches. For example, Rick Warren who is such a great preacher and writer does not believe in speaking in tongues. My Church believes in speaking in tongues as direct communication with God and wishes everyone to speak in tongues, but there are a few people who have still not yet spoken in tongues.[2]

They link 'baptism in the Spirit' with the biblical discourse of the occurrence of the 'Pentecost' event, during which the Holy Spirit came down upon the disciples in the form of tongues of fire (Acts 2:1–4), by citing other texts such as Acts 2:38–39 to point out that once a person is baptized, he or she will receive the gifts of the Holy spirit. Some members do not link glossolalia with baptism in the spirit, but cite other gifts of the spirit such as preaching, teaching, and healing as actualization of the grace received when one is baptized in the spirit. At the same time, they have high regard for glossolalia and expect everyone baptized in the spirit to speak in tongues. Glossolalia is also a very common practice not just in their prayer meetings, but also in their

---

[2] Interview with the pastor's wife, who is also a member of the ROLC, on 20 September 2008.

everyday life. A woman who has faced a lot of trouble from her husband for becoming a neo-Pentecostal found that whenever she could not pray openly in the house, she would pray in tongues and that gave her a lot of strength. Another woman sat in her bedroom and asked God for the baptism of the Holy Spirit and then for more than an hour she was speaking in tongues.

Marriages Are Made in Heaven

Latter-day anthropologists writing on religion have come to view religious systems as constituting virtually autonomous cultural domains, to be understood in their own terms (Caplan 1987a: 4). It is with this understanding of religion as an aspect of culture that shapes and conditions social processes and everyday rituals and practices, that the social institution of marriage will be analysed. Marriage as a 'ritual drama' or a 'cultural text' needs to be understood as an outcome of the interpenetration of the Charismatic habitus and the local sociocultural codes.

Marriage is viewed by the Catholic Church primarily as a relationship between consenting adults—'the consent of the parties makes a marriage' (Pope Paul VI quoted in Lobo 1983: 15)—rather than one between families or kinship groups. Therefore, according to canon law, a girl can marry only after puberty, that is, after 14 years, while a boy is permitted to marry after 16 years. The common age for marriage is kept very low due to the wide diversity of social customs and sociocultural situations. The neo-Pentecostals also regard marriage as a union between two consenting adults. They do not have any fixed age of marriage though they generally accept the minimum age of 21 for boys and 18 for girls prescribed by the Indian government in the Child Marriage Restraint Act, 1929. By focussing on the husband–wife relationship, the Catholics and neo-Pentecostals have, intentionally or otherwise, promoted the formation of nuclear families. The aim of viewing marriage as primarily between two adult individual Christians is also to loosen the hold of family and kinship ties, while situating the social institution of marriage within the Church. Thus, the biological rite of passage of marriage is elevated from the context of everyday life and placed in the sacred cosmic order, replacing the uncertainties, fears, and burden of expectations

connected with the rite of passage with divine reassurance and meaning. Besides the goal of uniting man and woman, Catholic marriage
promotes the preservation and progress of society and its culture
by enjoining upon the couple the procreation of children and their
proper upbringing.

Both the unitive and the procreative aims of marriage are accepted
by the neo-Pentecostals, who argue that these are drawn from the scriptures. Unlike the Catholic discourse on marriage, which has well-crafted,
theological aims and principles and has an elaborate set of rules in the
canon law, most of the neo-Pentecostal groups do not possess codified rules and regulations concerning marriage. Since many of the neo-
Pentecostals were Catholics before, they borrow a lot of Catholic ideas
concerning marriage, but after painting them with the brush of the
scriptures. In order to maintain their distinct identity from the Catholics,
the pastors and leaders of the neo-Pentecostal groups deny that these
ideas are borrowed from the Catholic doctrine, but claim that they are
taken from the Bible. The persistence of the religio-cultural influence of
Hinduism on contemporary Catholic life-cycle rituals in Goa indicates
that the missionaries probably allowed such rituals to be maintained
once they were, so to speak, Christianized (Robinson 1998).

The Charismatic habitus by emphasizing sayings such as 'marriages
are made in heaven' lead the neo-Pentecostals to believe that marriage is ordained by God and is not the creation of humans. It elevates
the social institution of marriage to the realm of the spiritual. For a
genuine Christian marriage, both the boy and the girl should ask God
to guide them to find the right spouse. Neo-Pentecostals stress that
marriage consists of three people—husband, wife, and the spirit of
God—who link and bind the marriage. Praying to God for a partner,
who is God-fearing and chosen by God, is the first step in an ideal
Christian marriage. Once the boy finds a girl, he should inform his
pastor whose duty is to guide him to choose a proper spouse. The girl
normally consults the wife of the pastor to guide her to choose the boy.
By leaving the responsibility of choosing a partner for marriage not on
the parents or blood relatives but on the prayer of the boy and girl to
God and the intervention of the pastor, his wife, or Church elders, the
neo-Pentecostal Church delinks the social institution of marriage from
its biological, kinship, or lineage ties and elevates it to the religious
domain. For the neo-Pentecostals, the community of Believers is their

real family with Christ as the head, and they maintain closer ties with members of their Church than with their own kin.

Marriage Ceremony among Neo-Pentecostals[3]

In the NFI Churches, a boy and girl who want to get married have to go through a marriage course, where the teachings of the Church are taught to them. Normally, the marriage course is for a period of three to four Sundays. Just like the Catholics, the neo-Pentecostals make the marriage course a mandatory prerequisite for marriage. As mentioned earlier, many of the customs followed by the neo-Pentecostals in their marriage are similar to those of the Catholics. Once they have decided to get married, banns are read in the Church to see if there are any objections to the marriage. Normally, three banns are read before the marriage. The boy and girl first perform a civil marriage and then get married by the pastor, according to the biblical tradition. The rites of Catholic marriage take place in the Church, generally during mass. There is a strict separation between the place of the marriage rite, which is a sacrament and is held in the sacred confines of the Church, and the place of the reception, which is a social function and is normally held in a wedding hall. On the other hand, the neo-Pentecostals have both the marriage rite and the reception at the same venue, usually a wedding hall.

A major difference between the Catholics and the neo-Pentecostals is regarding their sacramental theology. The Catholics have a well-developed sacramental theology that deals with the general nature and special characteristics of the seven sacraments. It establishes the common origin of all the seven sacraments in Jesus, while at the same time showing that they are specifically different realizations of Christian life in the recipient and of the Church's nature (Rahner and Vorgrimler 1983: 455). The Catholic Church has well-formulated liturgical rites for celebration of each sacrament. On the other hand, the neo-Pentecostals are non-sacramental and non-liturgical groups. When I interviewed the members of the ROLC, they told me that they accepted only two

---

[3] All the details about their marriage ceremony were gathered from my interviews with the individual members since they do not have any fixed written liturgical formula for the marriage rite.

sacraments—breaking of bread and water baptism. But they lack a developed sacramental theology or well-defined rites for celebrating the sacraments. They do not regard marriage as a sacrament and do not have any fixed formula for the marriage rite.

The officiating pastor for the marriage is normally from the boy's side. If any other pastor is brought to officiate the marriage, the permission of the local pastor is required. In the marriage ceremony, which does not have well-defined liturgical rites of celebration, and depends on the officiating pastor, the parents, through a public oath addressed to God, release their son/daughter. After the oath is taken by the parents, the couple exchanges rings and read out a public declaration of vows just like in the Catholic rite. The pastor then breaks the word of God by reading and preaching on a scriptural passage. It is followed by the breaking of bread. Two people from the boy's side and two from the girl's side (four in all) act as official witnesses as the boy and girl pronounce their marital vows and exchange rings. At the end, all the four witnesses besides the boy and girl have to sign the marriage covenant and the marriage records are kept with the officiating pastor.

Neo-Pentecostal Marriages Are Endogamous

Neo-Pentecostal marriages are strictly endogamous with regard to their own faith tradition. A Born-Again Christian cannot get married to someone who is not a Born-Again. Their understanding is that two adults get married only if their religious beliefs are common and match with each other. Marrying a person outside the Pentecostal fold is agreeable only if the non-Believer is ready to convert. So, endogamy is shifted from caste ties to religious ties. In fact, the neo-Pentecostals that I interviewed stressed on the absence of caste when it came to marriage. The pastor of the WRM, which has many Hindu converts belonging to the scheduled castes and other lower castes, said that in his Church a lower caste can get married to a higher caste. Parathazham's national survey of neo-Pentecostalism in India reveals that three-fourths of the sample did not approve of the members of their Church marrying anyone other than a Born-Again Christian (1996: 10). The justification for religious endogamy is drawn from biblical texts such as 1 Kings 11:1–9, which warns the Jews against taking foreign wives since they bring their own gods with them, or 2 Cor 6:14, where Paul warns the Corinthians not to be mismatched with non-Believers. The basis of religious endogamy is the understanding that the Born-Again Christians are religiously superior and ritually pure compared to the 'pagans'.

A Christian woman who married a Hindu man she loved, and later separated from him, felt that by marrying him she had betrayed her God, since she went down on her knees and worshipped her husband's gods. In her life, though she was a Christian, she was blinded by the Evil One and had opened herself to demonic spirits. When she joined the NFI Church, of which she is now a member, she had to undergo the Encounter with God programme, an induction technique of the NFI for new converts. She compared her encounter to a cleansing process wherein a lot of dirt came out of her, and at the end she was like a pure diamond, shining. Another woman from the NFI Church, who was a Hindu before, narrated how she had to go through a period of restoration before becoming a Born-Again Christian. When she was a Hindu, she had offered worship to idols, worn the bindi, which is regarded as the third eye of Shiva, and indulged in palmistry, horoscopes, and other practices. Therefore, during that period of restoration, she remembered all those past incidents and God helped her to be free from them. Thus, behind the insistence on marrying within their faith is the understanding that worship to pagan Gods pollutes and exposes a person to demonic spirits. Thus, notions of spiritual purity and pollution shape their practice of religious endogamy with respect to marriage.

This religious endogamy implies that the choice of partners for marriage is restricted to only the 7,000-odd neo-Pentecostals in Goa. Even the mainline Protestant Christians and Catholics are not considered suitable partners. Many of the neo-Pentecostal women whom I interviewed got married only in their 30s. Two of them had married men younger to them. There are also quite a few single mothers who have separated from their husbands. Coleman (2000: 137), in his fieldwork on Charismatic Protestantism in Sweden, describes the problems and conflicts that occur in the domestic realm when members of a family differ in their attitude towards Charismatic beliefs and practices. Strict adherence to biblical principles and evangelically sanctioned behaviours at home can lead to a collision of two worlds of perception and self-presentation (Coleman 2000). A strong emphasis on religious endogamy as the norm with little tolerance for inter-religious marriages distinguishes neo-Pentecostal marriages from contemporary Catholic marriages. The Catholic Church, too, used to prescribe that its followers marry within their own faith, which was in order to ensure the perpetuation of the Church through the social reproduction of its members. However, after Vatican II, which highlighted the positive values in other religions, the strong condemnation of mixed marriages has toned down and the Church accepts mixed marriages with dispensation and has a special section in canon law, under the title 'Disparity of Cult', devoted to inter-religious marriages (Canon 199–200). Inter-religious marriages are much more accepted among Catholics than among the Born-Again Christians.

Notions of Marriage among Catholic Charismatics[4]

As seen earlier, there are both similarities and differences between notions of marriage in the Catholic Church and in neo-Pentecostalism. Many of the founding fathers and leaders of the independent neo-Pentecostal groups, being Catholics before, were influenced by and borrowed from the Catholic doctrine on marriage by following a process of Christianization (painting the Catholic discourse with the brush of the scriptures). At the same time, notions of marriage among the Catholic Charismatics have been influenced by the Charismatic habitus and so tend to differ from the typical Catholic position on marriage. Almost all the Catholic Charismatics that I interviewed wanted a partner who matches them on the spiritual level. The criterion for choosing a marriage partner was not the social or economic status but the religious background of the person and his/her position towards the CCR. An unmarried Charismatic woman wanted a husband who is in the spirit, while a Charismatic man wanted a girl who is interested in prayer and in the Charismatic Renewal. For another woman, who felt that a lot of leaders' marriages were breaking up due to personality problems, an ideal partner would be one who is close to God, who understands her, and accompanies her to the prayer meetings. Another man was cautious that his would-be wife should not be someone who puts hurdles in his path of evangelization. Since none of the Catholic Charismatics

---

[4] The data on marriage in this section was collected from interviews with members of the Merces and Mapusa prayer groups.

mentioned that they wanted to marry only a Catholic, the notion of religious endogamy is not as vital to them as it is to the neo-Pentecostals. However, many of the Catholic Charismatics prefer a partner who will not oppose their Charismatic activities. Otherwise, the marriage may lead to what Coleman (2000: 137) describes as 'the collision of two worlds of perception and self-presentation'.

Many of the Catholic Charismatics found that the CCR has empowered spouses to handle marriage better and has led to a reduction of divorces. The Catholic Church strictly follows monogamous marriages and stresses on the absolute indissolubility of sacramental, consummated marriage (Canon 1056, 1141). The Catholic Charismatics opine that marriages break due to the absence of the word of God, the rosary, or the prayer; the lack of God's love; or failure on the part of the spouses in having an encounter of Christ. None of them mentioned socio-psychological or economic reasons for the breaking of marriages. The impact of the Charismatic habitus on the marriages of Catholic Charismatics and the manner in which they differ from other Catholic marriages is illustrated in the following rather unique case.

A Catholic Charismatic man, at the age of 43, got married to a female doctor, who was a few months younger to him and a member of the same prayer group. He did not want to get married, but rather join a monastic order and remain in the presence of God in silence. One day, God in a vision told him to get married. Like Jacob, he wrestled with the Lord arguing: 'I will do anything else but marry.' He finally agreed to get married but put a few conditions to God: his wife, like him, should keep God as her first love, she should allow him to go anywhere for the Lord's work, she should be able to play the keyboard, she should be a doctor ('when I go to preach the word of God in poor areas she will be able to look after their physical health'), and finally God should bring the woman into his life and prepare both their hearts to accept each other as husband and wife. He was, in a way, testing the Lord because he was sure that no doctor after knowing that he was a drug addict for nearly 25 years would marry him. After that vision of God, he did not think about marriage but got fully involved in the Renewal. Due to a lot of reading and studying the Bible, he began to get headaches and so went to see an ophthalmologist to check his eyes. He recognized the doctor, as she was a member of his prayer group. A little later, at one of the prayer meetings he felt God telling him that she was the one to whom he was to get married. When he approached her with this news, she said she would ask God for some sign during a retreat that she was going to attend. When she came back, she told him that God had spoken to her through the Book of Ruth—'Your God will be my God and your people will be my people' (1:16). This message was confirmed in another retreat, which she attended some months later. That is how they got married. He is very happy that he got married since they are both of the same mindset and she fulfilled all the conditions he had put before God. Thus, the Charismatic habitus does not only influence religious rituals and practices, but also shapes the everyday life of the individual Charismatic leading to ritualization of life.

Priesthood and Marriage

The neo-Pentecostals follow the Protestant position that there is no special calling or separate vocation for priesthood and that it is not a sacrament. They believe that all the faithful are called to be priests and they support this argument by referring to 1 Peter 2:9, 'But you are a chosen race, a royal priesthood, a holy nation.' They reject the ministerial aspect of priesthood and the distinction between the universal priesthood of all the faithful and the ministerial priesthood that the Catholic Church accepts.[5] Most of the neo-Pentecostal pastors are married men just like the other members of their congregation. Most of the neo-Pentecostals whom I interviewed reject the prerequisite of celibacy for priesthood and opine that their pastors should be married men. For them, the married state of life is a higher state of spirituality than the life of celibacy. They do not have a rule that every pastor should be married, though one hardly comes across a pastor who is unmarried. The study by Ignatius Fernandes (2007) on the leadership profile of pastors of evangelical groups in Goa shows that each of the 20 pastors he interviewed were married men. The neo-Pentecostal understanding is that if a pastor is not married and his family life is not secure, the Devil can use women to tempt him and pull him down. In addition, they claim that a wife is strength for the man in his spiritual journey. On the other

---

[5] For a brief description of the Catholic idea of priesthood, see Rahner and Vorgrimler 1983, 411–12.

hand, almost all the Catholic Charismatics that I interviewed were of the opinion that women should not get ordained as priests, while all of them felt that priests should not give up their celibacy. Most of them were also against married people being allowed to become priests. One of the female members of the CCR said, 'Priests getting married and married people getting ordained are not possible since scripturally it is not sanctioned. Women and married people can be helpers.'[6] Another man suggested that since celibacy does not seem to work today, systems of tackling and preserving the sanctity of a vocation in priesthood need to be developed in the Church. Thus, the CCR members hold on to the orthodox views of the Catholic Church regarding priesthood.

Many of the neo-Pentecostal pastors have no religious or theological training but are charismatic personalities who are excellent orators with a larger-than-life stage presence and competent leadership qualities. Most of them have emerged from the congregation and are not trained theologically. Only 20 per cent of the pastors he interviewed had a theological degree, while another 30 per cent had some ministry training of six months to one year (Fernandes 2007). Besides practical difficulties such as the lack of any accredited theological Bible college in Goa and the reluctance of married pastors with families to go for long-term theological training outside Goa, most of them did not feel the need for theological studies, as they were of the opinion that the Holy Spirit is the best teacher. On the other hand, it is mandatory for Classical Pentecostal pastors to have a formal degree in theology. Thus, the pastors of the older Pentecostal denominations are all trained theologically, just like the pastors of the mainline Churches.

While the neo-Pentecostals reject that their pastors are consecrated priests like the Catholic priests, at the same time their discourse on leadership elevates the office of pastor to a spiritual, sacred realm that earns the respect of the entire congregation, an essential requirement for the pastor to lead the group. Most of the people of the ROLC I interviewed had great respect for their pastor and considered him their spiritual father. The NFI Church teaches that becoming a pastor is a divine calling. God gives the revelation to particular persons to become

---

[6] Interview with a member of the CCR prayer group of Porvorim on 1 August 2007.

leaders and pastorship is not hereditary. A cursory glance at some of the pastors in Goa, however, shows that several of them have their kin as pastors. The pastor of the ROLC has two brothers who are also pastors. The procedure of becoming a pastor is long and requires a lot of prayer and commitment. The Assembly of God, consisting of anointed elders in the Church, watches over the behaviour of a would-be pastor, try to gauge his dispositions towards the Lord and people, and only after praying several times choose him to become the pastor. Thus, in the case of both the Catholic Charismatics and the neo-Pentecostals, priesthood is a divine calling, a liminal event that elevates the life-cycle ritual into a sacred order.

Church Leadership and Patriarchy

Early Pentecostalism taught that the same spirit who anointed men also empowered women. This resulted in a much higher proportion of women with charismatic gifts participating in Pentecostal ministry than in the historic Churches, which barred women from entering the ministry (Anderson 2004: 273). However, the early emphasis on the ministry of women reduced later in Classical Pentecostal missions and the importance of the experience of spirit baptism in the lives of female ministers had to take second place to the general patriarchal structure of Church and society (Anderson 2004: 275). However, even today Classical Pentecostal denominations surpass mainline Protestant Churches in the acceptance of women in ministry. But a pastor of the IPC whom I interviewed mentioned that there are no women pastors among the IPC in India due to cultural reasons. The followers at the grass-roots level do not accept a woman as a pastor.

Among the neo-Pentecostals in Goa, only married men can become pastors. There are no women pastors in the NFI. In my fieldwork, I did not meet any female neo-Pentecostal pastors though I have heard unconfirmed reports that there are one or two independent Charismatic groups started by women who continue as their founding leaders. Most likely, these groups are very small in number and consist mainly of women. Neo-Pentecostal women help out in various ministries such as those of charity, couples, or children, and the significant women in the Church are normally the pastors' wives. Most of the wives of pastors are actively involved in ministry work, but in the NFI Church women are not allowed to preach or become part of the group of elders. According to Hollenweger (1972: 487), the pastor's wife often has greater intellectual gifts than her husband, but is the gentle, tender, and brave but submissive helpmate of her husband. The pastor of the ROLC, while preaching about the qualities that elders of the Church should possess, said, 'I love women and have no quarrel with them, but the Bible is so very clear that the leadership role in the Church is for men alone. In today's world, there is a fight for equality between man and woman, but there is an order in the Church of God which does not change because of the culture today.'[7] Since the interpretation of the Bible is equivocal, the neo-Pentecostal groups selectively choose certain biblical passages, especially from the letters of St Paul, that define the role of women as confined to the domestic sphere and not in Church leadership while ignoring passages that have revolutionary potential in their interpretation of gender roles.

Women can lead praise and worship, make announcements, give testimonies, make intercessions, help in organizing the hall, teach in Sunday Catechism school, and prepare and serve coffee and snacks at the end of the Sunday service, but the neo-Pentecostal Churches believe that biblical evidence[8] points to God ordaining men to lead and so women cannot become pastors. While their official position is clear-cut and categorical, the views of the individual members I interviewed are divided. In the Pentecostal movement, there are informal systems of values in existence, which are in contradiction to the official doctrine that is preached (Hollenweger 1972: 489). The view of the majority is that God made men to lead and so women cannot become pastors. The view of the minority holds that the choice of a woman pastor is a grey area. They agree that according to the word of God a woman cannot be a pastor, but acknowledge that times are changing and if God decides, he can make a woman a pastor. This view of the minority group is a reflection of the changing patriarchal values in present-day society and the dynamic nature of the Pentecostal–Charismatic movement that changes under the influence of the Holy Spirit. On the other hand, the identification with the NTC and its patriarchal values is noticed in all

---

[7] Interview with the pastor of the ROLC on 23 December 2006.

[8] Texts such as 1 Timothy 2:11–15; 3:1–13 are quoted to justify their patriarchal system.

the women I interviewed, who readily agreed with the majority view that women cannot become pastors. One woman said, 'If women lead prayer cells with men in it, then men have to submit to the authority of women, which is not biblically correct,'[9] while another woman tried to rationally defend the denial of leadership positions in the Church to women by saying, 'To manage you need a position, but to lead you don't need a position. You can be in the lowermost position and yet be a leader.'[10] The Charismatic habitus embodies biblical texts in social practices, resulting in the dispositions and biases of the society of the New Testament shaping the neo-Pentecostal discourse on patriarchy more than the gender sensitization of contemporary society.

Family and Position of Women

The neo-Pentecostal Churches teach that the roles of different members of the family are derived from the New Testament model of family. The father is the head of the family and he has to teach his family about God and the Bible. The mother's role, which is a supplement-ing role, is to take care of the children. The wife has to submit to the husband and become the head of the family only in his absence. The gender roles sanctioned by the New Testament model of idealized womanhood complement the existing patriarchal biases in present-day society. Thus, the women of the ROLC are taught that most marriages today are breaking since the biblical model of marriage is not followed. Women nowadays are well-educated, hold good jobs, and so want to head the family. They are not willing to submit to their husbands, lead-ing to clashes and divorces. The neo-Pentecostals teach that even if the husband is educationally less qualified than the wife, the wife cannot become the man, that is, the head of the family. She should have faith in God that he will empower her husband to be the head. Thus, the discourse of the neo-Pentecostal Churches on gendered family roles superimposes the biblical sociocultural codes with its patriarchal val-ues on to the present-day social institution of family with its existing patriarchal biases. Heta Pandit (2008: 51), in her work on Goan houses, mentions that while a woman was allowed to carry out a certain act

---

[9]   Interview with a member of the ROLC on 20 September 2008.
[10]   Interview with a member of the ROLC on 7 September 2008.

within the house, she was expected to follow the dictates and traditions of the house, which were often laid down by the male head of the
house (Malekandathil and Dias 2008: 51–9).

The neo-Pentecostal Churches insist on an idealized New Testament
model of family, with strict adherence to biblical principles and
patterns of family behaviour and roles sanctioned by a Charismatic
habitus. However, in the comforting and familiar environment of the
home, there is a lot of negotiation between the strict principles of the
Church and the exigencies of daily life that result in the relaxation or
compromise of biblical roles and duties. One young neo-Pentecostal
man recounted to me his difficulty to follow faithfully the biblical
roles and positions. When he is out, his wife takes over his role and
does things that he as the head should be doing. Some neo-Pentecostal
groups teach that only the head of the family can pray over the children,
but his wife does that. While his Church emphasizes that the wife's
role is in the kitchen, whenever she is sick he does all the cooking and
washing. Since she is allergic to dust, he does all the cleaning in the
house. His wife admitted to me that her husband cooked better than
she did and whenever guests came he cooked the main dishes, while
she entertained them.

There is a lot of hidden dissent and opposition from the neo-
Pentecostal women to the patriarchal roles legitimized by the
Charismatic habitus. But since the family system of patriarchal roles,
rights, and duties has religious scriptural sanction, this dissent is normally covert and women through the process of socialization have
largely internalized these values. A young woman, who had seen her
father being very authoritative towards her mother and forcing her to
do everything that he ordered, was reluctant to say the word 'submit' in
the pronouncement of her wedding vows. She has been always battling
the Church's teaching that women should submit to their husbands.
This conflict within the self develops when two worlds of perception
and self-presentation collide (Coleman 2000: 137). In the case of the
above-mentioned woman, her world of a confident, well-educated,
independent working woman clashes with the submissive, domes-
ticated New Testament woman. Her struggle to live up to the ideal
standards of the biblical woman is noticed in her decision to give up
her job and look after her children. Initially, she found it very difficult
to adjust, since she had worked so hard and studied so much to be

something in life, but now she justifies her decision saying that the Lord has richly rewarded her. As Coleman says, Believers use rationalizing arguments with explicitly articulated expressions of Charismatic 'logic' to explain apparent failures (Coleman 2000: 138). There are many neo-Pentecostal women like her who have voluntarily given up their jobs and are housewives. Joseph (2005: 23) while quoting Fiorenza notes, 'The alleged "voluntarism" of the imposed submission in Christian patriarchy has turned women against themselves more deeply than ever, disguising and reinforcing the internalization process.'

The wife of the pastor of the ROLC had a well-paying job in a reputed company and was earning more than her husband, but she quit it when her first child arrived. She decided to quit her job to look after the children. She was well experienced in keeping accounts, very good at calculations having graduated in mathematics, and also good at repair and maintenance work in the house. Though she was more experienced and efficient than her husband, she stepped back and allowed him to learn and take charge of the house since their Church teaches them that the wife, however qualified she may be, cannot be the head of the family. She feels that whatever he is today is because of that decision of hers to step back and allow him to take charge of the house. The intense socialization into the biblical model of womanhood and the desire to meet the ideal standards of the iconic self-image produced by the Charismatic habitus is noticed in the above case. Such decisions to shift from the public to the domestic sphere are due to the internalization of the myth of Indian womanhood (the *Bharatiya nari*), which portrays the woman as a selfless giver, someone who gives endlessly, gracefully, and smilingly, however unreasonable the demands may be, and even if they are harmful to the woman herself (Joseph 2005).

The children of a neo-Pentecostal couple are looked at as God's children. The father and mother are caretakers and they need to treat their children well as if they are someone else's property. God has a plan of growth for each child and the parents' role is to help God achieve that growth. A father has to play his role and give happiness, joy, and the fear of God to the children. The role of the child, if he wants to live a long and happy life, is to honour his father and mother. The child, however smart he or she may be, has to submit to the father. For the neo-Pentecostals, the spiritual birth, that is, being born again in the spirit is more important than the biological birth. Thus, life as a neo-Pentecostal begins only after one is baptized as a Born-Again Christian and this occurs when one is an adult. Therefore, children are not regarded as members of the Church community and do not have much status or role to play in Church-related activities. The Charismatic habitus emphasizes the idea that the Church, which is the community of Believers, is their family more than their own kith and kin. Through water baptism, the converts become part of God's family and these spiritual ties are closer than their blood and kinship ties. This is reinforced by the idea that their children are the property of God and they are only caretakers. This discourse, which is reinforced by the fact that many of the new converts are forced to sever their blood ties after conversion, ensures that their allegiance to the Church community is stronger than any other bonding.

Death and Funeral

The inability of the human self to match up to the idealized Charismatic persona built on an ideology driven by triumphalist prosperity gospel can lead to considerable inner conflict (Coleman 2000). This also leads the neo-Pentecostals in Goa to downplay suffering, bodily imperfection, and death in their discourses. Rarely does one get to hear or see images or metaphors of human weakness, suffering, and death in their prayer meetings since these would weaken the idealized image of 'an omni-competent Charismatic persona' (Coleman 2000: 138). Coleman's ethnographic findings in Sweden also show that funerals do not have a prominent role in Word of Life (the group that he was studying) literature or other forms of public discourse. He also mentions stories of Believers being unable to accept the death of younger members of the group. Most of my respondents did not have much to say on the topic of death except that they should not be frightened about death. Instead, they were much more concerned about what will happen after death—either everlasting life or everlasting death. The whole purpose of the ritual of birth and death is to define each birth or death, from an accidental, contingent event to one that is part of a cosmic design (Das 1976: 252). The neo-Pentecostals explain death not as the end but as a transition to a better life. Since they are all certain about their salvation and like other Born-Again Christians are sure that they will be going to heaven, death does not frighten them. They are more preoccupied with the times to come in the world, 'when Antichrist will be revealed, the seal of the Antichrist "666" will be put on you and Believers will not be allowed to preach about Christ, times are coming when people will point a gun at you and tell you to give up your faith in Jesus', according to a neo-Pentecostal.[11]

Thus, the neo-Pentecostals integrate death into the divine cosmic plan of God. Those people who have not accepted Jesus in their lives and are not Born-Again have to fear death since they do not know if they will be saved. Death is a minor event in the cosmic cycle, which leads the Believer to the much more important event of the last judgement, where all people—those who have died in Christ and those who have not died in Christ—will be judged. This is a more liminal experience than death for the neo-Pentecostals as the terrifying possibility of not being saved and being condemned to eternal damnation 'threatens the basic assumption of order on which human society rests' much more than the event of death (Das 1976). The more the liminality of the life-cycle event, the more elaborate is the ritual. Since the neo-Pentecostals do not find death very threatening, they have brief funeral ceremonies similar to the mainline Protestant Churches. Normally, there is a prayer service of around half an hour either at the house of the dead person or in the Church to which that person belonged. In case neither of the above two options is possible, the entire funeral service is conducted at the cemetery. Though they do not have a funeral liturgy, they have a fixed format, wherein some scriptural passages pertaining to life after death and resurrection are taken. Apart from singing a few songs, the pastor and some from the congregation say a few prayers. Their prayers do not focus on the dead person and how he or she suffered, but on the eternal bliss that is awaiting the person in heaven. Besides the prayer service in the house or Church, the pastor also conducts a short service at the cemetery.

Life Plan

Compared to the mainline denominations, the independent non-denominational Christian sects demand a lot of time and commitment

---

[11] Interview with ROLC member on 26 July 2008.

from their adherents. They combine intense indoctrination in the faith with the comforting and reassuring structure of the community of Believers that provides support and fellowship to the individual Believer tossed in the stormy world controlled by worldly powers and principalities. Thus, for the besieged Believer, cut off from all blood and kinship ties, the Church (its teachings, practices, and support system) is the only raft on which one can steer through the storms of daily life. The Church provides a life plan, a Charismatic blueprint to the individual Believer, to deal with all that life throws at him or her. This life plan or Charismatic habitus is a set of guidelines or unconscious rules and regulations that help individual Believers strategize and negotiate social structures and practices by taking the Believer beyond the realities of everyday life to wider ones, which correct and complete them (Geertz 1973).

Pain and Suffering: Testing Gold in the Fire

Something that has always puzzled Believers all over the world is the presence of evil, pain, and suffering in the world, in spite of the presence of a good and loving God. On this issue, the Catholic Charismatic movement teaches its members that pain and suffering are not from God, but are often man-made and sometimes it is the Devil who sends illnesses, pain, or suffering. The course of action suggested by the CCR to its followers who are affected by the curses of the Devil is to participate in adoration before the Blessed Sacrament, make a good confession, and pray and fast. Some Charismatics hold the view that pain and suffering comes from God, who punishes them for their sins. The predominant view is that God neither punishes nor desires to give human beings any pain. Suffering comes because people have strayed from God's protection and think that there is no God and they can do anything. God allows suffering to test people to make them stronger in their faith and give them more graces.

Related to the above understanding of pain and suffering is the idea that after every trial God gives them a blessing. Therefore, their daily problems and difficulties are construed as punishment from God but are reinterpreted by the Charismatic habitus as a ladder to a higher state of life with more blessings and increased prosperity and well-being. Pain and suffering are, thus, viewed through the metaphor of refining gold in the fire, a type of building up that leads the person closer to God. This attitude towards pain and suffering is illustrated by the case of a neo-Pentecostal woman whose finances were hit very badly and who, thus, found herself in a lot of debt. She was staying in the hostel of the institute where she was teaching, but one day she was asked by the principal to vacate the place. As a single parent, she did not know where to go and what to do. She attributed all these problems to her checking horoscope on the Internet when she was blinded by the Evil One. Due to that activity, she exposed herself to demonic spirits and thereafter all the troubles followed. After two months of struggling to find proper accommodation, during which she kept God as her anchor, she got a well-furnished, spacious two-bedroom flat in the new staff quarters.

For the neo-Pentecostals, their Church modelled on the NTC is a wider reality, which influences and reconstitutes the present-day reality of individual Believers. They are taught that God has a life plan for each one of them, especially regarding the choice of his/her state of life. If God's plan for a Believer is to remain single then that person should remain single, but if God wants him to get married and he decides to remain single then a lot of misfortunes will befall him. A widow, who is in her 30s, has received several marriage proposals in the last few years, but since she did not get any definitive answer from the Lord she has not accepted them. Her Charismatic habitus that reassures her of the 'real' presence of God in her life, often in the role of a husband, has helped her cope with the catastrophic situation of losing her husband at a young age.

Finding the Supernatural in Their Daily Lives

A key and crucial belief of their habitus is the belief that the supernatural, the power of God, will triumph over the natural, the logic and rationality of the world, in their daily lives. The ROLC has been in existence for more than nine years, but they still do not have a place of their own and meet in a rented hall in a hotel. However, the pastor is certain that God will give them land in Panaji city to build their Church. The reason for his certitude is that a prophetic woman, who was praying over him, found the word 'land' coming repeatedly in her mind, and a paper being stamped in the 'heavenlies' (a word coined by the pastor, which means the wider divine reality). Though land in Panaji is very expensive, just like gold, and the Church cannot afford it, the pastor is sure that they will have a Church of their own soon. This example illustrates what Coleman (2000: 136) calls 'the process of externalization that involves focussing of language on to a specific recipient or object'. The pastor's certitude of acquiring land for the Church is the transfer of language from the prophetic woman's 'word' to its physical representation in the paper being stamped in the heavenlies, which becomes an embodied reality through the pastor's internalization.

This aspect of the Charismatic habitus makes the ROLC believe that though their Church membership is just over 100, they soon expect to see 1,000 people thronging the venue of their Sunday service. It also generates specific patterns of behaviour when they visit hospitals. When they go to the hospital to pray for somebody, they do not look at the tubes or machines or at the doctor's report, but just say, 'Thank you Lord and by your stripes [wounds] we are healed' (taken from Isaiah 53:5). They do not pay attention to the findings of medical science, but they believe in God for a miracle. When any of the neo-Pentecostals are sick, they usually follow this course of action—consulting a doctor, taking the prescribed medication, and being hospitalized if needed, besides interceding to God to guide the physician and bring about a cure. A few neo-Pentecostals refuse to see a doctor or take medication, insisting that they have more faith in Jesus, who is the greatest physician, than in the human doctor. This axiom of trusting in God and not in human strength guides the way they approach any difficulty or problem in their day-to-day lives. Their faith gives them a life plan that guides them in choosing careers, marriage partners, managing their finances and their families, and dealing with illnesses. At the same time, since many of the neo-Pentecostals are estranged from their kith and kin, and cannot turn to them in times of difficulty, the neo-Pentecostal Church compensates this need at two levels. It generates the discourse of putting their trust in God and not in man and at the same time it reconstitutes the spiritual community of Believers as a family support system that provides space for socializing and recreational purposes, and psychological and material support for those in difficulty. Thus, when any of the members are in difficulty, apart from turning to God in prayer, they also immediately telephone other members of their Church to request for prayers or other kinds of assistance.

Finding the supernatural in their day-to-day activities, trusting in God and not in man, also influences their attitude towards riches and wealth. The husband and wife in a neo-Pentecostal family from the ROLC work for a voluntary Christian organization, but draw no salaries and are dependent on support from families, friends, and the Church. Everything in their rented house has been donated by others. They believe that in spite of a lot of financial difficulties, God provides things to them miraculously. This attitude towards riches is guided by a key financial principle taught by the Church to its followers, namely Jehovah Jireh (God provides). When the woman was hospitalized for more than two months during the delivery of her second child, the medical expenses came to around ₹250,000. The insurance covered only ₹10,000, while the rest of the money was donated by different people. The couple confessed that they really did not know where the money came from. Thus, the Church not only provides a life plan for its members, but also gives social, psychological, and financial support, ensuring that its economically marginalized members are taken care of.

The life plan provided by the Charismatic habitus teaches them that they can either serve God or Mammon, because money is one thing that can very quickly take away one's devotion to God. Finances break marriages and affect one's relationship with God. If one's finances are in a mess, it reflects one's spiritual state. To handle their finances properly, the members are urged to seek counsel not from the best financial management people, but from the Bible and godly people. The advice they get from their pastor is to spend wisely and to repay what they have borrowed and remain out of debt. The Church also teaches its followers not to covet and run after riches, but to be content in every situation since Earthly riches are not as valuable as the riches in heaven. Thus, we find that many of the neo-Pentecostals spend a lot of their time and energy in Church-related activities and are content with the job they have and the income they get.

A woman who teaches in an educational institute and is not financially well off does not offer tuitions in the evenings to supplement her income. She feels her biblical duty as a mother is towards her son and so she refuses such offers. Her belief is that her Lord will satisfy her needs and she refuses to run after money. Many of the Catholic

Charismatics and neo-Pentecostals I interviewed mentioned how their religious beliefs have given them a blueprint for life and helped them work better, be more honest and sincere in their work, and deal with people in a better manner. In a study of the reasons for the growth of Pentecostalism in central Kerala, Oommen (2001: 143) concludes that the taboos imposed by the Church on the mainly Dalit converts in terms of dealing with money and the accountability of their earnings trained them to spend what they earned for the maximum benefit of the family, leading to economic mobility.

* * *

The creation of a distinct Charismatic habitus has led to the life-cycle rituals of the neo-Pentecostals differing from the biological clock and from other religious traditions. Life-cycle rituals such as birth, marriage, priesthood, and death were analysed in the light of notions of the Born-Again Christian community being elevated to a spiritual community of Believers, elevated from its biological and kinship moorings. The rite of baptism is a bridge-burning act for the new converts, who sever all ties with their old faith community and publicly declare their allegiance to the new faith. Neo-Pentecostals distinguish between water baptism and the baptism in the spirit, both important for their religious life. On the other hand, the Catholic Charismatics equate baptism in the spirit with water baptism and link it with the rites of initiation. Baptism in the spirit, which has no particular rite or place, is linked with glossolalia and is a distinguishing external characteristic of Pentecostalism. Like the Catholic Charismatics, the neo-Pentecostals reject the Classical Pentecostal position on the necessity of glossolalia. Water baptism, wherein the new convert is immersed completely in water, like circumcision, is a ritual marker of the new convert's membership in the Born-Again Christian community. The neo-Pentecostals connect birth with death through the notion of baptism being a funeral service, a liminal experience wherein the neophyte buries his or her old self and is born again in Christ. By accepting only adult baptism, which stresses on the free and deliberate choice of the individual to become a Christian, the neo-Pentecostals' life cycle begins not with biological birth but spiritual birth (being baptized in the spirit).

Catholic ideas and practices of marriage such as the unitive and procreative aims of marriage and the idea of marriage as a relationship between consenting adults, after being suitably 'Christianized', are found among the neo-Pentecostals in Goa. Neo-Pentecostalism believes that marriages are made in heaven and they involve three people—the husband, the wife, and the spirit of God, which links and binds the marriage. It shifts the practice of endogamy from caste ties to religious ties, behind which is the idea of spiritual purity and pollution. The marriage ceremony among neo-Pentecostals, which is similar to the Catholic ceremony, includes a mandatory marriage course, reading of banns, release of the bride and bridegroom by their parents, exchange of rings, public declaration of marital vows, and signing of the marriage register.

The profile of the Pentecostal pastor in Goa differs from the Catholic priesthood in that he is a married man with charismatic qualities and with very little theological training. Both the CCR and the neo-Pentecostals accept the patriarchal notion of only men becoming pastors and support it with scriptural sanction. The patriarchal biases in the choosing of pastors reflect the gendered roles of the neo-Pentecostal family based on the New Testament model of the idealized family. In keeping with the prescribed role of women as housewives assisting the man who is the head of the family, many of the neo-Pentecostal women have given up their jobs and are engaged in household work. Children who are still not Born-Again Christians do not have much status or role to play in the neo-Pentecostal Church. The last judgement is a more liminal experience than death for the eschatologically concerned neo-Pentecostals, who follow a different biological clock. Therefore, their funeral services are not very important and elaborate. For the neo-Pentecostals, most of whom are cut off from all blood and kinship ties, the teachings and structures of the Church provide a life plan, a habitus for the individual Believer to cope with pain, suffering, and the difficulties of everyday life. The usage of the Charismatic habitus, with its exclusive symbols and their underlying notions of sacred and profane, has serious ramifications for the sociocultural space in the state of Goa. The resultant power struggles and religious contestations will be taken up in the next chapter.

6 Power, Inequality, and Terrains of Conflict

In the preceding chapters, we have journeyed through the world of symbols of the Pentecostal–Charismatic movement based on the model of the NTC, which has shed light on how these identities are separate and distinct from other religions in the post-liberation history of Goa. By selectively emphasizing on certain religious beliefs and symbols and downplaying others, these new Christian movements have articulated new modes of religiosity that show signs of discontinuity with the traditional Catholic religious beliefs and traditions, which have been the dominant form of Christianity in Goa for centuries. Newman (2001: 164–91), in a study on Christ Ashram, a Goan Catholic–Hindu sect, points out that after 1961, due to economic upheaval, emergent urbanization, and migration, Catholic–Hindu syncretic cults gained prominence, co-existing with and adding to the diversity of mainline Christianity. He even coined the term 'Goan religion', meaning a continuum which is not only recognizably Catholic at one end and 'standard' Hindu at the other but also having a mixture of Catholic and Hindu rituals, saintly figures, symbols, and beliefs in the middle. While Goan Catholicism has seen forms and beliefs that are syncretic in nature, those have been found on the margins of mainline Catholicism, posing a very minor threat to the Church hierarchy. However, the entry of the Pentecostal–Charismatic movement has seriously challenged the monopoly of the Catholic Church and reworked the concept of Christianity in Goa.

In Goa, after conversion the village Church has replaced the village temple as the focus of the socio-religious life of the community and has become the centre of the relations of power and hierarchy within the Catholic community (Robinson 1998). Bayly, quoting from David Mosse, identifies ways in which Christianity has become embedded in the indigenous social and religious order of a Hindu–Christian village in South India (1989: 5, 6). Thus, the Church articulates, maintains, and redefines these relations based on caste status, ownership of land, or control within the local panchayat. The conflict among the Catholics of Cuncolim[1] over *confraria*[2] membership and the roles of the members of different castes is an example of how the Church redefined caste relations in Cuncolim (Newman 2001: 141–2). The Church, through the strong action of the Archbishop of Goa, closed the Cuncolim Church and forced the Catholic Gauncars[3] to relinquish their exclusive control over the confraria. This strong action opened up membership in all Church associations and organizations to Catholics of all backgrounds. In this chapter, we shall look at how concepts such as social stratification and unequal power relations that are prevalent in the local society are manifested, modified, or rejected in the rituals of the Pentecostal–Charismatic movement. This movement is often viewed by the lower sections of society as a means of asserting themselves and gaining power and social privileges. Throughout India, the domains of religion and politics are inextricably intertwined and, therefore, religion in Goan society cannot be studied in isolation. Bayly (1989) shows how conversion in the lower castes was not so much an attempt to avoid caste-based disabilities in everyday life as it was to create a ritual arena, which allowed them to improve their status within the region's wider caste hierarchy of ritual purity and pollution by adopting a Christianity-based caste lifestyle. Apart from analysing the CCR as a protest movement in the Church and a means of upward social mobility, we shall also study how the entry of these new movements with their strong fundamentalist ideas, an exclusive sense of identity,

---

[1] Cuncolim is a village in Salcete taluka in South Goa, with a total population of 16,623 (2011 Census) of which 37.6 per cent are Christians.

[2] Confraria or confraternity is an association of lay Catholics in Goa, formed for religious purposes.

[3] Founder members of a village community.

and the financial backing of foreign Church-planting organizations has led to a polarization of the religious space in Goa, with an increase in religious contestation and conflict.

Foucault and the Idea of Pastoral Power

To analyse the power relations within the Pentecostal–Charismatic movement, we borrow from Foucault's ideas on power, especially his idea of pastoral power. In *The History of Sexuality* (1980), Foucault presents a series of propositions about power, which are cautionary rules of thumb. Power is a general matrix of force relations operating at a given time, in a given society. Power relations are rooted in the system of social networks. Power is, therefore, found working in multiple different sites of social relationships and networks. Thus, for Foucault, power is not an absolute, universal thing that can be equated to political institutions and which acts on people and situations uniformly; there are various localized sites of power (Dreyfus and Rabinow 1982: 186). Power is multi-directional, operating top-down and also bottom-up and we are all enmeshed in it. Thus, power is exercised upon the dominant as well as on the dominated.

The characteristics of pastoral power, an old power technique which originated in Christian institutions, are (Foucault 1986: 213–15):

1. It is a form of power, whose ultimate aim is to assure individual salvation in the next world.
2. It is a power, which does not merely command, but is also prepared to sacrifice itself for the life and salvation of the flock.
3. It is a form of power, which does not just look after the community as a whole, but also looks after each individual person throughout their entire life.
4. This power cannot be exercised without knowing the thoughts inside people's minds, without exploring their souls. It presupposes knowledge of the conscience and an ability to direct it.

To sum up, this power is aimed towards salvation, it is seen as an offering to God, it is individual-oriented, it is coextensive and continuous with life, and it is linked with the production of truth—the truth of the individual himself. Thus, pastoral power is different from other forms of power such as political, legal, and so on.

Power Relations among the Neo-Pentecostals

According to the neo-Pentecostals, the Charismatic movement is the earthen vessel, through which the supernatural power is channelized and the power of God is made manifest in the world. The neo-Pentecostals derive their power from the powers of the Holy Spirit, which are manifested in the form of miracles, healings, exorcisms, and speaking in tongues. This supernatural power is boundless and anyone who is connected to the Holy Spirit and acknowledges Christ as their saviour can tap into this power. The neo-Pentecostals distinguish between 'good' power, which comes from the Holy Spirit and 'evil' power, which comes from Satan. The distinction between good power and evil power is not so much regarding quantity, as regarding quality. Thus, both good power and evil power are not fixed or constant. Neo-Pentecostalism teaches its followers to firmly believe that Christ has brought them complete victory by triumphing over the forces of evil. They also believe that all power struggles in the world are only a reflection of this spiritual warfare. Caplan (1987a: 256) argues that fundamentalists attribute many if not most everyday problems and misfortunes to the operation of occult evil forces, and so it is not surprising that the appropriation and control of supernatural power becomes a vital concern.

For Charismatics, the source of power in society lies in the spiritual infrastructure, which is in contrast with the Marxian theory of power that traces the source of power to the economic base of society. Depending on the level of their relationship with the forces of salvation, individuals or groups enjoy power in society. Thus, neo-Pentecostals who have accepted Christ as their personal saviour are sure of their salvation and are convinced that they enjoy more power and prosperity in society as compared to the pagans who worship the forces of darkness and are not sure of their salvation. The knowledge that they are empowered by the Holy Spirit makes the neo-Pentecostals bold and aggressive in their evangelization drive. Their belief that all the sociopolitical and historical forces in the world are under the power of their God makes them emboldened to preach the gospel even more powerfully, particularly in the face of opposition and persecution. They believe that all such oppositions and persecutions against the Born-Again Christians are nothing but signs of spiritual warfare leading to the advancement of the Kingdom of God and the triumphant victory of Christ.

'Pastoral Power' in the Charismatic Movement

The type of power found among the neo-Pentecostals and the Charismatic movement in Goa can be compared with Foucault's idea of pastoral power. It is intricately linked with the production of truth and the mediation of grace. The final decision-making authority in the neo-Pentecostal sects lies in the hands of the pastor, who is generally a married man. Women pastors heading sects are not found in Goa and this exclusion is justified by the Pentecostal–Charismatic movement on the basis of certain patriarchal biblical texts, which restrict women to the domestic sphere. Consonant with the Foucaultian understanding of pastoral power, the neo-Pentecostals believe that God has given only men the power to know the inside of people's minds, to explore their souls, and direct their conscience.

The pastor consults his team of elders for any important decisions, but is not always bound to follow their views. The model of power generally found in the neo-Pentecostal Churches in Goa is a pyramidal model, with either one man at the pinnacle—a one-man Church—or one man with a few elders, who are often just puppets. Since the pastor selects the team of elders and there is no election, he can ensure that the team of elders constitute those who agree with his views, people who will not challenge his charismatic authority. The pastor of the ROLC articulated this model of power during one of the Sunday prayer meetings, saying: 'The Church is not ruled by a democracy, where everybody will vote on what happens in Church. It does not work like that. They [pastor and team of elders] hear God and they do it.'

The Authority of the Pastor

The unequal power relations between the pastor and the rest of the congregation are clearly manifested in the ritual of the Sunday prayer meetings. When the pastor criticizes and berates the congregation for various shortcomings such as their lack of faith—'Hello, are you listening? Our foolish Christians go to the babas and gurus as if some pearls of wisdom are falling from heaven, when the babas are taking it all from the Bible, changing and twisting here and there'—or lack of attendance for the Sunday prayer meetings—'It is the devil who keeps you from Sunday worship'—or lack of courage to preach the gospel—'God has given us thousands of occasions to open our mouths for the 1.5 million people in Goa, but we have been afraid and reluctant to come out from our comfort zones'—the people listen quietly without any contestation. This is because the Believers accept the authority of their pastor, which is derived from their belief that the pastor is someone who is able to show the true path to every individual Believer and, thus, assure each of them salvation in the next world. They also believe the pastor is willing to sacrifice himself for the well-being of his members and for the salvation of the flock, all characteristics identified in Foucault's idea of pastoral power. When the ROLC celebrated eight years of their existence, the pastor and his wife were escorted to the stage and two members from the congregation came up and prayed for them. While praying for them, they described the pastor and his wife as their spiritual father and mother who first accepted faith and showed others the way to salvation.

While a lot of congregants participate in the religious rituals of the NFI Church, the practice of breaking of the word of God or preaching is the prerogative of the pastor. He may allow some other pastor or an elder of his Church to preach, but he keeps a strict control on the content of the sermon. Between December 2006 and January 2009, I attended 17 Sunday prayer meetings of the ROLC. Only once was the pastor not present for the meeting and in his place a pastor from another NFI Church officiated. In the remaining 16 meetings, the local pastor preached on 11 occasions, while on the other 5 occasions other NFI pastors or certain chosen members of his congregation broke the word of God. The pastor, by inviting other pastors or members from his congregation, well known to him, controls and monitors the production of truth for his congregation. Asad (1993) argues that religious symbols and the 'truths' they convey cannot be understood without reference to power, which give them authoritative status. While the neo-Pentecostals point out that they do not accept any teaching unless it is in agreement with the Bible, they accept without question interpretations of scriptural texts and their implications, when they come from their pastor or from preachers chosen by the pastor. The pastor of the WRM keeps strict control on the production of truth by not inviting other pastors to preach at the Sunday worship. His reluctance to invite other pastors is due to his understanding that different congregations are growing at different levels and he wants to ensure his congregation does not get the 'wrong' message.

At the WRM, which follows the model of a one-man Church, the physical structure of the hall reflects the power relations between the pastor and his congregation. At a usual Sunday prayer meeting, the small hall is packed with nearly 150 people. The hall is built like an amphitheatre. At one end is a marble stage, which is pretty high, and facing the stage are two levels with both the ground and upper levels packed with people sitting close to one another. The pastor, standing next to his well-designed marble lectern, with one glance is able to see all the people seated on both levels. It gives the impression that no one is able to escape the piercing gaze of the pastor, who is able to scrutinize even their souls. The sophisticated music system with sound mixers, electric guitars, a huge temple drum, and microphones with high treble are designed to have maximum impact on the crowd. The pastor's sermons are highly amplified and blasted through huge speakers arranged at strategic places in the hall to ensure that none in the audience can escape their deep psychological impact. There is no doubt that the pastor on the stage is supposed to be the centre of attraction and the entire architecture is designed to suit that purpose (see Figure 6.1). The careful utilization of the physical space of the WRM Church to construct a social space that reflects and reiterates the unequal power relations between the pastor and his flock is in keeping with Lefebvre's (1991) conception of space: space is always social, always produced, and there can never be any neutral or merely physical space.

The authority of the pastors is derived from the neo-Pentecostal belief that their appointment comes from God. At the same time, since many of the neo-Pentecostal pastors are self-appointed, questions are often raised about the legitimacy of their office. The proof of their divine authority to lead a Church is normally manifested in the form of different charisms such as preaching, prophesizing, healing, or exorcizing demons. To demonstrate their closeness to God, the pastors often cite various examples of how troubles of the people over whom they had prayed subsequently disappeared. Often, competing claims to the office of pastor by other charismatic members lead to schisms and a splintering of the sect. The Foucaultian pastoral power, from which the pastor draws his authority, is undermined when the pastor's claim

Figure 6.1   Structure of World Revival's Ministry Church
Source: Drawn by Raul D'Souza based on author's observations.

to lead his followers to salvation or his ability to know and direct the conscience of the individual are challenged. This is illustrated in the historical narrative of the ROLC. The Church, which began in 2000, saw steady growth over the years, and after six years, the strength of the group had gone up to around 50. Then one of the men who was assisting the pastor in running the Church started questioning him and dividing the people and this led to a crisis. For nearly a year, the crisis continued in spite of the pastor's best efforts to resolve the issue. The pastor was at last able to resolve the crisis by changing his entire leadership team and inducting new members. Sect fission is quite common among neo-Pentecostal Churches and mainly occurs due to disputes over the power to control the production of truth.

Catholic Charismatic Renewal: Changing Power Equations for Women

Chapter 3 described the socio-economic profile of the CCR in Goa, which revealed that the Charismatic movement is dominated by women. About 86.5 per cent of the Catholic Charismatics in Goa were female, but this numerical dominance was not reflected in the decision-making and governing bodies of the CCR. While the power relations in the CCR are skewed in favour of men, with few women being involved in decision-making structures, it is also true that the Charismatic movement has brought rural women out from the domestic sphere and into the public domain. Robinson (1998) in her study of Catholicism in rural Goa had predicted that a strengthening of the Charismatic and Pentecostal movements could shift the religious affiliation of the lower castes and Shudras from the established Churches to these movements, since they were being denied privileges in the rituals of the established Churches. She had cited an incident, in which, for some 'lower-caste' Catholics, involvement in the Charismatic movement became a means by which they were able to challenge the so-called 'high' castes on their own ground, that is, within the Church (Robinson 1998: 205–6).

My study shows that more than the lower castes, the CCR has provided liberation for its female members from the sense of exclusion that they have experienced in the predominantly male Church ritual. The CCR has provided the space and the way for women to enter mainstream Catholicism. The following case studies are examples of women who, through participation in the CCR, have acquired a certain degree of power, status, recognition, and liberation in the patriarchal public religious sphere.

Case 1: Alzira

She is 74 years old and an unmarried, retired schoolteacher. She has been a teacher all her life and has taught in different government schools. One of the schools she taught in was the government primary school in Merces and that is where she started the Merces Charismatic prayer group, the first Konkani prayer group in Goa. She has been involved with the Renewal since 1978 and can be rightly called the mother of the Konkani Charismatic Renewal in Goa. Alzira was born and brought up in Panaji, though her parents were from Benaulim, Salcete.

As an ordinary schoolteacher involved in the Charismatic Renewal, she had no ambition to take up leadership, but she felt God telling her repeatedly: 'Open a group and teach my people.' So, she collected all the women in Merces who were willing and interested in experiencing Jesus and knowing about the Holy Spirit. Her Konkani was not very good and she would tell the people that hers was Portuguese Konkani. Around the same time, a woman named Olga opened a Charismatic group in the neighbouring Santa Cruz village and requested Alzira to help her. Alzira was already busy since she was teaching in an English medium school though her education was in Portuguese. Thus, besides having to learning English and teach it to the students, she also had to study the Konkani Bible and teach the Santa Cruz and Merces prayer groups. At the same time, she attended a Bible course conducted by a Jesuit scripture scholar. She was completely confused by the different quotations and found it difficult to grasp the Bible, but that course gave her confidence and she started learning the scriptures by reading and memorizing. She also began attending many other Bible courses.

The news about the Charismatic movement spread rapidly and soon there was a lot of demand for Konkani retreats. So, Alzira got together with some other Charismatic members and started the Konkani retreats in different places in Goa. Since many of the people to whom she gave these Life in the Spirit retreats belonged to the Gauda and Kunbi communities (tribal communities) and did not know how to read or write, she would write the Bible quotations on the board. She also prepared lots of material in the form of charts, pictures, paintings, and other visuals to teach them. She walked miles and miles to different villages in Goa to give Charismatic Konkani retreats to the people. In the 1980s, it was unheard of for a woman, especially a layperson, to be actively involved in the public domain of religion, teaching Christian doctrine to villagers, both men and women. The fact that she spoke Portuguese well and was from the city of Panaji gave her an exalted status among the simple village folk and they addressed her as 'sister'.

She also got the status of being a 'holy woman' due to incidents such as the following: She used to go to Neura Church every day for the proclamation of the gospel during the novenas. Before the novena, she would spend time praying in the Church before the Blessed Sacrament. She was once praying for a miracle for the people. She asked for the Holy Spirit and suddenly water fell on the altar like a fountain gushing down. Another time she laid her hands on a child who was sick and the child became all right. Due to such miracles, people began to come to her and ask her to pray over them. Using such powerful signs, she was able to exercise Foucault's pastoral power by convincing the people who came to her that she was able to perform miracles in their lives and, thus, lead them on the path of eternal salvation. While analysing the political and cultural meaning of a miracle that occurred in Velim, Goa, Newman (2001: 147–63) interprets miracles and visions as a powerful tool that can mobilize people and focus their aspirations, especially those who have been powerless and exploited for long. Stirrat (1992) related demonic possession to gender roles saying that possession is not just a manifestation of the subordinate role of women; it is also a means through which such subordination is produced. Alzira, a layperson, by performing miracles and healing people who were sick or possessed by evil spirits challenged the subordinate role of women in the religious sphere and made a case for superior identity and higher status.

Besides starting new prayer groups, Alzira also occupied several positions in the Charismatic Renewal. Due to her long and active involvement in the Renewal, she came into contact with several well-known Charismatic evangelists and got a chance to go to Rome in 1988 and meet the Pope. An ordinary schoolteacher with elementary Portuguese education, who taught in government schools all her life, through her involvement in the Charismatic movement, was able to appropriate Foucault's pastoral power and, thus, influence the lives of many village folk in Goa. She is, therefore, highly regarded as 'sister', 'holy woman', and the mother of the Konkani Charismatic movement.

Case 2: Flory

Flory, a married, 41-year-old housewife with two daughters, has been in the Charismatic Renewal for the last 17 years and was also the leader of the Merces prayer group. Before her wedding, she was part of a Charismatic group led by the well-known Charismatic preacher Fr Savio Gama. He had at that time prophesized that Flory would start a Charismatic prayer group. When Flory joined the Merces prayer group, it was going through tough times and hardly anyone was attending the meetings. With the support of the parish priest and another woman, Flory was able to revive the prayer group and the membership gradually increased. In 1992, when they had elections, she was chosen as the leader and remained the leader until 2000, when she was advised bed rest due to the delivery of her daughter. This housewife with only secondary schooling and despite her household duties and family responsibilities learnt how to study the Bible and comprehend the word of God. She was guided and counselled in learning the Bible by the Merces parish priest, who taught her how to change her life.

Initially, as the leader of the prayer group, all the group work used to fall on her. As the leader, she had to arrange for people to go for different Charismatic meetings and programmes. People were reluctant to go and often she had to go alone for these meetings and programmes. Only because her in-laws and husband supported her involvement in the CCR by looking after the children when she was out, was she able to take part in these activities. Through the Life in the Spirit seminars and other Charismatic programmes, Flory learnt a lot and was able to persuade many people to join the prayer group. She also had a natural flair for preaching and teaching and was able to convince people using persuasive arguments and formulating reasonable and plausible explanations. For example, initially many of the Catholic women would not come to the Charismatic prayer meetings because they were offended by the clapping and dancing. Flory explained this practice in the following innovative manner: 'If a minister comes here, will you not clap? Then what about Jesus, who is the biggest minister, the king of kings? Why should we feel shy about clapping and dancing to him in our prayer meetings?'

Besides her responsibility as group leader, the parish priest also made her a Eucharistic minister (one who assists the priest during liturgical services by distributing communion) and she was also elected to the Parish Pastoral Council of Merces. According to Foucault, power is multi-directional, operating top-down and also bottom-up. This is seen in the case of Flory who, despite being only a housewife, was able to influence and impact many people in her prayer group, her parish, and the wider Charismatic movement in Goa.

Despite being only a housewife, she was able to exercise power in the family by inculcating the Charismatic disposition in her family members through various practices such as reading and explaining the Bible, teaching Charismatic ideas, and making them all do praise and worship, the Pentecostal style of prayer. Often, her husband would get frustrated with his work and complain that God was not answering their prayers and was sending evil on them, but she would correct him by telling him that God does not send evil on them. She taught him that it was due to their sins that pain and suffering was befalling them. Also, in her natal family, her three brothers were unemployed. She taught them the Bible. All three began reading the Bible regularly, and subsequently all of them were employed. Thus, this housewife, Flory, got power and recognition through the CCR as a lay religious leader in the public religious sphere. She was entrusted with important responsibilities in the Charismatic movement and in the parish Church, and has been able to realize and develop her natural gifts of preaching, teaching, and leadership, which she would not have been able to do in the liturgical rituals of the Catholic Church.

Terrains of Conflict

Both the CCR and the neo-Pentecostal Churches that have emerged in contemporary Goa have been movements that have attempted to reform the way Christianity is being practised in Goa. In Portuguese Goa, the Catholic Church enjoyed state patronage and aligned with the colonial power, manifesting and articulating colonial biases against the natives both in Church ritual and in appointments to the Church hierarchy. After liberation, the Church lost its state patronage, but continued to be the focus of the socio-religious life of the Catholic community in the villages. The Church continued to maintain and articulate the relations of power and hierarchy within the Catholic community based on caste status, ownership of land, or control within the local panchayat (Robinson 1998).

The new Christian movements in contemporary Goa have been liberating in the sense that they have reformed Church liturgical services to allow the lower strata of society and also women greater access to and participation in Church rituals, which they were denied in the Catholic Church. Their attempts to reform Church ritual and challenge certain beliefs, practices, and traditions of the Catholic Church have led to contestations and conflicts in the religious terrain of Goa. In addition, their evangelistic agenda of proselytizing, combined with a strong 'exclusivist' position and a hyper-critical attitude towards other religious traditions, has led to conflicts with both the Catholic and Hindu communities. The opposition from the Catholic and Hindu communities to the new Christian movements has often spiralled into specific sites of conflict rooted in particular socio-historical contexts. Drawing from the Foucaultian argument that power relations are intentional and non-subjective, I argue that these sites of contestations between the Born-Again Christians and the Catholic and Hindu communities do not fit into a grand overall plan hatched by the Pentecostal–Charismatic movement to capture the socio-religious and political space in Goa, but specific socio-historical contexts and local power relations have led to these contestations. According to Foucault (1986: 220), both consensus and violence are the instruments or the results of power, but they do not constitute the basic nature of power. The exercise of power is not violence or struggle, but a mode of action acting upon the actions of others. Power is exercised only over free subjects and more than violence, resistance, or domination, freedom is the condition for the exercise of power (Foucault 1986: 221).

According to Robinson (1998) and Newman (2001), in the changing agrarian economy of post-liberation Goa, the Catholic Church has become the arena of a variety of conflicts between socially mobile caste groups that are attempting to translate their newly acquired wealth into honour and respect by seeking ritual privileges within the Church. My contention is that in a changing global economy where local identities are getting reworked and religious, ethnic, and regional fissures are widening, the arena of contestation in Goa has shifted from the Catholic Church to the wider religious space in Goa, from the local village community to the global Christian community, and from intra-Church to inter-Church conflicts. These contestations are manifested in different areas—family, village, schools, cemeteries, and media—and cover various spaces—social, spiritual or metaphysical, physical, and economic.

Social Space

Many of the neo-Pentecostals in Goa are former Catholics and so most of their kin are still Catholics. Thus, change of religious identity has resulted in ruptures in family and kinship ties, and in many cases, the hurts and wounds caused by this change have not healed over time. In most of the cases, change of religion has been the initial cause for family disputes, but other factors such as inheritance, family honour, and social pressures have aggravated the situation and led to bitterness, conflicts, and social boycott. This is illustrated through the case of Augustine (name changed) from Sanguem, who became a Born-Again Christian, while the rest of his family remained Catholic. Soon after joining the ROLC, he was called one night by his eldest brother to his parents' place, where they questioned him about leaving the Catholic faith. His sister-in-law harshly accused him of harming the marriage prospects of her daughters, saying that because of his indiscretion the entire family would suffer and everyone in the village would look down on them. According to social convention, a married woman is expected to behave politely with her husband's male kin such as his father and brothers since in the family power hierarchy she is subordinate to her male in-laws. Augustine was very upset at the harsh accusations of his sister-in-law and felt like retaliating, even using physical means, but according to him, by the grace of God, he did not react even though she accused him of many things.

Augustine got married in May 2007 to a girl from another neo-Pentecostal Church. Even though his marriage banns were read in the Catholic Church at Sanguem, his father did not want to attend his wedding, but his mother persuaded him by saying that they should just attend it as if attending a drama. Normally, just prior to the marriage, a ceremony called Bhikaranchem Jevon or Bhikranjevan is held to honour the dead ancestors of the bride and groom (Gracias 2007: 32; Robinson 1998: 161–3). Food is cooked and served to poor people in the name of the deceased ancestors and this custom had been followed at each of his three siblings' weddings. However, in his case, since he had betrayed the Catholic faith his family did not follow this custom. Only his sister, who was close to him and one of his brothers, besides a few of his friends and colleagues attended his wedding since the news spread that it was a 'Believer's wedding'. The Catholic parishioners of Sanguem sought the parish priest's advice on whether they could attend Augustine's marriage since he had arranged a bus for them to come. He was deeply hurt by this social boycott of his wedding.

Many Catholic families in Goa have been split down the middle because of people such as Augustine leaving the Catholic Church and joining the neo-Pentecostal Churches. Due to the strained social relations, the Catholics do not allow the neo-Pentecostals to meet in their village neighbourhoods and, therefore, most of the neo-Pentecostal Churches in Goa conduct their meetings in towns or cities. The social boycott experienced by individual neo-Pentecostals in their family and neighbourhood also extends to the venue of their Sunday prayer meetings. Many of the neo-Pentecostal Churches have to keep shifting from place to place for their Sunday praise and worship since people are reluctant to rent out their place for their prayer meetings. The pastor of the IPC in Porvorim shared how his group used to meet in a particular hotel in Porvorim, but the local parish priest warned the owner, a Catholic, and he stopped their meetings. Up till now, they have moved to three or four different venues for their prayer meetings. The same pastor, who had taken up residence in a housing society in Porvorim was forced to move out within a few months since there was strong objection from some of the neighbours, who were pro-Hindutva. They claimed that he was using his place for conversion activities. The above examples illustrate how the physical space of the neo-Pentecostals has shrunk due to the restrictions being placed on their social space as a result of the Catholics ostracizing them.

Another illustration of the shrinking social space for the neo-Pentecostals is the attempt of the pastor of the WRM to organize a large Christian prayer meeting at a well-known wedding hall in Parra village, involving world famous evangelists preaching to thousands of people. However, the matter reached the ears of the pro-Hindutva BJP government ruling the state of Goa at that time, and he was denied permission to have it on security grounds. The conflict in the social sphere also extends to schools. When it comes to admission to Catholic schools, many of the neo-Pentecostals face difficulties and are sometimes even denied admission. Since the Catholic Archdiocese and the Catholic religious orders run many schools in Goa (122 high schools and higher secondary schools),[4] of which many are well-known for the standard of education and discipline they impart, parents normally make a beeline for these schools first. Since there are hardly any Protestant schools in Goa, the neo-Pentecostals are forced to seek admission either in government or private schools.

Spiritual or Metaphysical Space

For Robinson (1998), conflict in the Catholic Church was primarily centred around caste relations, whereas over the course of this study of new Christian movements, we see that conflict is centred around the production of truth and mediation of grace. The neo-Pentecostals understand conflict on two levels: at the heart of the matter is the primal clash taking place in the spiritual realm between the forces of good and evil, and at another level is the conflict occurring in the social space of Goa between the neo-Pentecostals and the Catholics and the right-wing Hindutva forces. The neo-Pentecostals believe that the conflict in the latter sphere is a reflection of the warfare taking place in the former metaphysical realm and that victory in the spiritual warfare will ensure victory in the social sphere. According to Caplan (1987a: 255), the saving mission of Christ can be understood only in terms of its opposition to the power of the Devil. Stirrat (1992) shows that as long as Catholic shrines could provide a visible and audible display of the battle between the forces of good and evil they could prosper, but their popularity began to decline as soon as they failed to supply such visible proof. The curing of the demonically possessed was taken as proof that the shrine was a sacred place.

In the 1970s, when the CCR began, and also during the 1980s, the focus of the Renewal was not on healing. As the trend of going to the Divine Retreat Centre, Potta, began, the focus of the CCR shifted from spiritual Renewal to physical and psychological healing. The idea developed that people had to go to Potta since the power and glory of God was manifest there in a spectacular manner, through miracles, healings, and exorcisms. It was envisaged that people who went to

---

[4] Statistics taken from *The Catholic Directory of India 2005–06* (2013).

Potta would come back and exercise the gifts of the spirit in their neighbourhood. Therefore, the CCR started becoming a place where only healings took place. Various independent Charismatic centres and individual ministries that came up tried to emulate the Divine Retreat Centre and provide a visible, dramatic display of people being healed, cured of possession, and slain in the spirit in their prayer meetings and programmes to attract people. This image of the CCR has influenced all its members, especially those from rural areas and belonging to the poor and lower middle classes, who view the Renewal not as a place for Christian growth and Renewal, but as a place for the visible display of the triumph of the supernatural over evil forces. As mentioned earlier, Newman (2001) interprets a vision that occurred at Velim as producing a discourse of identity that acknowledged and emphasized the self-worth of the illiterate or semi-educated, the poor and the powerless.

At the same time, in the 1990s, the neo-Pentecostal sects burst on the Goan religious scene in a big way with a clear emphasis on super-natural signs and wonders occurring in daily life. Thus, stories about great signs and wonders started making the rounds and competition grew between the different neo-Pentecostal sects and the independent Catholic Charismatic centres and individuals in providing proof of each one's sacred power in the form of prophecies, healings, slaying in the spirit (explained later in the chapter), and exorcisms, in order to attract people. The following account from a member of the CCR from Mapusa illustrates this growing competition to claim access to spiritual resources from the neo-Pentecostal Churches:

> I heard from a Catholic Charismatic that the presence of God came in the form of thunder and lightning and there was a visible cloud in a par-ticular Pentecostal Church. Nearly 3,000 people saw the mighty presence of God in that Church. In another born-again Protestant Church, God told the people to fill up jars with water and after one week when they opened the jars at a communion service, they found to their surprise that the water had changed to wine. Where is the fellowship, presence of God in the Catholic Church?[5]

---

[5] Interview with a member of the CCR prayer group of Mapusa on 18 September 2007.

Often, the arena for the spiritual warfare between the forces of good and evil is the neo-Pentecostal prayer service and this is illustrated below. A well-known evangelist gave a talk on idolatry and witchcraft in Panaji on 28 June 2007. He said that as long as there is witchcraft and idolatry there can be no peace. He mentioned that by believing in different types of fortune telling such as Ouija boards, tarot cards, palm reading, crystal ball gazing, and tea leaf reading, and by turning to mediums and wizards, people place themselves under curses. He considered horoscope (star gazing) also a form of idolatry. He described a story of how he had liberated a family that was involved in crystal ball gazing through the blood of Jesus. The evangelist then asked people from the congregation who were under the curse of idolatry and witchcraft to come forward and become free from it. Many people came forward and the evangelist and his team began praying over each person, rebuking the evil spirits and commanding them to come out in the name of Jesus. This action of the evangelist and his team, which restrains the actions of the evil spirits is what Foucault explains as the exercise of power, namely a mode of action acting upon the actions of others. While praying over them several persons swayed and fell on the ground, some very slowly and gently, others rather abruptly (stricken in the spirit). There were volunteers standing behind them ready to hold them as they began to fall. After lying on the ground for some time with their eyes closed, they got up and stood again. Most of them were women.

Neo-Pentecostalism teaches that the practice of idolatry and witchcraft leads people to bondage under the authority of evil spirits, which, in turn, leads to all sorts of problems and illnesses. Therefore, a man of God, filled with spiritual power and operating with the gifts of the Holy Spirit 'like the ritual specialist with mediatory links with the Hindu divinities' (Caplan 1987a: 255), can exorcise the evil spirits. This act is dramatized in the form of a spiritual conflict, where the protagonist, using the powerful weapons of the 'blood of Jesus' and the 'name of Jesus', is able to drive away the evil spirits. As the conflict rages on within the afflicted person and the evil spirits are chased out, the person sways and falls to the ground, starts crying loudly, or starts twitching and rolling on the ground, which are external signs of the internal spiritual battle. This ritual of healing people afflicted by demons, accompanied by the afflicted person's falling to the ground, is referred to as being 'slain or stricken in the spirit'. This practice is described by Coleman (2000: 135) as a form of internalization, a verbal practice found in the Charismatic habitus. Here, internalization involves surrendering to a power that is too strong for normal human consciousness to bear.

Omenyo (2002: 252–77), while analysing the rapid growth of Charismatic Churches in Ghana, found that the Charismatics, due to their familiarity with the supernatural world view, explicitly responded to the issues raised by the African primal world view. The Charismatic response to issues such as witchcraft, evil spirits, or affliction was to label all of them as the manifestation of evil, caused by Satan and demons. The Charismatic response led them to embrace issues such as healing, deliverance, prosperity, and miracles. Like Omenyo, who found that the supernatural world view of the Charismatics fitted perfectly with the African primal world view, Caplan (1987a: 254–5), too, found that at the phenomenological level, there is a wide measure of overlap between Hinduism and Protestant fundamentalism since both the worlds are populated by a host of maleficent forces—human and superhuman—and both have place for a prophet, the divinely inspired miracle worker. In Goa too, the dualistic spiritual world view of the Born-Again Christian sects that emphasizes healings and miracles, fits at the phenomenological level with the world view of the poor and lower middle class Catholics and Hindus.

In the beginning of this section, I had stated that conflict in neo-Pentecostalism is centred around the production of truth and the mediation and dispensation of grace. Similar causes for conflict are noticed in the Catholic Church too. In the long-term history of the Catholic Church, there has always been a tension between the institutional Church and individual holy people (saints) that centres on the workings of grace. The institution of the Church claims to be the mediator between humans and God on the ground of apostolic succession, the Church of Rome being the direct successor to Christ and his apostles. Through the rituals of ordination, special supernatural powers are transferred to bishops and priests, powers which can be traced down through the centuries to Christ himself. Furthermore, through what Weber called the 'routinization and depersonalization of charisma', these powers adhere to the office of the priest, not his person. While on the one hand the Church has attempted to monopolize mediation of grace between humans and God through the liturgy and sacraments, at the same time it has always recognized that particular persons can be imbued with, or have a special relationship with, the divine. Such personalization of grace and creation of channels of communication with the divine outside priestly control constitute a challenge to the Church's authority over the mediation of grace. Historically, there has been continuous tension between these two channels of mediation, that is, the Church/priest and the holy person/prophet. Institutionalized grace and personalized grace form two poles in a fluctuating and dialectical process (Stirrat 1992: 134–6).

Independent Charismatic Preachers and the Dialectics of Grace

Ever since the CCR began in Goa, there has been an uneasy relationship between it and the Church hierarchy, marked by doubt and suspicion on the side of the clergy and a critical attitude towards the clergy and Church ritual on the side of the Charismatics. This often-fractious relationship between the CCR and the clergy has been discussed in Chapter 4. This suspicion gets aggravated when it comes to the Church hierarchy's relationship with the independent Charismatic centres and individual ministries. The conflicts between the Church hierarchy and the independent Charismatic evangelists revolve around the dialectics of 'institutionalized grace' and 'personalized grace' on the one hand and 'orthodox truth' and 'heterodox truth' on the other.

Who is an independent Catholic Charismatic preacher? Any Charismatic individual or group in the Archdiocese of Goa that is not registered with the GST, which is part of the worldwide ICCRS, is considered as independent. Many of the independent charismatic preachers in Goa are diocesan priests and they believe that their Charismatic activities are under their capacity as parish priest. So, they do not find it necessary to submit themselves to the GST, which is primarily a body of lay people, since as diocesan clergy they are under the bishop. Therefore, the bishop appointed a Diocesan Charismatic Service Team (DCST) to animate and monitor the use of charisms in the Archdiocese through clear norms and guidelines, based on the teaching of the Catholic Church and with special reference to public healing services and public evangelization programmes. All CCR ministries and centres in the Archdiocese of Goa come under the purview of this team. Unlike the GST, where only two members are priests while the rest are lay people, in the DCST all the members are priests, except one lay person, who is a member of the National Service Team.

The reports of the DCST meetings with priests involved in the Renewal reveal that these meetings discussed the various so-called 'aberrations' taking place during the charismatic services held in different parishes and the steps to be taken to stop these aberrations and pave the way for genuine Renewal. The minutes of the meetings held on 25 November 2002 and 16 December 2002 reveal the tug of war that took place between some of the priests involved in the Renewal and the DCST. The aberrations discussed in the meetings focussed on the issues of 'healthy' practices of healing and penance, pastoral jurisdiction and violation of territorial boundaries, proper use of the gift of knowledge, proper use of liturgical symbols and elements, commercialization of spiritual programmes, and use of trained counsellors. The main issue underlying all the above-mentioned aberrations was the regulation of the production of truth and mediation of grace in the Charismatic services of some independent Charismatic priests by the DCST, which is the monitoring body of all CCR phenomena in the Archdiocese of Goa.

Thus, forcing people to repeatedly come to a particular place at regular intervals for the purpose of 'healing' was deemed to not be a 'healthy' and accepted Catholic practice by the DCST. Similarly, the DCST also judged that the practice of blessing large amounts of water and distributing it to the people for the purpose of healing was not in accordance with the Church's view of the proper use of holy water by the faithful. It also considered the practice of drinking water mixed with blessed salt as being harmful to health. The DCST also discouraged the use of noisy, loud, 'unhealthy', and even 'hysterical' expressions during Charismatic religious services. Asad (1993) argues that it is power and not merely religious symbols that controls the production of truth and implants true Christian dispositions. The DCST, by censuring the priests involved in the CCR for their 'aberrations' and laying down clear guidelines for the proper rituals and practices to be followed in the CCR services, ensured that the production of truth and mediation of grace in the CCR would be under the control of the Church leadership. As seen earlier, Foucault defines the exercise of power not in relation to violence or struggle but as a mode of action acting upon and structuring the possible field of action of others. This is seen clearly in the manner in which the DCST, without the use of violence or force, acted upon the practices of the Charismatic priests and, through clear-cut guidelines, restricted and restrained their possible field of future action in the CCR services.

While the Charismatic priests come under the authority of the bishop, there are some lay people in the Charismatic movement in Goa who function independent of any authority. Two prominent lay preachers in Goa are Br Johnson from Mumbai and Br Edmund from Vasco. While both of them are lay person, their followers address them as 'brother', a title given to show that though they are not ordained as priests they have the same charisma and supernatural powers that bishops and priests have through the ritual of ordination. Johnson who has a regular Charismatic ministry in Mumbai comes often to Goa to conduct Charismatic services. He has a weekly Charismatic service in Porvorim, which is managed by his team. Since Johnson functions independent of the GST and also the DCST, his group has had to shift venues often due to lack of permission from the ecclesiastical authorities. Initially, they used to meet in a retreat house at Porvorim, then they began meeting in a Catholic school, then in a wedding hall, and now in their own place donated to him by his followers.

In the 2006 CCR Leaders' Camp in Goa, all the prayer group leaders were warned by the GST not to call Johnson for any of their meetings. The bishop of Mumbai had sent a letter which stated that Johnson was not allowed to preach outside Mumbai, and even within Mumbai only with his permission. However, Johnson continues to preach in many places in Goa, drawing huge crowds, and is often invited by diocesan priests who are involved in the CCR. In 2008, Johnson had preached at a Charismatic retreat held at an open ground in Porvorim, attended by more than 500 people, most of them Catholics. The Foucaultian concept of power as multi-directional, from top to bottom and also bottom to top, is noticed in the charismatic activities of Johnson. The Church hierarchy uses its power over the GST and the prayer group leaders to dissuade them from calling Johnson for their Charismatic programmes. At the same time, power is brought to bear on the independent Charismatic priests, the GST, and the prayer group leaders by the grass–root level members of the CCR to invite Johnson due to his popularity and charisma as a preacher and healer.

Br Edmond, unlike Johnson, is based in Goa and is the founding leader of a Charismatic group called The Association of Crusaders for

Jesus with Mary (popularly known as the Crusaders) since March 2001. Edmond left his job as a lawyer after going to the Potta Charismatic Retreat Centre for a retreat. He now works full-time doing God's work and is looked upon as a 'holy man' by many people in his group. The Crusaders have prayer groups in the cities of Panaji, Margao, and Vasco and offices in Vasco and Panaji. The Vasco office has a media centre where they sell Christian devotional audio cassettes, CDs, and other literature. They also have teams that go to give Charismatic retreats in remote parts of Goa such as Pernem and various parts of the world.

From the beginning, the Crusaders had the Pallottine[6] priests in Chicalim as their spiritual guides and the Pallotine provincial had requested the bishop of the Archdiocese of Goa to give them recognition. According to one of the core group members of the Crusaders, the leader and some other members of the group had also met the bishop to ask for official recognition, but he refused saying that if he recognized them he would have to grant recognition to many other independent groups. Another reason why 'the Crusaders' do not have official recognition is because they do not want to be under the GST. Every prayer group that wants to be part of the official CCR has to register itself under the GST and submit to the rules and regulations of the GST, which include having elections every three years and submitting accounts of their financial transactions for audit. It appears that the Crusaders are not ready for that. Besides these two prominent preachers, there are many other Charismatic preachers and ministries operating independently in Goa.

The CCR was started by lay people, independent of the Church hierarchy, but over time the ecclesiastical authorities have tried to regulate, institutionalize, and set clear guidelines for the functioning of the Renewal. The CCR has always preached channels of communication, in which the divine is outside priestly control—a form of personalized grace—and thus comes across as challenging the authority of the Church in the mediation of grace. With the establishment of parish-based prayer groups that are regulated by the local parish priest and other

[6] The Pallottines Society of the Catholic Apostolate is a religious institute of the Catholic Church founded in 1835 by the Roman priest Vincent Pallotti (hence the name 'Pallottines). They are involved in social and pastoral ministries with a special emphasis on lay ministry.

monitoring bodies such as the GST and the NST at the national level, the ecclesiastical authorities have ensured some control over the personalized charisma of the CCR. The power of the disciplining activities of social institutions such as family, school, and Church and ecclesiastical laws implant 'true' Christian dispositions (Asad 1993: 35). However, independent Charismatic preachers such as Johnson and Edmund have defied the Church's attempt to implant these true Catholic dispositions and control the mediation of grace between humans and God. This has resulted in sanctions against them such as barring them from preaching in parishes or at GST-sponsored Charismatic programmes, refusing them official recognition, and denying them other facilities and privileges accorded to the 'official' Charismatic preachers. The tussle between the Church authorities and independent Charismatic preachers is a reflection of the dialectical process involving institutionalized and personalized grace. This tussle is illustrated in the incident that took place in the village of Sao Joao de Areal in South Goa.

Conflict in Sao Joao de Areal

Sao Joao de Areal is a village in Salcete taluka having a population of 10,229, of which more than 51 per cent are Christians (according to the 2011 Census). In June 2007, on the invitation of a female Catholic parishioner of Sao Joao de Areal, a lay Charismatic preacher tried to organize a retreat in her house. The Catholics in her neighbourhood on noticing the tent erected outside her house and the gospel music coming from the loudspeakers reacted angrily because they thought that the Believers were having a prayer meeting in their locality. As the news spread about the Believers' prayer meeting, the local Catholics gathered and forcefully removed the tent and the sound system arranged for the prayer meeting. Police had to rush to the scene, as the entire area became tense and some policemen guarded the woman's house for several days as a precautionary measure. The independent preacher wanted to organize the meeting at any cost, while the local Catholics threatened to disrupt the meeting if it took place. Finally, the police resolved the case by denying permission to the preacher to have the programme there due to security reasons.

Fr Joseph Silva, the convenor of the DCST who later went on a fact-finding mission, found that the independent preacher had several beliefs that were in contradiction to the Catholic faith such as regarding the Blessed Sacrament as an idol, not accepting the 'Holy Mary' prayer since it is not in the Bible, and not going for mass on Sundays. Citing these reasons, Fr Joseph reported to the bishop that he was not a Catholic preacher. The above exercise shows that deciding who is a Catholic on the ground is not an easy matter! The bishop issued a statement that that independent preacher should not be called to preach in any of the Catholic parishes or institutions. The Church establishment, by defining this man as a 'counterfeit' Catholic and passing sanctions against him, seems to be indicating that Foucault's pastoral power, which is able to guide people to salvation, is not present in him. According to Fr Joseph, the preacher used to organize several meetings in different places and many people used to attend them, but after this incident even the independent Charismatic preachers who used to call him for their programmes, stopped calling him since the Church hierarchy had officially declared that he was not a Catholic preacher.

The Sao Joao de Areal controversy was an eye-opener for the Church authorities who, after careful study of the Church doctrine, came up with clear-cut guidelines regulating retreats preached by independent preachers, which was published in the press. The independent preachers have to be invited by the bishop or priests to preach a retreat. They cannot preach independent of the Church. The Church maintains that the mandate of the priests is to preach, since their whole training and formation prepares them to preach the word of God. Through the sacraments of baptism and confirmation, lay people are duty-bound to be witnesses to Jesus through the priest's words, actions, and life, but not have the right to preach. According to Canon Law, lay people can be invited to preach, but it is not their right. This dispute has prompted the ecclesiastical authorities to issue these guidelines in which the basic principle is that lay people have to be called by the parish priest, as they cannot, on their own, organize services in the Churches. When the independent Charismatic preachers organize their programmes without the consent of the Church, the guidelines state that they cannot have mass and confessions in those programmes.

The Sao Joao de Areal dispute and the resultant stand of the ecclesiastical authorities illustrate the struggle between independent Charismatic preachers and the Church authorities concerning production of truth and mediation of grace. On the one hand, the non-clerical

Charismatic preachers believe that having received the baptism of the Holy Spirit they have the divine sanction to preach and teach wherever they wish to, and the Catholic Church has no right to decide who can or cannot preach. But on the other, the ecclesiastical authorities, while not aspiring for total uniformity within the CCR, try to regulate and control the production of religious truth by the lay Charismatic preachers to certain specified and well-defined orthodox patterns. This regulation of various Charismatic practices into categories of orthodoxy and heresy, noticed in the above-mentioned dispute, are also seen in Asad's description of the role of authorizing discourses in the creation of religion in the Middle Ages that rejected or accepted pagan practices, authenticated particular miracles and relics, authorized shrines, regularized popular social movements into rule-following orders (for example the Franciscans), or denounced them as heresy (Asad 1993: 37–8). The struggle of the medieval Church to subject all practice to the unified authority of the one true Church, and the Sao Joao de Areal incident, in which the Church tried to regulate the practice of independent lay Charismatic preachers, both illustrate the larger tussle over control of the production of truth and mediation and dispensation of grace.

Physical Space

Often, religious conflicts begin with disputes over physical entities such as land, finances, and so on. It has been discussed earlier how the neo-Pentecostal sects struggle to find a suitable permanent venue for their Church rituals, having to move from place to place due to various reasons, especially due to opposition from the dominant Catholic and Hindu communities. Besides getting place for conducting their Sunday rituals, the neo-Pentecostals also find it difficult to bury their dead. A cemetery, which is the Christian resting place of the dead and is associated with the saying 'rest in peace', is ironically a place where there is no peace even for the dead. Religious wars have often been fought on the turf of cemeteries and gruesome acts such as exhuming bodies of the dead and damaging graves have been part of such conflicts.

In Goa, too, the cemetery has been the site of conflict, illustrated through the Gauncar–non-Gauncar tussle in the Catholic Church in Cuncolim village. Several despicable acts were committed by both sides such as the exhuming and desecrating of the body of a non-Gauncar, the assault and molestation of a non-Gauncar woman by a Gauncar, and the boycott of the novenas and feast of Our Lady of Health by non-Gauncars (Miranda 2000). When a neo-Pentecostal died in the village of Mandur in the 1990s, Jacinto Vaz, the late Konkani dramatist—and a most amiable character on stage—led a movement to deny the 'apostate' burial in the parish cemetery (Cabral 1994). Julie D'Silva, a 'certified pioneer' (a prized title of the congregation) of the Jehovah's Witnesses had difficulty burying her husband, James, also a Witness, in the Catholic cemetery (Cabral 1994). Finally, she paid ₹10,000 and bought two graves in the St Inez cemetery in Panaji, which is a municipal burial ground, so that she also could be buried by her husband's side.

Since the Catholic Church does not allow its cemeteries to be used for the burial of non-Catholics, the Pentecostals do not bury their dead in Catholic cemeteries, which are normally attached to the parish Church. In the 1970s, when the neo-Pentecostal sect Vasco Brethren Assembly came up, they had no place to bury their dead and so petitioned the government, who gave them land for a cemetery. Since then all the Protestant denominations, including the Born-Again Christians, bury their dead in that cemetery in Vasco. Some of them also bury their dead in the St Inez municipal burial ground in Panaji.

Another religious conflict that was fought over land and territory was the conflict at Batim, a village in Tiswadi taluka with a strong Catholic presence. The Youth with a Mission (YWAM), an inter-denominational Christian organization, had bought property adjoining the Catholic Church in Batim from a Catholic priest, with whom the leader of YWAM was acquainted. The place was used by YWAM as a training centre for all their youth programmes. Once the local Catholics came to know that they were Born-Again Christians, they warned them to close the place and leave, saying that Born-Again Christians were like a disease, and so before they became a plague that spread to all the Catholics, they should get out of there.

The Christians refused to leave Batim since they had bought the place. They tried to reason with the Catholics, assuring them that they would not share the gospel with anybody there, but only have their training centre. But the Catholics were not convinced and one Sunday after mass, all the Catholic parishioners, young, old, women, and children, came to the YWAM centre and broke everything in the house, including the vehicles, and beat up all the Christians. The Catholics also threatened them that they would attack any Christian who came to that place for training. Due to the destruction of their house and property and the fear of being attacked in the future, they sold the place and moved out from Batim. While the main reason for this conflict was the issue of religious jurisdiction and territory (Born-Again Christians moving into a Catholic territory), the visibility and physical proximity of the Christians (the YWAM property was just adjoining the Catholic Church) played an important role in aggravating the issue. In addition, the fact that many people, especially youngsters, were coming to the YWAM centre for training, which was perceived by the Catholics as a proselytizing activity, increased their anxiety that they would be targeted next. Melton (2004: 16–35), while enumerating behaviour patterns of new religious groups that are found to be unacceptable to the religious establishment, picks out aggressive proselytization as the main action that causes a group to be declared a cult, especially if the proselytizing efforts target older mainline religious groups (a practice known as sheep stealing).

Both of the above-mentioned cases, the cemetery of the Catholic Church and YWAM land in Batim, involved a bitter dispute over physical space resulting from the collision of two worlds of perception and self-presentation (Coleman 2000: 137). According to Lefebvre, any given local space is a tripartite synthesis of physical, mental, and social spaces that operate simultaneously. In the case of denying burial in Catholic cemeteries to those Catholics who left the Church and joined neo-Pentecostal sects, the notion of the neo-Pentecostal as an apostate or betrayer of the faith leads to the transformation of the physical space of the cemetery into an external marker of Catholic identity meant exclusively for dead Catholics. Similarly, in the case of the land belonging to the YWAM in Batim, the perception among the local Catholics that the neo-Pentecostals are aggressive evangelizers and a threat to the Catholic community charged and transformed that physical space into an arena of religious contestation.

Religious Contestations between Neo-Pentecostals and Catholics in Siolim

A religious battle has been going on for several years between the WRM Church and the Catholic Church in Tropa, Siolim, spanning across physical, social, and spiritual or metaphysical spaces, and involving ecclesiastical, civil and law enforcement authorities, and the media. The pastor of the WRM was the leader of the Konkani Catholic Charismatic prayer group in Mapusa, before he broke away in 1998 and formed his own sect, taking many members of the prayer group with him. While many healings, miracles, and instances of people falling down were reported from the prayer group, according to the local Catholics he was not practising Catholic teachings and was influenced by neo-Pentecostal beliefs. When the parish priest tried to stop this, he, with several other group members, left the Church. This illustrates the struggle between the independent, lay Charismatic preachers and the Catholic Church hierarchy over who controls of the production of truth and mediation of grace.

Unlike most of the neo-Pentecostal Churches, who are based in the cities and conduct their prayer meetings there, the WRM pastor converted his old residence, where he used to run a bar and restaurant, into what is now the Church of Five Pillars, which is very close to a Catholic Church, Our Lady of Consolation for the Persecuted Church, Tropa (see Figure 6.2). The name of his Church comes from the five white pillars under the cross at the front symbolizing Christ's stigmata. His boast was that nowhere in Goa would anyone find a Believer's Church

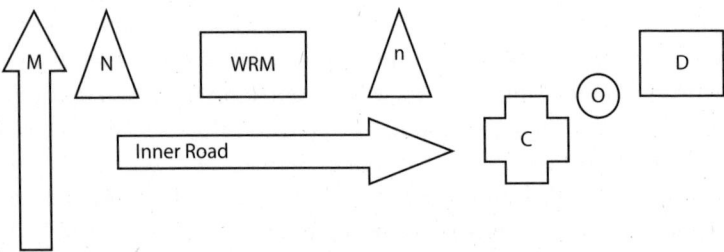

Figure 6.2   Map of Worship Place of Neo-Pentecostals and Catholics in Siolim

Note: M = main road of Tropa, Siolim; N = Hindu neighbour; WRM = the pastor's old house, which has been converted into the WRM Church, the venue of their prayer meetings and containing the pastor's office; n = another Hindu neighbour; C = Church of Our Lady of Consolation for the Persecuted, Tropa (Catholic Church); D = the pastor's residence; and O = disputed area.

Source: Based on author's observations and interviews with the WRM pastor and the parish priest of Tropa.

so close to a Catholic Church, given the antagonistic attitude the two groups has for one another.

Wounded history and injured memory play an important role in understanding this conflict. The Catholics in the village felt doubly betrayed since the WRM pastor not only left the Catholic Church, but as leader of the CCR prayer group he also persuaded other members of the group to leave and join his new sect. This sense of betrayal increased when he converted his old residence into a Church and began conducting prayer meetings there, right under the nose of the Catholic Church. Since his prayer meetings began more or less at the same time as the Sunday mass in the Catholic Church, the frustration of the local Catholics grew seeing so many neo-Pentecostals coming for the services and having to bear with the loud music coming from the WRM Church. As the parish priest of Tropa Church mentioned, 'Since the two places are so close to each other, their loud music would disturb us.' The physical proximity and the larger visibility of the neo-Pentecostal place further contributed to the conflict between the two groups. Perera (1998: 48–9) describes two incidents of members of some new Christian groups distributing Bible tracts and other literature at a temple festival in Nepal and a government-sponsored Buddhist exhibition in Sri Lanka to highlight the inability or the lack of interest of some evangelical groups to pay attention to how religious competitions may be perceived by people on the basis of historical memory and issues such as sacred space. This lack of sensitivity or disregard for the perception of other religious communities is noticeable in the above instance of the neo-Pentecostals conducting their religious services so close in space and time to the Catholic Sunday service, given the prevailing tension between them.

The first conflict between the Catholics and neo-Pentecostals in Siolim took place on the night of 31 December 2000. The WRM was having an open-air prayer service, which was supposed to end before the midnight mass began in the Catholic Church, so that there would be no disturbance. However, just before the worship began, a group of Catholics barged into the place and attacked the worshippers. The Catholics, who were led by the Sarpanch of the village, also vandalized the place. The WRM pastor immediately filed an FIR with the police and took recourse to legal means to resolve the issue. After some time, things cooled down and for several years peace prevailed between the two communities, until another dispute broke out in 2007 over a piece of land located between the Church property and the pastor's house (marked as O in Figure 6.2). While the pastor claimed the land belonged to him and had the Portuguese ownership papers to prove it, the Catholic priest argued that according to the panchayat records the land was a common pathway for people to walk. The trouble began when the Church authorities opened a gate from their compound wall onto the disputed land and in retaliation the pastor dug a trench in front of the gate to block them. Some of the parishioners (members of the parish council and *fabrica*[7]) reacted to this by assaulting his workers and threatening his wife.

According to the pastor, in the ensuing standoff he approached some members of the parish council to ask for a meeting with the Church authorities, but in vain. He also wrote letters to the archbishop, the panchayat, and the priest in charge of the fabrica, describing the attack on their workers and the abusive language used. Since that incident, there has been an uneasy truce between the neo-Pentecostals and the Catholics in Siolim. In the light of the repeated disputes with the WRM sect, the priest argues that the entry of born-again sects in the village has disrupted its religious space, which had remained peaceful for centuries. Therefore, such groups should be banned from entering at all.

Another issue that has fed into the above-mentioned conflict is the insider–outsider tussle. According to the priest, while most of those who came to WRM services were outsiders (from outside Siolim, besides many non-Goans), the Catholic services were for the local parishioners. The entry of the Born-Again Christian groups into Goa is linked with the influx of outsiders into Goa, who came to work in construction, mining, tourism, fishing, and other industries that emerged in post-liberation Goa. This large influx of workers from neighbouring states has led to Goans feeling outnumbered and disadvantaged in their own region. The resultant 'anti-outsider' feeling and 'Goa for Goans' sentiment (Newman 2001: 69) has translated into anger and resentment against the new Christian groups, which are often headed by non-Goans, with a substantial number of its members being outsiders,

---

[7] A fabrica is a trust that manages the revenue and property of a Church.

and are viewed by the local Catholics as catering primarily to the poor migrant labourers from beyond Goa's borders.

Besides the control of religious and physical space in Siolim, the conflict between the neo-Pentecostals and the Catholic Church is also played out in the landscape of media. The neo-Pentecostals are convinced that the daily newspaper *Herald* is pro-Catholic, with a strong anti-Believer bias. Hence, they feel the newspaper blows up any small controversy concerning the neo-Pentecostals and never publishes anything positive about them. The neo-Pentecostals accuse the Catholic Church of using media and culture to target them, citing the example of a Konkani drama titled 'He Polloi Mhoji Mai' (Look, this is my mother), based on Mother Mary, which was staged at the Catholic Church in Tropa and contained some derogatory remarks against them.

The 'Renewal', the pastoral bulletin of the Archdiocese of Goa, has repeatedly espoused the official views of the Catholic Church in Goa and the views of individual Catholics on the issue of the emergence of the neo-Pentecostal sects. It devoted an entire issue, dated 1–15 October 1997, to the topic of sects and cults and the general tone of the articles and views was one of criticism and condemnation of the new sects as creating divisions, leading to fundamentalism and fanaticism. The official position of the Catholic Church viewing the neo-Pentecostals as divisive and harmful in Goa is similar to the situation in the Philippines (85 per cent of the people are Roman Catholics), where the Catholic Bishops' Conference of the Philippines issued a pastoral letter titled, 'Hold fast to what is good' in January 1989 forewarning their folk against fundamentalist groups. Like the conflict in Siolim, there are other such tussles taking place between the dominant Catholic community and the neo-Pentecostals in different villages of Goa, and media and culture play an important role in these disputes. Seul (1999: 564) points out that religion does not cause conflicts between religious groups, but it frequently supplies the fault-lines along which inter-group identity and resource competition occurs. In the case of the Siolim conflict too, issues of ownership of land, the insider–outsider notion, the threat to village peace, memories of the wounds inflicted, and claims over use of public utilities have led to the conflict that developed on the fault-lines of a Catholic–Believer religious divide. The above conflict has been fought on different terrains and factors such as caste rivalry, class equations, family disputes, insider outsider differences, and language and identity politics have played an important role in igniting and aggravating such conflicts, thus echoing the Foucaultian position that power is not an absolute, universal thing that acts on people and situations uniformly, but is found working in different, multiple sites of social relationships and networks.

Christian Fundamentalism

In the discussion so far, we have noticed that the entry of neo-Pentecostal groups into Goa has led to increased religious polarization and disputes. This has also led to the fragmentation of the religious space in Goa. The Catholic priest of Siolim argues that the religious space of the village, which has been peaceful for centuries, has been disrupted thanks to the entry of the neo-Pentecostal groups. This raises the question of whether the entry of neo-Pentecostal groups into any religious space is disruptive due to their fundamentalist nature. Today, more than ever before, fundamentalist movements of various types are highly visible and active in the world. Religious fundamentalism has generally been understood in the Western academic world as a form of Protestant Christianity that promotes the inerrancy of the Bible and the imminent Second Coming of Christ and this template has been used to understand all other fundamentalisms (Almond, Appleby, and Sivan 2003). The origin of the term 'fundamentalism' is traced by Almond, Appleby, and Sivan (2003: 1–2) to the 1920 edition of the Northern Baptist periodical *The Watchman-Examiner* in the USA, whose editor described himself and a group of conservative evangelical Protestants as militants willing to have a battle royale to preserve what they perceive as the fundamentals of the Christian faith from the evolutionists and biblical critics infecting mainline seminaries and colleges. Fundamentalism was the name given to this religious–ideological movement that sprang up in the USA before World War I, aiming at a strictly literal understanding of the Bible (especially of Genesis), which developed into a collective conservative Protestant movement. Their resistance to modern forms of secularization and concern about the erosion of religion is a defining common feature of religious fundamentalism shared across religious, cultural, and political boundaries. Fundamentalist movements form in reaction to, and in defence against, the processes and consequences of secularization and modernization, which have penetrated the larger religious community.

Almond, Appleby, and Sivan (2003: 90) classify fundamentalist movements into three categories—unmixed religious movements such as Abrahamic fundamentalism, whose primary interest is protection of a religious way of life; ethno-religious and nationalist movements that have mixed memberships and goals such as the Hindu and Buddhist movements; and finally movements that are identified as fundamentalist by the media because of their religious trappings, militance, and visibility, but do not qualify as fundamentalisms according to their definition. Various forms of Pentecostalism in Latin America are included in the last category. N. Ammerman (Almond, Appleby, and Sivan 2003: 93–7) gives four characteristics of North American Protestant fundamentalism. These Bible-inspired core tenets are: evangelism aimed at salvation of souls, belief in the inerrancy of Scripture, belief in pre-millennialism (Bible-based knowledge of the End Times), and separatism (separation from those whose beliefs and lives are suspect). Christian fundamentalisms, strictly speaking, do not include Pentecostal Churches or movements, which rely a lot on the inspiration and guidance of the Holy Spirit. However, the twentieth century has been characterized by new syncretic forms of fundamentalism, in which Christian Pentecostals and Bible-believing fundamentalists find common ground for political purposes. While some authors analytically distinguish between Pentecostals and fundamentalists on the grounds that the latter aim to preserve the canon and the fundamentals, while the emphasis of the former is on the charismata of the spirit, my findings from this research match with Thomas's (2008) work in Chennai, which found that Christian triumphalism was present in both the more traditional as well as the recent Pentecostal ministries.

Thus, Thomas expands the definition of Christian fundamentalism to include not only those who ratify an unwavering, strict interpretation of the scriptures, but all those Christian groups and sects that are united in their belief that Christian triumphalism is mandated in the gospels and that Christians are duty-bound to translate this vision into political reality by various possible means, including engaging in and supporting Christian conversions. Drawing from the above definitions of Almond, Appleby and Sivan, Ammerman, and Thomas, the distinct characteristics that Christian fundamentalists exhibit are the following:

1. Belief in the inerrancy of scripture.
2. Evangelism aimed at conversions and salvation of souls.

3. Concern with erosion of Christianity in society, which leads to a vision of a Christian state and a Christian world.
4. Belief in pre-millennialism and Christian triumphalism found in the gospels.

We will now investigate whether the above-mentioned four characteristics are present in the neo-Pentecostal movement in Goa, and if the neo-Pentecostal Churches fit into Almond's category of new syncretic forms of fundamentalism.

A strict biblical fundamentalism is characteristic of the neo-Pentecostal sects in Goa as discussed earlier in Chapter 5. They follow a strictly literal understanding of the Bible and do not accept scientific biblical exegesis. The biblical fundamentalism of neo-Pentecostals in Goa leads them to regard their scriptural tradition as God-inspired while all other religious traditions are human-inspired. This leads them to aggressive and urgent evangelization and proselytization in a bid to save others who are lost, which polarizes the socio-religious space of Goa, leading to conflict situations with the Catholic and Hindu communities. The religious views of the neo-Pentecostals concerning salvation, other religious communities and sacred texts, and inter-religious dialogue are strictly non-syncretic, exclusivist, and extreme.

The neo-Pentecostals are against inter-religious dialogue, which they feel will not achieve anything and this is illustrated in the view of one of the members of the NFI Church:

> We are evangelists at heart and so we will share about God's love. I know I have the true God, I have God's salvation. I will directly tell the Hindus and Muslims about the gospel and that will crash the whole dialogue. There is no meeting point. I believe that my religion is the only true one and the Bible is the only word of God. There is no doubt at all. So where do we meet? I feel I will not be able to dialogue. Paul did not try to dialogue with the heathens or the Gods of the Roman Empire. Like Paul, I, too, say, 'Woe to me if I don't preach the gospel.' Finally we have to go and tell them the gospel. That is our commission.[8]

The neo-Pentecostals, beside their concern for the salvation of the pagans, are very much concerned with the decline of the Catholic

---

[8] Interview with a member of the NFI Church, Panaji, on 25 September 2008.

Church, which over history has degenerated into man-made traditions. This leads them to envisage planting a Born-Again Church in every village of Goa by 2010 and capturing Goa and India for Christ. At the same time, the minority status of Christians in Goa and in India implies that any pan-Indian Christian political project will remain a case of wishful thinking. Though the neo-Pentecostals deny that there is any political agenda to their purely religious, soteriological movement, their ethno-national goals are noticeable in how their pastors often exhort their congregations to dream big dreams, such as seeing the whole of India following Christ or seeing their ideological enemies from the Hindu right-wing such as Thackeray and Advani chanting the name of Christ. This political thrust was also noticeable in the efforts made by the entire congregation of the ROLC, including the pastor, in the campaign of one of the ROLC members, who stood for the Municipal Corporation elections. Besides accompanying the candidate every evening after work for door-to-door campaigning, the members of the Church also helped out on the election day.

The eschatological vision of the neo-Pentecostals that envisages them living in the End Times, and the vivid description of the End Times and the Final Judgement reveal that they are a pre-millennial movement. They believe that these End Times are a period of blessings and by public positive confession of scriptural texts they can unlock the triumphalism found in the gospels and acquire healings, good health, prosperity, and wealth for themselves. On the one hand, the Born-Again Christian groups in Goa show Pentecostal characteristics of ecstatic and emotive forms of worship, orality of tradition, and explicit manifestations of the gifts and charisms of the Holy Spirit, and on the other hand, they follow a strictly literal understanding of the Bible with aggressive proselytizing aimed at expansion of their organization and realizing the vision of a Christian Goa and India. The neo-Pentecostal groups in Goa show all the above-mentioned characteristics of Christian fundamentalism and thus fit into Almond's category of new syncretic forms of fundamentalism.

* * *

In this chapter, we have explored notions of power, authority, hierarchy, difference, and conflict in the context of the CCR and neo-Pentecostalism in Goa. Foucault's propositions about power as an aspect of social relations, which are found in multiple localized sites of social networks, and his pastoral power, which is soteriological, individualizing, coextensive and continuous with life and linked with the production of truth, are used as the theoretical yardstick to analyse the power relations among the neo-Pentecostals and Catholic Charismatics. The power relations among the neo-Pentecostals are intricately linked with the production of truth and mediation of grace and, thus, fit in with Foucault's pastoral power. Power in neo-Pentecostalism is derived from the working of the Holy Spirit and all power struggles in society are only a reflection of the spiritual warfare between good and evil forces. Neo-Pentecostals make a qualitative distinction between the good power of Christ and the evil power of Satan.

Human history is construed as the creation of human beings by God with dominion over the Earth, which is followed by their fall and resultant loss of the dominion over the Earth. This fall is offset by the entry of Jesus Christ, the son of God, who by his own sacrifice disarms the authority of Satan and restores the former pristine glory of humankind. Thus, neo-Pentecostals become powerful when they submit to the authority of Jesus, the King, and these images of power and authority empower them to aggressively evangelize and proselytize, even in the face of persecution and opposition and despite their small numbers.

The pastor is the final decision-making authority in the neo-Pentecostal sect since the faithful believe that God has given him special access to the production of truth and the mediation of grace. In spite of greater participation by the people in Church ritual, compared to the mainline Churches, the neo-Pentecostal pastor controls key areas of the ritual such as breaking the word of God, which involves production and interpretation of religious truth. Competing claims and disputes over the extent and legitimacy of the power and authority of the pastor leads to sect fission. The construction of the physical space in the WRM Church reflects the authoritative status of the pastor in relation to the congregation.

The two cases of Catholic Charismatic women illustrate the, though rather limited and still regulated, liberating space provided by the CCR for women to enter in the predominantly male Church ritual. One woman, an ordinary government schoolteacher with no religious or theological training, through her involvement in the Charismatic

Renewal, was able to reach out to so many village folk in Goa through the Life in the Spirit retreats and is regarded as the mother of the Konkani Charismatic movement in Goa. The other woman, a house-wife with only high-school education, was able to develop her natural gifts of preaching, teaching, and leadership without any formal theo-logical training. She was also entrusted with important responsibilities in the parish and in the Charismatic movement.

The Pentecostal–Charismatic movement, by entering the religious sphere of Goa has attempted to reform Church rituals, challenge the traditions of the Catholic Church, and also promote an evangelistic agenda of preaching and proselytizing. This has led to contestations and conflicts with both the Catholic and Hindu communities. We have explored these contestations that have occurred in a rapidly changing Goan society in different spaces such as social, spiritual or metaphysical, and physical and that have covered different terrains such as family, village, school, cemetery, and media, by studying specific instances of conflict in Sao Joao de Areal, Batim, and Siolim villages. These conflicts have centred round the production of truth and mediation of grace and have resulted in the shrinking of the physical space, the social boycott of the neo-Pentecostals, and even violent acts in the name of religion. These conflicts have emphasized healings and exorcisms, highlighted the insider–outsider issue, and have curbed the practices of independent CCR preachers.

Neo-Pentecostal sects in Goa, which exhibit Pentecostal character-istics of inspiration of the Holy Spirit, a literal and fundamentalist understanding of the Bible, aggressive, provocative, and urgent evan-gelization with ethno-national goals of a Christian state, and belief in pre-millennialism and Christian triumphalism can be characterized as fundamentalist, according to the definitions of Almond, Appleby, and Sivan, Thomas, and Ammerman. The neo-Pentecostal notion of a militant Church with strict non-syncretic and exclusivist views on salva-tion and other religions led to the churning up of the religious space of Goa. As Perera (1998: 46) pertinently notes: The mere non-existence of visibly destructive processes of conflict or violence emanating from the competitiveness between new evangelical religions on the one hand, and Hinduism, Buddhism, or more established Christianities on the other, does not mean the non-existence of tension and violence in times to come.

7 Tying Loose Ends
Concluding Remarks

Though every chapter has some concluding remarks, there is a need to reinforce, qualify, and tie together the different strands of thought in order to assemble together a mosaic of the contemporary Pentecostal–Charismatic movement in Goa. However, this picture of the movement may soon be outdated, given 'the state of flux in which the movement finds itself' (Wright 1997: 61). This work on the advent and progress of Pentecostalism in contemporary Goan society has made forays into the area of sociology of religion known as 'new religious movements'. Since new religious movements are generally pitted against the mainstream religious establishment and occupy a contested religious space, this work has revolved around themes such as power, identity, evangelization, authoritative discourses, sacred and profane symbols, production of truth and mediation of grace, and terrains of conflict. The mission, the NTC, the dualistic spiritual world view, and the formation of a Charismatic habitus that structures and guides the everyday life practices and processes of individual Believers are also important strands woven into this book to create a tapestry of Pentecostalism.

The first theme explored in this study was the question of the paternity of the neo-Pentecostal and Catholic Charismatic groups in Goa. While many features of these religious groups show signs of Pentecostal paternity, the creation of these groups has been shaped by specific socio-historical changes and processes in post-colonial Goan society such as rapid urbanization, economic development, massive in-migration, changing religious demography, and the changing face of the Catholic Church. The difficulties and dilemmas faced by the new state of Goa as it cut its umbilical cord with Portugal and tried to find its footing within the vast terrain of India led to the emergence of questions on Goan culture and identity and the insider–outsider tussle, which formed the signposts guided by which the global Pentecostal–Charismatic movement entered Goa. The history of the Pentecostal–Charismatic movement, from its origin in the revival movements of the nineteenth and twentieth centuries to present-day Goa, has revealed the polycentric origins and the global dimension of the movement—it is not just a Western American religious phenomenon. Thus, both the CCR and the neo-Pentecostal Churches in Goa distance themselves from global Pentecostalism and claim to be indigenous. In addition, the emergence of the post-denominational neo-Pentecostal Churches in contemporary Goan society represents a distinct break from the traditional Goan Catholic faith of nearly five centuries.

It is important to note that the CCR began in India not through priests, nuns, or theologians, but through laypeople and, in the case of Goa, through housewives. The emergence of the Pentecostal–Charismatic movement is an indication that ever since institutionalized religion has lost its monopoly on the sacred, individuals and communities who had previously enjoyed very little in the way of spiritual gifts or charisma have been claiming direct access to the sacred without the mediation of religious professionals. While the CCR is a movement mostly of natives and with an indigenous Goan identity, the entry of the neo-Pentecostal groups into Goa is linked with the influx of migrants who came to work in various industries that emerged in post-liberation Goa. The resultant assertion of Goan identity and the anti-outsider sentiment have led to the new groups occupying a turbulent and heavily contested religious space.

The entry of Catholicism into the state was facilitated by a conjunction of missionary activities, the political and military interests of the Portuguese, and a system of privileges that allowed the new faith to piggyback on the political clout of the colonial rulers. On the other hand, the sociology of conversion and expansion of Pentecostal–Charismatic Christianity that entered the region through the migrants reveals a different trajectory. While Catholicism in Goa until 1961 was identified as the powerful colonizer's religion and changed the political equations and local societal norms and cultural mores, Pentecostalism, which is not explicitly political in its orientation, slipped in rather unobtrusively. However, it must be noted that Pentecostalism's entry into Goa was facilitated by the changing face of the post-colonial Catholic Church and the changing religious composition and caste equations. Martin (2002: 167) terms Pentecostalism as a cultural revolution undertaken from below with no political theory to guide it, no political ideology to promote it, and no political system to protect it.

At the same time, the central themes of this movement such as spirit-empowerment, exclusive religious identity, and an expansionist agenda of proselytization with a pan-Indian Christian vision exhibit political overtones. Additionally, the fact that Pentecostalism sees itself as Christ's militant army, ready to venture to any part of India in order to counter and convert the Hindu fundamentalist forces that propagate anti-Christian, ethnonational goals of a Hindu India, contradicts the idea that it is merely a cultural revolution or a pietistic movement. The studies of Thomas (2008), Caplan (1987a), and my discussion in Chapter 7 reveal the potential of Christian fundamentalist groups and sects to create conflict, even though the minority status of Born-Again Christians in Goa and in India makes any pan-Indian Christian political project simply wishful thinking. Increasingly, Pentecostal–Charismatic groups in various parts of India have been blamed over the issue of conversions and their members and institutions have been targeted in attacks by Hindu fundamentalist forces. Three broad factors are involved in the disproportionate targeting of Pentecostals in the violence against Christians in India: (*a*) evangelical assertion and enthusiasm; (*b*) greater presence and participation of marginalized and vulnerable peoples in the movement; and (*c*) its counter-cultural posture (Bauman 2015: 71). This is also noticed in the numerous conflict situations between neo-Pentecostals and other religious communities and the resultant rupture of the peaceful religious space in Goa, which has been discussed in Chapter 7. That chapter has explored the contestations and conflicts occurring in a rapidly changing Goan society in different spaces such as social, spiritual or metaphysical, and physical, and covering different terrains such as family, village, school, cemetery, and media by studying specific instances of conflict in Sao Joao de Areal, Batim, and Siolim. While my book has tried to highlight this theme, more studies of new Christian groups and sects in other parts of India are required to generate a more nuanced and broader understanding of Christian fundamentalism.

This study, at the anthropological level, is an ethnographic exploration of the entire world—the real world and the world of symbols—of the neo-Pentecostals and Catholic Charismatics in Goa, following the multi-sited mode of ethnography. It charts the religious journey of a neophyte right from conversion and initiation into the new organization, exploring patterns of worship, world view, rites and rituals, and especially life-cycle rituals, till death. Thus the cultural patterns of any religion such as Pentecostal–Charismatic Christianity and its systems and complexes of symbols, discussed in Chapters 5 and 6, give meaning to and constitute the social and psychological reality of the adherents, both by shaping themselves to it and by shaping it to themselves (Geertz 1973). The attraction of Pentecostalism to new members, who are situated in a globalized world wherein 'times and seasonal rotations have been ruptured' is its religious image of being a 'Church on the move' or 'a going people', which corresponds to the circumstances of people migrating to cities (Martin 2002: 168). It is not surprising that the Pentecostal–Charismatic movement originated in the urban centres of India, as changes across space (geographic mobility) and changes over time (adaptation, assimilation) produce new religious forms (Williams 2005: 239–42).

The new supportive spiritual community of brothers and sisters born again in the spirit is like a raft in a stormy ocean. It also compensates for the rupture of kinship ties as well as the social and cultural ostracization invariably brought on by conversion. In the discussion in Chapter 3 on conversions and adherence to new Christian sects, the various cases examined revealed that no single causal factor could account for conversions, but that a combination of leading and facilitating factors, generally situated in the context of everyday life, led people to join these sects. While poorer neo-Pentecostals are helped financially either by the Church or by other richer members, it does not follow that money and inducements are the main pull factors for conversion.

In the case of both neo-Pentecostals and Catholic Charismatics, members were recruited through public and private evangelism, healings, crisis events, and micro-social networks of kinship relations and personal contacts. Coleman (2000) suggests that the motivations of people for joining a group may differ from those that keep them within the religious community and he points to the development of a globalizing Charismatic habitus as one of the key reasons for remaining in the group. This habitus, in the case of neo-Pentecostals in Goa, was formed through intensive socializing during their weekly praise and worship, prayer cell meetings, and the Encounter with God programme and in the case of Catholic Charismatics was formed during their prayer group meetings, charismatic programmes, and retreats such as the Potta retreat and Life in the Spirit seminar.

Members of the neo-Pentecostal movement shaped by the Charismatic habitus, based on the New Testament values, perceive the world in dualistic and spiritual terms. God provides a life plan for each member, complete with a 'spiritual career' or 'a calling' (Coleman 2000: 231). Activities such as 'service to the Church', the Sunday praise and worship, and preaching and listening to the word of God (regarded as both canon and charisma) are elevated to the level of sacred activity, while Hindu practices such as yoga and Indian forms of meditation, worldly music, inter-religious dialogue, and certain lifestyle habits and practices are taboo. These hard-line and counter-cultural beliefs and practices backed by the charismatic authority of the pastorate are not uniformly accepted by all the Charismatics. Among the neo-Pentecostal Churches and especially in the CCR, these beliefs are forced to engage in complex negotiations with competing discourses, emerging from the older tradition of ecumenical and inter-religious dialogue found in the post-Vatican II Catholic Church and mainline Protestant denominations.

This habitus, on the one hand, orients them to think that they are in the world but not of the world, and leads them to seek spiritual solutions for the material problems of everyday life. On the other hand, it encourages Believers not to retreat from the world, but to appropriate its institutions and assets; and not to avoid consumerism, but to incorporate it within expansive modes of religious attachment, thus blurring the boundaries between the material and the spiritual (Coleman 2000: 236). The prosperity gospel that gives spiritual legitimation to practices of consumption and downplays suffering and the imagery of the cross is promoted along with miracles, visions, prophecies, and exorcisms in a Pentecostal world of spirits and demons drawn from the biblical times.

The dualistic spiritual world view of the Believers also influences their notions of divinity, which is discussed in Chapter 5. They worship a God who is at once both loving and vengeful, a God of wrath juxtaposed with a loving, emotional, and jealous God, a God who is both within the self, thus the temple of the Holy Spirit, and a powerful, active force intervening all over the world. Jesus Christ occupies the highest position in the divine hierarchy of Charismatic Christianity, though devotion to Mary has crept into the CCR prayer groups in response to the criticism that they were more Protestant than Catholic. Their dualistic world also comprises a pantheon of the demonic that includes Satan and his fallen angels as well as the gods of the non-Christian divine pantheons. This dualism is also noticed in the Pentecostal mapping of the universe into reached (Christian) and unreached (demonic) territories, a global system of sacralized and demonic societies and the reading of history as an epic cosmic battle between the forces of good and evil, highlighting only the Christological periods of the New Testament Age and the present End Times.

Due to the Charismatic habitus, the neo-Pentecostal life-cycle rituals are not celebrated in accordance with the biological clock and so differ from other religious traditions. At the same time, the findings of the fieldwork indicate that rituals persist because certain Catholic notions and practices regarding birth, marriage, and death as well as kinship patterns are retained by the neo-Pentecostals after being suitably 'Christianized'. The neo-Pentecostals connect birth with death through the understanding of baptism as a funeral service, wherein the neophyte buries their old self and is born again in Christ. The presence of religious endogamy in neo-Pentecostal marriages reveals how they have adapted Hindu practices of purity and pollution, but the notion of caste pollution has been replaced by notions of religious pollution. Since the neo-Pentecostals follow a different biological clock, the last judgement is a more liminal experience than death and so their funeral services are not very important and elaborate.

Besides being an ethnographic exploration of the everyday lived-out reality of the Pentecostal–Charismatic world, this research also focused on the factors responsible for the growth and success of the

Pentecostal–Charismatic movement and its impact on Goan society and culture. Some anthropological studies on societies in which Christianity has entered recently analyse Christianity as an organic reality living within the social structure: it both impacts and is reinterpreted within the local system of meanings and religious world views. It is within this paradigm that this study is also a comparative analysis of two different living strands of the Pentecostal–Charismatic movement in Goa, namely neo-Pentecostalism and the CCR.

As mentioned in the first chapter, the factors that contributed to the growth and success of Pentecostal–Charismatic Christianity are varied and complex. Its strength has been in its flexibility and adaptability, which has allowed it to constantly negotiate between its local identity as an autonomous Born-Again Church and its global corporate identity as the universal Church of Christ; its fundamentalist and anti-modern trends and its globalized, thoroughly modern, and even postmodern ideas. Additionally, in order to maintain a spiritual world view that appeals to and maintains continuity with local, indigenous religious world views, Pentecostal–Charismatic Christianity has had to dilute its strong anti-syncretic stance that emphasizes the exclusive and the bounded. Another important factor that has contributed to the rise of neo-Pentecostalism in Goa has been its success in portraying itself as a viable alternative to other religious models: a faith that is more traditional, and faithful to the scriptures and the original divine revelation than other faiths. It has also succeeded in offering rites and rituals, liturgy, and modes of worship that are more animated, spontaneous, and participative. These practices celebrate experiences and provide group therapy and spiritual succour to today's working people, overloaded with responsibility and stress and struggling to find meaning in modern de-sacralized societies. Given that Pentecostal beliefs and practices are experientialist and oral in nature, Hollenweger in the late 1970s contrasted the oral forms of Pentecostal theology that were promulgated via songs, poems, testimonies, and dances with the standard, literary Western forms of theology. However, in recent years, Pentecostal denominations have codified their theological beliefs in dogmatic statements of faith and this written tradition has led to an explosion of Pentecostal theological scholarship. Many of these theological reflections are generated from a triad of sources: the texts of scriptures, the community of the

Church, and pneumatology (Mark Cartledge in Robeck and Young 2011: 254–72).

The guiding aim of the NTC, according to them, informs the corporate identity of the neo-Pentecostal movement and the construction of individual identities, which are built around their everyday life practices. This identity formation involves marking of clear-cut boundaries with the Hindu and Catholic communities. Neo-Pentecostals elevate their identity over the mainline religious identities through the appropriation and application to the present times of the dualistic spiritual world view of the biblical times. According to this dualistic spiritual world view, on the one hand they identify themselves as a besieged and persecuted community with strong intra-group solidarity and fellowship, and on the other they understand their mission as being urgent, aggressive proselytization aimed at rapid expansion. The identity of the neo-Pentecostals is constituted through the realization of their mission of saving the lost, illustrated by expressions such as 'expanding Church', 'Church on the move', and 'a going people'. Unlike the Catholic community in Goa that is embedded in the regional culture and whose practices and rituals are informed by local mores and ritual codes (Robinson 1998), the lives of the neo-Pentecostals involve 'constant, complex interplays between representations of a generic religious belonging, the articulation of a regional and national identity and the embodied appropriation of spiritual power whose origins are often traced to contexts far distant in both space and time' (Coleman 2000: 239).

Thus, the distinct and paradoxical identity of neo-Pentecostalism is of it having a wide global outlook of a universal biblical Church having an authentic, trans-cultural Christian spirituality that cannot be confined to societal or sectarian borders combined with the notion of belonging to a local, autonomous, Christian fellowship. The glossolalia characteristic of the movement transcends the 'babel' of conflicting languages and disparate cults leading to a global language that unites all humanity. On the other hand, the understanding of speaking in tongues as a liminal experience with emphasis on individual charisma and the empowerment of the ignorant, unlearned self gives the impression that it is tailored to the individual needs and interests of the local community. The global in the local and vice versa are not separate, conflicting ideas but rather blend and merge into a single identity, which is the strength of neo-Pentecostalism. This merging is not always smooth, but includes bumps and uncertainty, and this book has tried to capture something of them in its highlighting of the global–local neo-Pentecostal identity in the religious rites and rituals and social practices of individual Believers. Indigenization and autonomy are essential elements of this process.

The new Christian identity is instilled in the Believer and inscribed on the individual body through strict moral codes that prohibit certain lifestyle habits such as drinking, smoking, and taking drugs, and promote the disciplining of the human body through activities such as fasting, prayer, and obedience. This instilling of the Pentecostal identity involves elevating the physical body of the Believer from the realm of the profane to the sacred and emphasizing the spiritual aspect of the body. Neo-Pentecostalism teaches that a Believer is better placed to survive the exigencies of life and to grab whatever economic and social opportunities that may present themselves, if the spirit is released by animated and ecstatic participation within the controlled and protective atmosphere of the Sunday worship and the adherent adopts a discipline of life and family.

On the other hand, a key reason for the rapid growth of the CCR all over the world and especially in Goa is the 'Catholicization' of the Pentecostal movement—the CCR has acquired the identity of an indigenous Catholic movement, different from both Pentecostalism and traditional Catholicism. The CCR has provided a safe and acceptable space for spirit-empowered and spiritually educated lay Charismatics to be critical of the mass reproduction of religious experience and the role of the clergy in the Catholic Church and yet, at the same time, maintain a safe distance from the Born-Again Christians outside the Catholic fold. However, the tussle between some independent CCR preachers and the diocesan-level ecclesiastical authority over the production of truth and mediation of grace indicates a breaching of this safe space. While the flourishing of local parish-based prayer groups under the guidance of the GST has led to the creation of a strong local Catholic Charismatic identity, the presence of independent centres and ministries in the CCR point to the autonomous nature of the CCR and the Pentecostalization of the Catholic Church.

Both the CCR and the neo-Pentecostal Churches emerged around the same time in Goa. The non-hierarchical and web-like organization of the CCR, with emphasis on the free movement of the spirit has flourished within the hierarchical and highly-structured confines of the Catholic Church, spreading to almost every parish in Goa. In the process, it transformed the charisma of the original Pentecostal experience of a few into a permanent possession of the entire movement. The autonomous neo-Pentecostal Churches, based on the New Testament model that calls no one father or master, abolished all symbols of hierarchies and mediations of the clergy, but, on the other hand, exchanged the clerical authority for the charismatic authority of the pastorate, making it the final decision-making authority in their Church. Relations of power within neo-Pentecostal Churches are intricately linked with the production of truth and the mediation of grace, which the faithful believe has been entrusted to the pastor by God. These relations of power resemble Foucault's pastoral power, which is soteriological, individualizing, coextensive and continuous with life, and linked with the production of truth (Dreyfus and Rabinow 1982: 213–15).

On a crowded highway in the midst of chaotic traffic, the chances of survival and reaching one's destination depend on unquestioning obedience to authority, and so members of neo-Pentecostal sects willingly accept new markers of identity and disciplining activities that tend to have an element of rigour (Martin 2002: 168). The leadership model found in the CCR and in neo-Pentecostalism reflect Weber's idea of charismatic authority routinized into rational–legal authority, which is at the same time a release from previously established Church leadership and an acceptance of a new form of discipline and authority. This new form of authority is a result of the personalization of grace, providing a direct channel of communication between the holy person or prophet and the divine, outside priestly control. Given the transitory and fluid nature of the organization of neo-Pentecostalism, which runs riot in numerous small, autonomous ministries, structures, and networks, there is no universally acceptable and undisputed hierarchy—unlike the mainline historic Churches, canalizing and controlling the resources for its own ends. Competing claims and disputes over the extent and legitimacy of the authority of the pastor results in schisms and sect fission, a characteristic of the Pentecostal–Charismatic movement.

Both the CCR and the neo-Pentecostal Churches have a high prevalence of women clientele, most of whom are married and come from the middle classes. Right from the beginning, the Pentecostal–Charismatic movement has been a women's movement and women have actively participated and played important roles in the mobilization and growth of the movement in its initial stages. However, as a result of the patriarchal biases in society, women practically disappeared from influential roles and the ministry in the later stages of the Pentecostal–Charismatic movement, resulting in the gender paradox analysed by many researchers of Pentecostalism (Martin 2002: 169). Both the CCR and the neo-Pentecostal Churches have a high proportion of female members. As the cases of Catholic Charismatic women analysed in the previous chapter reveal, the movement has provided a liberating space for the individual Believer to experience the self as 'both a receptacle for and transmitter of generic power' (Coleman 2000: 233). The gender paradox is that the construction of social and ritual life on biblical precedent has resulted in the office of the pastorate and leadership roles being predominantly male-controlled and women being confined to the private, domestic domain.

So, what is the final word on the mosaic of the Pentecostal–Charismatic movement? Is it its glossolalia and revivalist character, its fundamentalist and evangelical foundations, its ecstatic and emotive forms of worship, its orality of tradition, its aggressive and direct evangelization, or its global–local identity? It is all the above characteristics and much more, because this work cannot claim to be the final word on neo-Pentecostalism given the state of flux of the movement and the constant rupture of sects and formation of new groupings with new theological orientations. The impact of Pentecostal–Charismatic Christianity—born amidst rapid social change in post-colonial Indian society—on the religious space is noticeable in how the mainstream Churches have become progressively more charismatic and informal and the religious domain has become increasingly polarized. The latter has led to a surge in violence against Christians in recent times. The disproportionate targeting of Indian Pentecostals in instances of violence is a manifestation of a more chronic tension in secular democracies. Pentecostals in India, by being at the forefront of the conversion movement, threaten to provoke radical social change and exacerbate fears about its impact by preaching a gospel of radical cultural discontinuity (Bauman 2015: 193). The field of NRMs in India, with their distinct modes of interaction with mainstream religious establishments; their processes of influencing and being shaped by socio-economic change, modernization, secularization, and globalization; and their specific religious identities, beliefs, rites, and rituals will take shape and grow as more studies on new religions in various parts of India are conducted. My earnest hope is that many more similar ethnographic studies are done in the future so as to contribute to this important field of NRMs in India.

Bibliography

Books and Articles

Abreu, Savio. 2007. 'Popular Religiosity and Syncretic Practices in Goa—Western and Eastern Influences'. In *St. Francis Xavier: His Times and Legacy*, edited by K. Acharya and C. Mata, pp. 181–97. Mumbai, New Delhi: Somaiya Publications Pvt. Ltd.

———. 2009. 'The Making of a Christian Minority'. *Seminar* 602(October): 64–9.

Almond, G., R.S. Appleby, and E. Sivan. 2003. *Strong Religion: The Rise of Fundamentalisms around the World*. Chicago and London: The University of Chicago Press.

Alva, Reginald. 2014. *The Spirituality of the Catholic Charismatic Renewal Movement*. New Delhi: Christian World Imprints.

Alvarez, C.E. 1987. 'Latin American Pentecostals: Ecumenical and Evangelicals'. *One in Christ* 23(1–2): 93–6.

Anderson, Allan. 2001. 'The Globalization of Pentecostalism and the Reshaping of Christianity in the Twenty-first Century'. *Missionalia* 29(3): 423–43.

———. 2004. *An Introduction to Pentecostalism: Global Charismatic Christianity*. Cambridge: Cambridge University Press.

———. 2007. *Spreading Fires: The Missionary Nature of Early Pentecostalism*. New York: Orbis Books.

Anuario Estatistico. 1950. Cidade de Goa: India Portuguesa Reparticao Central de Estatistica e Informacao.

Anuario Estatistico. 1955. Cidade de Goa: India Portuguesa Reparticao Central de Estatistica e Informacao.

Archdiocese of Goa and Daman Directory 2006. 2006. Panjim, Goa: Diocesan Center for Social Communications Media.

Archer, Francis. 1998. 'New Pentecost'. *Renewal* XXVII(5): 109.

Arulsamy, S. (ed.). 1996. *Neo-Pentecostalism: A Study*. New Delhi: CBCI Secretariat.

Asad, Talal. 1993. *Genealogies of Religion*. Baltimore: John Hopkins University Press.

Barbosa, Alexandre. 2004. 'Church in Transition'. *Goa Today* XXXVIII(8): 26–30.

Barrett, David B., George T. Kurian, and Todd M. Johnson (eds). 2001. *World Christian Encyclopedia: A Comparative Survey of Churches and Religions in the Modern World*, Vol. I. Oxford: Oxford University Press.

Bauman, Chad. 2015. *Pentecostals, Proselytisation, and Anti-Christian Violence in Contemporary India*. New York: Oxford University Press.

Bayly, Susan. 1989. *Saints, Goddesses and Kings: Muslims and Christians in South Indian Society 1700–1900*. Cambridge: Cambridge University Press.

———. 1994. 'Christianity and Competing Fundamentalisms in South Indian Society'. In *Accounting for Fundamentalisms*, edited by M. Marty and R. Appleby, pp. 726–69. Chicago: Chicago University Press.

Bernard, Jessie. 1976. *The Future of Marriage*. Harmondsworth: Penguin Books.

Bhandari, Romesh. 1999. *Goa*. New Delhi: Roli Books.

Bird, Frederick B., and F. Westley. 1985. 'The Economic Strategies of New Religious Movements'. *Sociological Analysis* 46(2): 157–90.

Bottomore, T.B., and M. Rubel (eds). 1963. *Karl Marx: Selected Writings in Sociology and Social Philosophy*. Harmondsworth: Penguin Books.

Bourdieu, Pierre. 1984. *Distinction: A Social Critique of the Judgement of Taste*. London: Routledge & Kegan Paul.

———. 1990. *The Logic of Practice*, translated by Richard Nice. Cambridge: Polity Press.

Brockway, A.R. (ed.) 1987. *New Religious Movements and the Churches*. Geneva: WCC.

Burgess, S.M., and E.M. van de Maas (eds). 2003. *The New International Dictionary of Pentecostal and Charismatic Movements*. Michigan, USA: Zondervan.

Cabral, Mario e Sa, ed. 1986. *Winds of Change*. Goa: Department of Information, Government of Goa, Daman & Diu.

———. 1994. 'Stairways to Heaven'. *Goa Today* XXVIII(7): 12–20.

Caplan, Lionel. 1983. 'Popular Christianity in Urban South India'. *Religion and Society* XXX(2): 28–44.

———. 1987a. *Class and Culture in Urban India: Fundamentalism in a Christian Community*. Oxford: Clarendon Press.

——— (ed.). 1987b. *Studies in Religious Fundamentalism*. Albany: State University of New York Press.

Carr, E.H. 1964. *What Is History?* Middlesex, England: Penguin Books.

The Catholic Directory of India. 2013. Bangalore: Claretian Publications.

Censo da Populacao do Estado da India em 1 de Dezembro 1900, Vol. I. 1903. Nova Goa: Imprensa Nacional.

Censo da Populacao do Estado da India em 1 de Dezembro de 1910, Vol. I. 1916. Nova Goa: Imprensa Nacional.

Choi, Syn-Duk. 1986. 'A Comparative Study of Two New Religious Movements in the Republic of Korea: The Unification Church and the Full Gospel Central Church'. In *New Religious Movements and Rapid Change*, edited by James A. Beckford, pp. 113–145. New Delhi: Sage Publications.

The Code of Canon Law. 1983. Bangalore: Collins for Theological Publications in India.

Coleman, Simon. 2000. *The Globalisation of Charismatic Christianity: Spreading the Gospel of Prosperity*. Cambridge: Cambridge University Press.

Costa, Cosme J. 2002. *The Heritage of Govapuri (A Study of the Artifacts in and around the Pilar Seminary Museum)*. Pilar, Goa: Pilar Publications.

Cox, Harvey. 1996. *Fire from Heaven*. London: A Cassell imprint.

Das, Veena. 1976. 'The Uses of Liminality: Society and Cosmos in Hinduism'. *Contributions to Indian Sociology* 10(2): 245–63.

Dawson, Lorne. 1998. 'Anti-modernism, Modernism and Postmodernism: Struggling with the Cultural Significance of New Religious Movements'. *Sociology of Religion* 59(2): 131–56.

D'Costa, Anthony. 1965. *The Christianisation of the Goa Islands*. Bombay: St. Xavier's College.

D'Epinay, C. L. 1969. *Haven of the Masses: A Study of the Pentecostal Movement in Chile*. London: Lutterworth.

Dinges, W.D. 1986. 'The Vatican Report on Sects, Cults and New Religious Movements'. *America* 155(7): 145–54.

The Documents of Vatican II with Notes and Analytical Index. 1966. New Delhi: St. Paul Publications.

Dreyfus, H., and P. Rabinow. 1982. *Michel Foucault: Beyond Structuralism and Hermeneutics*. Great Britain: The Harvester Press.

D'Souza, B.G. 1975. *Goan Society in Transition: A Study in Social Change*. Bombay: Popular Prakashan.

D'Souza, Joel. 1988. 'Siolim Panorama'. *Goa Today* XXIII(4): 22–6.

———. 1991. 'Mushrooming Mapusa'. *Goa Today* XXV(10): 48–51.

D'Souza, Leela. 1996. 'The Charismatic Movement—A Religious Experience'. *Word & Worship* 29(8): 305–16.

Dunn, J.D.G. 1977. *Unity and Diversity in the New Testament: An Inquiry into the Character of Earliest Christianity*. London: SCM Press Ltd.

Durkheim, Emile. 1976 [1912]. *The Elementary Forms of the Religious Life*, translated by J. Swain. London: Allen & Unwin.

———— 1995. *The Elementary Forms of Religious Life,* translated by K.E. Fields. New York: The Free Press.

Eister, Allan. 1967. 'Towards a Radical Critique of Church–Sect Typologizing'. *Journal for the Scientific Study of Religion* 6(1): 85–90.

Engineer, Minoo. 2008a. 'CCR in India—A Reflection on the Beginnings'. *Charisindia* VII(4): 8–11.

————. 2008b. 'CCR in India—A Reflection on the Beginnings'. *Charisindia* VII(8): 28–30.

Fastiggi, R.L. 1990. 'New Religious Movements within the Catholic Church'. *Jeevadhara* 20(119): 365–89.

Fenn, Richard, ed. 2001. *The Blackwell Companion to Sociology of Religion.* Oxford: Blackwell Publishers.

Fichter, Joseph. 1975. *The Catholic Cult of the Paraclete.* New York: Sheed & Ward.

Finke, R., and R. Stark. 2001. 'The New Holy Clubs: Testing Church-to-Sect Propositions'. *Sociology of Religion,* 62(2): 175–89.

Fonseca, Jose N. 1878. *An Historical and Archaeological Sketch of the City of Goa.* Bombay: Thacker & Co. Limited.

Foucault, Michel. 1980. *The History of Sexuality, Volume I: An Introduction,* translated by R. Hurley. New York: Vintage/Random House.

————. 1986. 'Afterword'. In *Michel Foucault: Beyond Structuralism and Hermeneutics,* by H. Dreyfus and P. Rabinow, pp. 208–28. Great Britain: The Harvester Press.

Fuss, Michael (ed.). 1998. *Rethinking New Religious Movements.* Rome: Pontifical Gregorian University.

Geertz, Clifford. 1973. 'Religion as a Cultural System'. In *The Interpretation of Cultures,* edited by Clifford Geertz, pp. 87–125. New York: Basic Books.

Gerlach, L.P., and V.H. Hine. 1968. 'Five Factors Crucial to the Growth and Spread of a Modern Religious Movement'. *Journal for the Scientific Study of Religion* 1(Spring): 23–40.

———— (eds). 1970. *People, Power and Change: Movements of Social Transformation.* New York: Bobbs-Merrill.

Godbey, W.B. 1896. *Commentary on the New Testament.* Cincinnati, USA: Revivalist Office.

Gomes, Olivinho. 2003. *The Religious Orders in Goa (XVIth—XVIIth Centuries).* Chandor, Goa: Konkani Sorospot Prakashan.

————. 2004. *Goa.* New Delhi: National Book Trust, India.

Gowalkar, M.S. 1966. *Bunch of Thoughts.* Bangalore: Vikram Prakashan.

Gracias, Fatima. 2007. *The Many Faces of Sundorem: Women in Goa.* Panjim, Goa: Surya Publications.

Gune, V.T. (ed.). 1979. *Gazetteer of the Union Territory Goa, Daman & Diu, Part I, Goa*. Panaji, Goa: Gazetteer Department of Govt. of Goa, Daman and Diu.

Heras, H. 1935. *The Conversion Policy of the Jesuits in India*. Bombay: Indian Historical Research Institute.

Hollenweger, Walter. 1972. *The Pentecostals*. London: SCM Press Ltd.

———. 1986. 'After Twenty Years' Research on Pentecostalism'. *International Review of Mission* 75(297): 3–13.

———. 1996. 'From Azusa Street to the Toronto Phenomenon: Historical Roots of the Pentecostal Movement'. *Concilium* 3: 3–13.

———. 1998. 'Pentecostalism, Growth and Ecumenism'. *Priests & People* 12(4): 153–6.

Hunt, Stephen, Tony Walter, and Malcolm Hamilton (eds). 1997. *Charismatic Christianity: Sociological Perspectives*. Hampshire: Macmillan Press.

Iragui, Marcelino. 1977. *Good News Today*. Alwaye, Kerala: Pontifical Seminary.

Jaffrelot, Christophe (ed.). 2017. *Hindu Nationalism: A Reader*. Ranikhet, India: Permanent Black.

Jebens, Holger. 2005. *Pathways to Heaven*. New York: Berghahn Books.

Jones, Robert. 1986. *Emile Durkheim: An Introduction to Four Major Works*. Beverly Hills, CA: Sage Publications.

Joseph, Pushpa. 2005. 'An Indian Critique of the Cult of Ideal Womanhood'. In *Ecclesia of Women in Asia: Gathering the Voices of the Silenced*, edited by E. Monteiro and A. Gutzler, pp. 22–41. Delhi: ISPCK.

Katre, S.M. 1966. *The Formation of Konkani*. Poona: Deccan College.

Kosambi, D.D. 1962. 'The Village Community in the "Old Conquests" of Goa'. In *Myth and Reality: Studies in the Formation of Indian Culture*, edited by D.D Kosambi, pp. 152–88. Bombay: Popular Prakashan.

Larsen, Karin. 1998. *Faces of Goa*. New Delhi: Gyan Publishing House.

Lederle, H.I. 1986. 'The Charismatic Movement—The Ambiguous Challenge'. *Missionalia* 14(2): 61–5.

———. 1990. 'The Pentecostal and Charismatic Movements: An Ambiguous Renewal of the Christian Church?' *Ministerial Formation* 50(July): 35–43.

Lefebvre, Henri. 1991. *The Production of Space*, translated by Donald Nicholson-Smith. Oxford: Blackwell Publishing.

Lobo, George V. 1983. *The New Marriage Law*. Bandra, Mumbai: St Pauls.

Lucas, Phillip C. 1992. 'The New Age Movement and the Pentecostal/Charismatic Revival: Distinct Yet Parallel Phases of a Fourth Generation Awakening'. In *Perspectoves on the New Age*, edited by James R. Lewis and J. Gordon Melton, pp. 189–212. New York: State University of New Yourk Press.

Madan T.N. 1989. *Family and Kinship: A Study of the Pandits of Rural Kashmir*, 2nd enlarged edition. Delhi: Oxford University Press.

Malekandathil, P., and R. Dias (eds). 2008. *Goa in the 20th Century: History & Culture*. Panaji, Goa: Institute Menezes Braganza.

Mani, K., and F. Noronha. 2008. *Picture-Postcard Poverty*. Goa: Goa, 1556.

Manney, Jim. 1973. 'Before Duquesne: Sources of the Renewal'. *New Covenant* 2(8): 12–17.

Marcus, George E. 1995. 'Ethnography in/of the World System: The Emergence of Multi-Sited Ethnography'. *Annual Review of Anthropology* 24: 95–117. Available at: http://www.jstor.org/stable/2155931 (accessed on 23 October 2019).

Martin, David. 2002. *Pentecostalism: The World Their Parish*. Oxford: Blackwell Publishers.

Marty, M.E. 1960. 'Sects and Cults'. *The Annals of the American Academy of Political and Social Science* 332(1): 125–34.

Mascarenhas, Fio. 1996. *A Handbook for Leaders*. Bangalore, India: National Charismatic Office.

Mascarenhas, Nascimento J. 2008. *Follow Me: Parish Priests of the Parishes of Bardez*. Goa: Nascimento J. Mascarenhas.

Mascarenhas-Keyes, S. 1987. 'The Native Anthropologist: Constraints and Strategies in Research'. In *Anthropology at Home*, edited by A. Jackson, pp. 180–95. London: Tavistock Publications.

Mathew, P.T. 2009. 'The Phenomenon of Catholics Joining Pentecostal Groups, and the Feasibility of Catholic–Pentecostal Dialogue: An Inquiry in the Kerala Context'. *Vidyajyoti Journal of Theological Reflection* 73(9): 692–710.

McAlister, Elizabeth. 2005. 'Globalization and the Religious Production of Space'. *Journal for the Scientific Study of Religion* 44(3): 249–55.

McDonnell, Kilian. 1975. 'A Sociologist Looks at the Catholic Charismatic Renewal'. *Worship* 49(7): 378–92.

———. 1976. *Charismatic Renewal & the Churches*. New York: The Seabury Press.

——— 1980. *Presence, Power, Praise: Documents on the Charismatic Renewal*, 3 Vols. Collegeville, MN: The Liturgical Press.

——— 1987. 'Catholic Charismatic Renewal and Classical Pentecostalism: Growth and the Critique of a Systematic Suspicion'. *One in Christ* 23(1–2): 36–61.

———. 1999. 'Pentecostals and Catholics on Evangelism and Sheep-Stealing'. *America* 180(7): 11–14.

McGee, G.B. 1994. 'Pentecostal Missiology: Moving beyond Triumphalism to Face the Issues'. *Pneuma* 16(2): 275–82.

McGuire, M.B. 1974. 'An Interpretive Comparison of Elements of the Pentecostal and Underground Church Movements in American Catholicism'. *Sociological Analysis* 35: 57–65.

Melton, J. Gordon. 1993. *The Encyclopedia of American Religions*, 4th edition. Detroit: Gale Research.

Melton, J. Gordon. 2004. 'An Introduction to New Religions'. In *The Oxford Handbook of New Religious Movements*, edited by James R. Lewis, pp. 16–35. New York: Oxford University Press.

Mendonca, Delio. 2002. *Conversions and Citizenry: Goa under Portugal 1510–1610*. New Delhi: Concept Publishing Co.

Miller, A.G. 1996. 'Pentecostalism as a Social Movement: Beyond the Theory of Deprivation'. *Journal of Pentecostal Theology* 4(9): 97–114.

Miranda, Alister. 2000. 'A Senseless Tussle'. *Goa Today* XXXIV(8): 30–2.

Moraes, G.M. 1964. *A History of Christianity in India: From Early Times to St. Francis Xavier: A.D. 52–1542*. Bombay: Manaktalas.

Mundadan, A.M. 1984. *History of Christianity in India: From the Beginning up to the Middle of the Sixteenth Century (up to 1542)*. Bangalore: Theological Publications in India.

The New American Bible. 1976. Iowa, USA: World Bible Publishers.

Narayan, Kirin. 1993. 'How Native Is a "Native" Anthropologist?' *American Anthropologist* 95(3): 671–86.

Newman, R.S. 2001. *Of Umbrellas, Goddesses & Dreams: Essays on Goan Culture and Society*. Mapusa, Goa: Other India Press.

Niebuhr, R.H. 1960. *The Social Sources of Denominationalism*. New York: Meridian Books, Inc.

Nwaobi, P.O. 1993. *Charismatics and the Church*. Ibadan, Nigeria: Shaneson C.I. Ltd.

Omenyo, Cephas. 2002. 'Charismatic Churches in Ghana and Contextualization'. *Exchange* 31(3): 252–77.

Oommen, George. 2001. 'Growth of Pentecostalism in Central Kerala from 1921–47: A Paradigm for Pentecostal Growth of Churches in North India'. *Indian Church History Review* XXXV(2): 131–46.

Pandit, Heta. 2003. *Walking in Goa*. Mumbai: Eminence Designs Pvt. Ltd.

———. 2008. 'Goan Houses—The Feminine Space'. In *Goa in the 20th Century: History & Culture*, edited by Pius Malekandathil and Remy Dias, pp. 51–9. Panaji, Goa: Institute Menezes Braganza.

Pereira, R.G. de. 1978. *Goa: Hindu Temples and Deities*. Panaji, Goa: Printwell Press.

Perera, Sasanka. 1998. *New Evangelical Movements and Conflict in South Asia: Sri Lanka and Nepal in Perspective*. Colombo, Sri Lanka: Regional Centre for Strategic Studies.

Phal, S.R. 1982. *Society in Goa*. Delhi: B.R. Publishing Co.

Pickering, W.S.F. 1984. *Durkheim's Sociology of Religion*. London: Routledge and Kegan Paul.

Pinto, Christovam. 1882. *Estado da India Recenseamento Geral, 1881*. Nova Goa: Imprensa Nacional.

Pinto, Rochelle. 2007. *Between Empires: Print and Politics in Goa*. New Delhi: Oxford University Press.

Priolkar, A.K. 1961. *The Goa Inquisition*. Bombay: Bombay University Press.

Rahner, Karl, and H. Vorgrimler. 1983. *Concise Theological Dictionary*, 2nd edition. London: Burns & Oates.

Reidy, M.T.V., and J.T. Richardson. 1978. 'Roman Catholic Neo-Pentecostalism: The New Zealand Experience'. *Journal of Sociology* 14(3): 222–30.

Renewal. 2007. 'Welcome Speech of Most Rev. Filipe Neri Ferrao at the Annual Civic Reception on the Occasion of Christmas'. XXXVI(2): 21–2.

Robbins, Thomas. 2000. '"Quo Vadis" the Scientific Study of New Religious Movements?'. *Journal for the Scientific Study of Religion* 39(4): 515–23.

Robeck, C.M. 1987. 'Pentecostals and the Apostolic Faith: Implications for Ecumenism'. *One in Christ* 23(1–2): 110–30.

Robeck, Cecil, and A. Young (eds). 2014. *The Cambridge Companion to Pentecostalism*. Cambridge: Cambridge University Press.

Robinson, Rowena. 1998. *Conversion, Continuity and Change: Lived Christianity in Southern Goa*. New Delhi: Sage Publications.

Robinson, Rowena, and S. Clarke. 2003. *Religious Conversion in India: Modes, Motivations and Meanings*. New Delhi: Oxford University Press.

Rodrigues, Maria de Lourdes. 2000. 'Mutant Merces'. *Goa Today* XXXIV(8): 50–3.

———. 2001. 'Marriage Traditions & Customs amongst the Catholics of Merces. In *Goa in the Indian Sub-Continent*, edited by S.K. Mhamai. Panaji, Goa: Directorate of Archives and Archaeology.

Saliba, John A. 1995. *Perspectives on New Religious Movements*. London: Geoffrey Chapman.

Seul, Jeffrey R. 1999. 'Ours Is the Way of God: Religion, Identity and Intergroup Conflict'. *Journal of Peace Research* 36(5): 553–69.

Singh, K.S. (ed.) 1993. *People of India: Goa*. Bombay: Popular Prakashan Pvt. Ltd.

Sinha, Arun. 2002. *Goa Indica: A Critical Portrait of Postcolonial Goa*. New Delhi: Bibliophile South Asia and Promilla & Co.

Stark, Rodney, and W.S. Bainbridge. 1985. *The Future of Religion: Secularization, Revival and Cult Formation*. Berkeley, CA: University of California Press.

Statistical Hand Book of Goa 2001. 2001. Panaji, Goa: Directorate of Planning, Statistics and Evaluation.

Stietencron, H.V. 2001. 'Charisma and Canon: The Dynamics of Legitimization and Innovation in Indian Religions'. In *Charisma and Canon: Essays on the Religious History of the Indian Subcontinent*, edited by V. Dalmia, A. Malinar, and M. Christof. New Delhi: Oxford University Press.

Stirrat, R.L. 1992. *Power and Religiosity in a Post-colonial Setting: Sinhala Catholics in Contemporary Sri Lanka*. Cambridge: Cambridge University Press.

Stolee, H.J. 1963. *Speaking in Tongues*. Aurora, Illinois, USA: Augsburg Publishing House.

Suico, Joseph R. 1999. 'Pentecostalism: Towards a Movement of Social Transformation in the Philippines'. *Journal of Asian Mission* 1(March): 7–19.

Synan, Vinson. 1973. 'The Classical Pentecostals'. *New Covenant* 2(11): 7–27.

———. 1982. 'Discerning the Charismatic Renewal'. *Theology Today* 39(2): 187–93.

——— 1987. 'Pentecostalism: Varieties and Contributions'. *One in Christ* 23(1–2): 97–109.

———. 1997. *The Holiness–Pentecostal Tradition: Charismatic Movements in the Twentieth Century*. Grand Rapids, Michigan: William B. Eerdmans Publishing Co.

Thomas, P.N. 2008. *Strong Religion, Zealous Media: Christian Fundamentalism and Communication in India*. New Delhi: Sage Publications.

Varghese, Alan. 2015. *Pentecostal Churches and Ecumenism in India*. Delhi: Indian Society for Promoting Christian Knowledge.

Visvanathan, Susan. 1999. *The Christians of Kerala: History, Belief and Ritual among the Yakoba*. Delhi: Oxford University Press.

Weber, Max. 1958. *The Protestant Ethic and the Spirit of Capitalism*. New York: Charles Scribner's Sons.

———. 1978. *Economy and Society—An Outline of Interpretive Sociology*, edited by Guenther Roth and Claus Wittich. Los Angeles: University of California Press.

Westley, Francis. 1983. *The Complex Forms of the Religious Life*. California: Scholars Press.

White, Alma. 1949. *Demons and Tongues*. New Jersey, USA: Pillar of Fire.

Williams, Rhys H. 2005. 'Introduction to a Forum on Religion and Place'. *Journal for the Scientific Study of Religion* 44(3): 239–42.

Wilson, B. 1970. *Religious Sects*. London: Weidenfeld and Nicolson.

Wright, Nigel. 1997. 'The Nature and Variety of Restorationism and the "House Church" Movement'. In *Charismatic Christianity: Sociological Perspectives*, edited by Stephen Hunt, Tony Walter, and Malcolm Hamilton, pp. 60–76. Hampshire: Macmillan Press.

Xavier, P.D. 1993. *Goa: A Social History*. Panaji, Goa: Rajhauns Vitaran.

Reports, Souvenirs, and Unpublished Theses

Census of India. 2011. 'Census_Data_Goa-ByReligions_2011'. Microsoft Excel file prepared by the Directorate of Census Operations.

———. 1991. *District Census Hand Book—North Goa*, Part XII-A & B. Goa: Directorate of Census Operations.

———. 2001. *Primary Census Abstract—Goa*. Goa: Directorate of Census Operations.

D'Souza, Leela. 1999. *The Return of Religion: A Reversal of the Secularisation Process*. PhD diss., Bombay University.

Fernandes, I. 2007. *Quest of Evangelical Church History of Goa*. Master of Divinity diss., New India Bible Seminary, Paippad, Kerala, India.

Gopinath, R. 2009. 'The History of the Middle Classes in India'. Paper presented at the 'The Middle Class in India', an international seminar organized by Indian Council for Social Science Research (Western Regional Centre), 12–14 June. Mumbai.

Open the Doors to the Redeemer. 1999. Souvenir of the 'Eleventh National Great Jubilee CCR Convention', Goa.

Parathazham, Paul. 1996. 'Neo-Pentecostalism in India: Report of a National Survey'. Paper presented at the Catholic Bishops' Conference of India, 13–21 February 1996. Thiruvananthapuram, Kerala.

Shukla, R. 2009. 'The Great Indian Middle Class: An Analysis through Their Purchasing Power'. Paper presented at 'The Middle Class in India', international seminar organized by Indian Council for Social Science Research (Western Regional Centre), 12–14 June, Mumbai.

Index

About the Author

Savio Abreu, a Catholic priest belonging to the Society of Jesus, is assistant professor of sociology and anthropology at St. Xavier's College, Mumbai. He was director of the Xavier Centre of Historical Research (XCHR), Goa, from 2011 to 2018. He has a PhD from Indian Institute of Technology Bombay for which he conducted a sociological study on new Christian movements in contemporary Goa. He has co-edited two books, *Goa 2011: Reviewing and Recovering Fifty Years*, 2014 (with R.C. Heredia), and *Public History of Goa: Evolving Politics, Culture and Identity*, 2019 (with A. da Silva and R. D'Souza).

Abreu has presented many papers at local, national, and international seminars and conferences and has published over 20 articles in edited volumes and academic journals. He is interested in the sociology of religion, especially new religious movements, cultural studies, Jesuit studies, issues of human rights, and social movements—topics he discusses on his blog: http://savioabreu.blogspot.in.